Who Should Decide?

Who Should Decide?
Paternalism in Health Care

James F. Childress

New York   Oxford
OXFORD UNIVERSITY PRESS

Oxford University Press

Oxford   New York   Toronto
Delhi   Bombay   Calcutta   Madras   Karachi
Kuala Lumpur   Singapore   Hong Kong   Tokyo
Nairobi   Dar es Salaam   Cape Town
Melbourne   Auckland

and associated companies in
Beirut   Berlin   Ibadan   Mexico City   Nicosia

Copyright © 1982 by Oxford University Press, Inc.

First published in 1982 by Oxford University Press, Inc.
200 Madison Avenue, New York, NY 10016
First issued as an Oxford University Press paperback, 1985

LIBRARY OF CONGRESS CATALOGING IN PUBLICATION DATA
Childress, James F.
   Who should decide?
   Bibliography: p.
   Includes index.
   1. Medical ethics.   2. Paternalism.   I. Title.
[DNLM: 1. Ethics, Medical.   2. Informed consent.
W 50 C536w]
R725.5.C48   1982   174'.2   82-7945
ISBN 0-19-503127-X   AACR2
ISBN 0-19-503976-9 (pbk.)

Printing (last digit): 9 8 7 6 5 4 3 2 1
Printed in the United States of America

For Georgia

Preface

The conflict between professional paternalism and patient autonomy pervades health care. It is not possible to understand or to resolve this conflict without examining the metaphors and principles that create it. In particular, it is necessary to examine the principles of beneficence and respect for persons and the metaphors of father or parent, drawn from family life, and autonomy, drawn originally from political life. In the first chapter, I indicate how the paternal metaphor structures much contemporary health care even when it is not consciously acknowledged, and I define paternalism as a refusal to acquiesce in a person's wishes, choices, or actions for that person's own benefit. After distinguishing paternalistic actions from other kinds of nonacquiescence, I analyze several types of paternalism: pure and impure, restricted and extended, soft and hard, direct and indirect, and active and passive.

In order to determine whether the paternal metaphor can adequately guide and direct health care, it is necessary to explore the principles that both support and limit paternalism. Thus, in the second chapter, I analyze several forms and levels of the principle of beneficence, concentrating on neighbor-love and care in religious traditions and on patient-benefit in the Hippocratic tradition of medicine. The principle of beneficence (prevent and remove harm or promote good) supports paternalistic interventions, but even on its own terms it suffers from serious limitations, especially in a pluralistic society. These limitations are distinct from the limits set by the principle of respect for persons— the subject of the third chapter. The principle of respect for persons limits and constrains acts of beneficence because it requires attention to the beneficiary's wishes and choices. But when the beneficiary is not autonomous, that is, cannot deliberate rationally or act freely, it is not a form of insult or disrespect to override his wishes or choices for his own benefit. The principle of respect for persons does not require identical treatment for autonomous and nonautonomous persons. Recognition of autonomy as a limit and constraint on actions of beneficence does not presuppose acceptance of autonomy as a goal or as an ideal; nor does it presuppose isolated selves, stripped of community and tradition.

Application of the principle of respect for persons is rarely easy because people are so complex. They may not only express different wishes at the same time, such as ambivalent responses to proposed medical treatment, but they may also make different choices at different times. What they choose in the present may differ from what they chose in the past or would probably choose in the future. In chapter IV, I explore these issues under the heading of "Consents," where I examine the nature of consent, varieties of consent—such as express, tacit, implied, and presumed consent—and different times of consent—past, present, and future. I argue that it is not sufficient to appeal to tacit, implicit, or presumed consent in order to override the express refusal of a competent patient. Furthermore, neither past consent nor probable future consent—which I call ratification—can justify interventions against a competent patient's refusal of such interventions. Past consent can indicate the values for "soft" paternalism (paternalism that appeals to the patient's own values over time) rather than "hard" paternalism (paternalism that imposes alien values), and it may assign some agents the responsibility to consider the patient's wishes, competence, and risks over time. But by itself past consent cannot justify overriding a competent patient's current voluntary choices. Likewise, a prediction that in the future a patient will ratify a current intervention will not justify that intervention, even though such a prediction may provide marginal evidence that it is justified.

Whatever the complexity of the principle of respect for persons, it rules out some forms of paternalism. It does not, however, exclude all paternalism. It is possible to develop a principle of limited paternalism, in which beneficence is constrained by the principle of respect for persons. Chapter V develops this principle of limited paternalism by examining the conditions under which paternalism can be justified. This chapter focuses on decision-making with passing attention to willing and acting. In order to justify paternalism within the limits set by the principle of respect for persons, it is essential, first, to rebut the presumption of an adult's competence to make his or her own decisions. The second condition for justified paternalism is the probability of harm unless there is intervention. The third condition is proportionality—the probable benefit of intervention should outweigh the probable harm of nonintervention. Fourth, it is necessary to assess modes of paternalistic action, such as deception and coercion. Effectiveness is not sufficient. In general, the least restrictive, least humiliating, and least insulting means should be employed. Whether the principle of limited paternalism can be implemented through actual or proposed procedures is an important question. To override a person's wishes, choices, or actions without "due process" is to deepen the affront to dignity. The sort of procedures required will vary according to the rights at stake, such as the deprivation of liberty. If it is not possible to develop reliable procedures that can express both care and respect, even limited paternalism may not be acceptable in practice.

In the final three chapters (VI–VIII), I indicate how this framework, particularly the principle of limited paternalism, can illuminate controversies regarding deception, lying, and nondisclosure of information in health care (chapter VI), suicide and refusal of lifesaving or lifeprolonging medical treatment (chapter VII), and prevention of ill health and early death through governmental intervention in personal lifestyles (chapter VIII).

Both paternalists and their critics are susceptible to various temptations. Paternalists are tempted by pride and self-righteousness. There is the arrogance of benevolence; as Nathaniel Hawthorne observed, "benevolence is here the twin of pride." Critics of paternalism are often tempted by sloth and even indifference. They stand back, frequently denying any responsibility for what happens to others, sometimes remaining unmoved by the needs of others. It is possible to avoid both temptations by properly defining and maintaining a tension between the principles of beneficence and respect. Our acts, policies, and practices in health care should express care and concern, on the one hand, and respect for persons, on the other—in short, limited or constrained paternalism.

Acknowledgments

In writing this book I have incurred many debts to colleagues, students, and institutions. I cannot identify all of them, but some deserve special mention. While I cannot expect to discharge my obligations through this acknowledgment of indebtedness, it is a gesture of my deep appreciation and gratitude.

Both the Kennedy Institute of Ethics, where I developed several of these ideas in preliminary form, and the University of Virginia, where this book was written, have provided excellent opportunities for intellectual stimulation and development through research and teaching, outstanding colleagues for discussion and debate, and excellent support staffs. I am also grateful to the University of Virginia for a grant to cover some of the costs of preparing the manuscript for publication and to Wanda Proffitt and LaRea Frazier for typing large portions of the book with great skill and efficiency. Both Steven Dalle-Mura and James Tubbs provided able research assistance, and the latter prepared the index with his usual efficiency.

Several former colleagues at the Kennedy Institute of Ethics have influenced my thinking over several years. In particular, I want to thank Tom Beauchamp, Tristram Engelhardt, Richard McCormick, S.J., and LeRoy Walters. Stanley Hauerwas of the University of Notre Dame has been a valuable and tireless conversation partner in twenty years of rich friendship. Oscar Thorup has taught me a lot during our three interdisciplinary and interprofessional seminars on Ethics and Public Policy in Health Care at the University of Virginia, while Kenneth Crispell has provided support and several valuable suggestions. Mark Siegler has been a stimulating and challenging colleague during the final stages of the preparation of this book. I am grateful to him as well as to Tris Engelhardt, Richard O'Neil, and Gene Outka for reading part or all of the manuscript at one stage or another. Their thoughtful suggestions made the book better.

Teachers often learn more than they teach. I have benefited greatly from teaching in several settings, particularly in summer seminars sponsored by the National Endowment for the Humanities for medical and health care teachers and for college teachers.

Georgia and our twin sons, James Frederic and Albert Franklin, have made me a better father by limiting my "paternalism" and expecting collegiality. I dedicate this book to Georgia as a feeble gesture of my gratitude for all that she has been and done over many years.

Charlottesville, Virginia   J.F.C.
May 1982

Contents

Who Should Decide?

I

Paternalism in Health Care

Metaphors and Models of Health Care Relationships

A woman injured in an automobile accident inquired about the condition of her daughter who was also injured. At the physician's insistence, the nurse, as reported in case #1, reassured the woman about her daughter's condition although the daughter was already dead. In order to prevent unnecessary anxiety, a radiologist in case #6 withheld information about the risk of death from a patient about to undergo urography. In case #22, a retarded woman was sterilized against her will, in part for her own good, while in case #10 a Jehovah's Witness refused a blood transfusion that might have saved her life. As case #14 indicates, a man suffering from frostbite developed gangrene, but he refused to allow his feet to be amputated. Medical efforts to obtain a court order to authorize the surgery failed.

As these cases suggest, conflicts between health care professionals and patients are not uncommon.[1] In all these cases, there is tension between what the patient wants and what the professional believes the patient needs. Sometimes the professional even overrides the patient's wishes for the patient's own benefit. Such actions are usually called "paternalistic," and I want to explore their nature and their justification. In this chapter I will examine the metaphor of father as applied to health care professionals, the nature of paternalism, and types of paternalism.

According to the *Oxford English Dictionary*, "paternalism" is "the principle and practice of paternal administration; government as by a father; the claim or attempt to supply the needs or to regulate the life of a nation or community in the same way as a father does those of his children."[2] Although the term "paternalism" only emerged in the 1880s, the idea of paternalism has had a long history. For example, in political thought, the related idea of "patriarchalism" has been very important in several different periods (such as 17th century England). Furthermore, the idea of paternalism is not limited to political thought. It is also prominent in health care.

It is sometimes held that paternalism involves the use of a "biological model of the caring parent."[3] But fatherhood is not merely biological; it is also a social role. In discussions of paternalism in politics or health care, the social role of father is used as an analogue for the social role of government or health care provider. This familial analogy is used to interpret or to legitimate another social role. When it is used normatively, the image of father is invoked to legitimate power outside the family. The legitimation of power is an exercise of imagination as well as an appeal to principles, rules, and values. And imagination is basically "reasoning in metaphors."[4]

Some similarities among social roles make images, metaphors, and analogies both appropriate and effective. Without some similarities, they could not function. When paternalism is used to illuminate or to legitimate the role of the professional or the state in health care, two features of the paternal role are prominent. First, the father's motives, intentions, and actions are assumed to be benevolent; they are aimed at his children's welfare. Second, he makes all or at least some of the decisions regarding their welfare rather than letting them make these decisions. These two features involve a distinction between acting on someone's *behalf* and acting at someone's *behest*. Paternalism is morally interesting and important because the paternalist claims to act on a person's behalf but not at that person's behest; indeed, the beneficiary of the paternalist's actions may even explicitly oppose those actions. In Arthur Kopit's play, *Oh Dad, Poor Dad, Mamma's Hung You in the Closet and I'm Feeling So Sad*, Jonathan reveals to Rosalie what she had suspected: his mother locks the front door when she leaves him in the house. Rosalie says, "I thought so." Jonathan responds, "No! You-you don't understand. It's not what you think. She doesn't lock the door to kaka-keep me in, which would be malicious. She . . . locks the door so I can't get out, which is for my own good and therefore . . . beneficent!"[5]

"A physician is a father to his patients."[6] Such a metaphor involves "seeing as." Indeed, the essence of metaphor is "understanding and expressing one kind of thing in terms of another."[7] Standard examples include, "man is a wolf," "argument is war," and "life is a game." According to the interaction view of metaphor, as developed by Max Black, meaning results from the intersection between the primary subject ("man") and the subsidiary subject ("wolf").[8] We see the principal subject through the subsidiary subject. The subsidiary subject, the metaphor, is not always dispensable or replaceable by literal expressions because it may add cognitive content and insights. The subsidiary subject serves as a "focus," a "filter," or a "screen" for the principal subject; it "organizes" our view of the principal subject by selecting and emphasizing certain features while subordinating others. It both highlights and hides features.

This interaction view rescues metaphors from attempts to replace them everywhere by more literal expressions. But this view may mislead insofar as it appears to hold that similarity or analogy only *results* from the interaction between the terms and is not *presupposed* by the interaction. Paul Ricouer argues that even the interaction view presupposes "resemblance," that is, seeing similarity in dissimilars. Resemblance, the ground of metaphor, involves both similarity and difference. It guides the metaphor. "Father" is used as a metaphor for "physician" precisely because of some resemblance. According to Ricouer, resemblance in metaphor "can be construed as the site of the clash between sameness and difference."[9] The physician is both similar and dissimilar to the father.

Metaphors highlight and hide features of the principal subject, such as physician, by their "system of associated commonplaces."[10] For example, thinking of a physician as a parent highlights some features of the medical relationship (care and control) while hiding others (payment of fees). Thus, when metaphors are used to interpret and illuminate roles and activities, they can be criticized if they distort more features than they illuminate. And when they are used to prescribe and direct roles and activities, they can be criticized if they highlight one moral consideration while hiding others. For example, paternalistic health care tends to highlight the professional's care while hiding the patient's rights.

Even when paternalism is held to be inadequate, either descriptively or normatively, alternative models of health care are also built on metaphors. In general, these are structural metaphors: a concept from one domain (such as family life) is used to structure a concept from another domain (such as medicine).[11] In addition to father, the physician has recently been seen as

> Priest
> Fiduciary
> Partner, collaborator, colleague
> Negotiator and accommodator
> Contractor
> Technician, engineer, plumber
> Friend
> Teacher
> Bureaucrat
> Captain

I have analyzed these metaphors and models in more detail elsewhere, and will implicitly evaluate several of them as I explore paternalism in subsequent chapters.[12] But several general points are important.

First, these metaphors are not mutually exclusive. For example, negotiation may precede a contract, and, according to the terms of the contract, the health care professional may be viewed as a technician or as a teacher. Indeed, critics of a contractual model of health care often argue that it tends to make the physician a mere technician, deprived of moral agency.[13]

Second, metaphors for health care professionals also imply metaphors for recipients of care, who may be viewed, for example, as contractors, partners, friends, pupils, and children. In recent years, the term "patient" has come under attack, because it often appears as the opposite of "agent." While its meaning and significance in health care can be seen in its Latin root (*pati*: to suffer), it appears to suggest passivity and thus to support paternalistic views of the health care professional. As a result, critics have proposed terms for the care-receiver that emphasize autonomy, such as "client" and "consumer." Nevertheless, among convenient terms, "patient" is the most neutral and widely-accepted. Thus,

I will continue to use it in this book, while recognizing that there are reasons to replace it.

Third, many conflicts in health care stem from the use of different metaphors. For example, if physicians see themselves as parents in relation to their patients, and patients see themselves as contractors or partners, conflict can be expected. Because "seeing as" may not be conscious or acknowledged, the source of the conflict may not be evident. A physician or a patient may fail to see the impact of metaphors on their interaction, even when it is difficult to interpret their actions without reference to these metaphors.[14] For example, paternalists may view "consent" mainly as *acceptance* of what they propose and may view "refusal" as a sign that the patient is incompetent. The contractor, by contrast, may view "consent" mainly as *decision*, which includes both acceptance and refusal.

Fourth, as the last two points suggest, metaphors often reverberate through patterns of thought, experience, and action. They have implications that are systematically related.[15] For example, viewing the physician as "captain of the team" usually reflects a military metaphor rather than a sports metaphor, though these two are often closely related. The military metaphor seems especially appropriate because of a conception of disease attacking the body. Thus, medicine is war. The physician as "captain" leads the "battle" against disease, ordering a "battery" of tests, developing a "plan of attack," calling on the "armamentarium" of medicine, directing "allied health personnel," issuing "orders" for "aggressive therapy," and expecting "compliance." Patients are expected to put up a "good fight," rather than "give up." "Victory" is sought, and "defeat" is feared. Only professionals who fight "in the trenches" or stand "on the firing line" can really appreciate the problems of health care; and they frequently have "war stories" to report. As medicine wages war against germs that "invade" the body and threaten its "defenses," the society may also declare "war on cancer," looking for a "magic bullet."[16] It is also easy to see how this military metaphor can support paternalism. After all, the attack on disease is viewed as a defense of the patient. It is in the patient's best interest.

Despite this reverberation of metaphors, it is not possible to defend a "principle of complete implication."[17] If someone says "that is paternalistic," he does not necessarily claim that the "likeness is complete." A single metaphor may not structure the whole pattern of thought, experience, and action.

Furthermore, usually only a portion of a metaphor is used.[18] One unused part of the paternal metaphor may be gender. Women also act paternalistically, whether they are physicians or nurses. Another unused part of the paternal metaphor may be the relation between the adults, mainly mother and father, who have responsibility for the children. The paternal metaphor does not imply any particular view of the relations among physicians and other health care professionals. Individually or collectively, they may act paternalistically toward the patient. Nevertheless, some nurses contend that paternalism is a form of sexism and male dominance that pervades relationships among health care professionals. Most physicians are men, and most nurses (95%) are women.[19] Thus, some nurses argue, the term "parentalism" should replace "paternalism."[20]

Other critics hold that the use of the metaphor "father" is inappropriate not because of changes in health care but because of changes in familial roles. Thus, they contend, dramatic changes in family structure in the last century have stripped the paternal role of the characteristics, such as dominance, that made it so useful for metaphorical constructions. Since women and children have gained new roles, rights, and independence, "paternalism" can only refer to bad fathers, not to good or even normal fathers. But even if fathers in our society do not generally act "paternalistically" (that is, the way the metaphor "father" appears to presuppose), the metaphor may still be useful because of what Max Black calls its "system of associated commonplaces." What is evoked by the metaphor "father" (or by the model of paternalism) is critical, not whether fathers currently act that way. As Black points out, "the important thing for the metaphor's effectiveness is not that the commonplaces shall be true, but that they should be readily and freely evoked."[21] The image of father in paternalism clearly antedates changes in family structure in this century.

In some settings, "parental" or even "maternal" may be preferable to "paternal." Although I will sometimes interchange "parental" and "paternal," and "parentalism" and "paternalism," I will use "paternalism" more frequently because it has a sharper and clearer "system of associated commonplaces." It is also hallowed by numerous practical and theoretical discussions. I will use it to identify a particular form of interaction, which I will define more precisely later in this chapter. But insofar as it tends to support sexism, it merits criticism beyond its implications for the relationship between health care professionals and patients.

Fifth, the choice of models and their assessment depend on the aspects of medical relationships that are emphasized. For the most part, the metaphors listed above have been used in practice and in the literature to identify the locus of decision-making within medical relationships, the valuational and technical components of decisions, and the professional's involvement and distance. Metaphors such as priest, parent, and captain emphasize the asymmetry of medical relationships: decision-making is hierarchical and the physician is at the apex. Other metaphors such as partner and friend emphasize the equality of both parties in the decision-making. Still other metaphors such as contractor or technician emphasize the primacy of the patient in decision-making. Similar points could be made about what these metaphors imply for the liberty of health care professionals and patients.

Finally, how we assess these different metaphors and models will depend on whether they are primarily descriptive and explanatory or primarily prescriptive and normative. For example, someone might concede that physicians are often seen as fathers, but contend that they should be seen as partners or contractors in order to create adequate moral relationships. If the models are designed to describe and explain health care interactions, the relevant tests should include whether they overlook important facts, whether they distort reality, and whether they illuminate practice better than alternative models. If they are viewed as prescriptive and normative, it is necessary to consider their moral adequacy and feasibility. Thus, it is important to evaluate paternalism in relation to principles of beneficence and respect for persons, the latter implying liberty and treatment as equals. Since I evaluate paternalism as a normative model throughout this book, I now want to consider some evidence regarding descriptive and explanatory models.

As I have already noted, these models vary in several ways, particularly according to whether they emphasize the mutual, free, and active participation of equals or professional dominance with hierarchy, inequality, patient passivity, and limits on the patient's freedom. Paternal, priestly, military, and some bureaucratic images express this professional dominance.[22] Dramatic evidence for professional dominance appears in the way some health care professionals approach their roles. Brian Bird, a physician, argues that the physician's authority is established not only by official documents but also by personal acceptance of the role of "being a doctor."

> Taking this extra step, accepting this role, is not always possible. Some doctors cannot do it. They refuse to be set apart, refuse to see themselves as exceptions. Some may go part way but retain a lingering uneasiness at being called "Doctor," at being revered or regarded in a special way by their patients. . . . They do not see that the role is necessary for both doctor and patient.
>
> Some doctors not only cannot accept this role for themselves, but they cannot tolerate it in other doctors. They argue that patients should be treated as "equals," that the "consumer" should decide how he should be treated. While it is easy to support wholeheartedly the consumer's right to decide what he consumes it is exceedingly dangerous, in my opinion, to do anything to destroy the doctor's sense of his special, even unique, attitude toward patient care, his sense of himself as an exception, someone who has been given the tremendous responsibility of doing to other human beings things that no one else is permitted normally to do. Only then, only when a doctor develops this benevolent but almost arrogant belief that it is right and proper for him to enter intimately into the life of his patients, will his medical skill, including talking with patients, reach a higher than ordinary level.[23]

A prominent descriptive-explanatory version of the paternalist model was developed over many years by the sociologist Talcott Parsons. One of his last statements is representative: "In many respects, the relational nexus which generally becomes involved in health care resembles that of the family, with the physician or other agent of care playing a quasi-parental role which emphasizes the adequate handling of the patient, and the latter playing a quasi-child role."[24] Parsons' classic description of the "sick role" presupposes and reinforces this conception of paternalism. The sick role is not merely a condition of the organism or personality; it is also a set of institutionalized expectations including several rights and responsibilities. The sick person is regarded as a victim of other forces and hence not at fault. He is exempted from ordinary daily responsibilities, and he is expected to seek help from health care agents. The patient's entry into the health care system is an implicit acknowledgement that health is a good and sickness an evil and that "measures should be taken to maximize the chances to facilitate recovery or, if the condition is chronic . . . to subject it to proper 'management.' "[25] By contrast, the fiduciary role of the health care professional is marked by presumptive competence, skills, and ability. The health care professional is "a genuine trustee of the health interests" of his patients; he or she is also assumed to have "moral authority, grounded in the common assumption of health care agents and sick people that health is a good thing and illness by and large a bad thing, and that the balance should, insofar as it is feasible, be altered in the direction of maximizing the levels of health and minimizing the incidence of illness." Indeed, since illness is viewed as a form of "deviance," the health care professional's role involves "social control." Although Parsons stresses that the "sick role" includes active participation (at least to the extent of seeking and cooperating in treatment), it is mainly passive. For Parsons, there is no way to eliminate this functionally specific hierarchy, this irreducible "element of inequality," that permits him to draw on the analogies with parent-child and teacher-pupil relationships.[26] While Parsons uses several metaphors to describe and interpret the relationships between health care professionals and patients, the parental metaphor is the most prominent.

The main difference between Parsons' interpretation of the physician-patient relationship and some other prominent theories such as Eliot Freidson's is not a dispute about hierarchy or inequality in decision-making. It is rather a dispute about legitimation. Parsons emphasizes that the system through shared values legitimates both the physician's and the patient's roles, while Freidson stresses their conflict.[27] In part, Parsons and Freidson disagree about whether the relationship is one of authority or authoritarianism.

Despite dramatic statements of professional dominance in decision-making (such as Bird's) and despite the emphasis on hierarchy and inequality in sociological interpretations, the empirical evidence about models in medical practice is inconclusive. It is impossible to determine with certainty whether the more egalitarian or the more authoritarian models are dominant. Although some data exist, sociologist Bernard Barber rightly concludes,

> we do not have enough specific and carefully collected data for a satisfactory answer. It is nevertheless our impression that the weight of the evidence leans more toward the dominance model. . . . For all the allegations of medical authoritarianism . . . when we look for systematic and solid evidence to support the charge, we do not find it. . . . We do not have direct evidence of physician authoritarianism; nobody has actually observed doctor-patient *interaction* on a systematic

and representative basis with this problem in view, nor has anyone made a systematic study of the *attitudes* of patients or physicians on the matter of authority.[28]

Neither patient dissatisfaction nor patient satisfaction will yield an answer, for either may be attributed, at least in part, to factors other than the mode of physician-patient interaction. Some trends may suggest an increase in free, mutual participation as equals; for example, some studies indicate a dramatic increase over the last twenty years in the number of physicians who have a policy of telling their cancer patients the truth.[29]

Several different metaphors may be required to illuminate physician-patient interactions in various settings. While a descriptive model may not accurately and adequately represent all health care relations, it may represent some aspects of such relations. Probably no single model can satisfactorily represent the whole of any single relationship (such as primary care, secondary care, tertiary care, preventive medicine, and clinical research) and, *a fortiori*, all these relationships. Difficulties sometimes emerge when interpreters try to extend one metaphor or model to the whole range of interactions in research, medicine, and health care. For example, the metaphor of partner or collaborator may be appropriate for some clinical research, while the metaphor of teacher may be more appropriate for some aspects of family practice.[30]

It is not necessary for my purposes to show that the paternal metaphor or the paternalistic model is dominant in health care, or, if it is, whether it is accepted by patients or imposed by professionals. Viewing the health care professional as a father or as a parent may illuminate some features or aspects of health care, but it may not illuminate the whole system. Nevertheless, the paternalistic model is often presupposed in the *justification* of practices, policies, and acts in medicine and health care. It is sometimes explicit, sometimes only implicit. My task is to determine the adequacy of paternalistic justifications in health care. It is thus necessary to define paternalism more precisely.

The Nature of Paternalism

Based on the paternal analogy, paternalism attempts to meet the needs of another person even against that person's wishes. The first feature of paternalism is altruistic beneficence—the aim to benefit another person.[31] The second feature is a refusal to accept that person's wishes, choices, and actions in some circumstances. Paternalism may be defined as a *refusal to accept or to acquiesce in another person's wishes, choices, and actions for that person's own benefit.* As a fusion of beneficence and power, it is prima facie right because it is intended to benefit another person, but, at least in certain modes, it is prima facie wrong because it refuses to acquiesce in that person's wishes, choices, and actions.[32] Whether it is actually wrong will depend on the meaning and weight of various moral principles, especially beneficence and respect for persons.

Following Thomas Szasz and Marc Hollender, we can distinguish two different versions of paternalism, based on two different prototypes.[33] If we take the *parent-infant* relationship as the prototype, the physician's role is active, while the patient's role is passive. The patient, like the infant, is primarily a recipient. This model has clinical applications in such cases as acute trauma, coma, and delirium. A second version takes the *parent-child* (especially adolescent) relationship as the prototype. In this version, the physician encounters a patient who may or may not cooperate. Obviously the patient is more active than in the first version; at least, he or she can obey or refuse to comply. My discussion of paternalism uses the parent-child rather than the parent-infant prototype. Even if the patient is seen as a child, he or she has wishes, makes choices, and acts. The difficult moral questions emerge when the patient's needs, as defined by the professional, conflict with the patient's wishes, choices, and actions. Such questions may arise, of course, even when the patient is in a coma—and thus in an infant-like condition—particularly if she has previously expressed her wishes, perhaps through a "living will," about her treatment under such conditions.

Many discussions and examples of paternalism focus on interference with liberty of action, particularly coercion. For the most part, they are shaped by the way John Stuart Mill formulated the issues in *On Liberty*, which argued against collective, especially legal, coercion except where other individuals are harmed.[34] Thus, philosophers tend to take legal coercion (i.e., the imposition of criminal sanctions) as the paradigmatic paternalistic intervention. For example, Gerald Dworkin defines paternalism as "roughly the interference with a person's liberty of action justified by reasons referring exclusively to the welfare, good, happiness, needs, interests or values of the person being coerced."[35] But the issues of paternalism, patricularly in health care, are broader than coercion, especially legal coercion. Some instances of paternalistic legal coercion are a compulsory sterilization and a court-ordered transfusion for a competent, adult Jehovah's Witness. However, not all interferences with liberty of action are coercive, as Dworkin's definition seems to imply. Coercion is only one mode of nonacquiescence in a person's wishes, choices, and actions. Although coercion is common and perhaps raises the most important and difficult moral questions, it is inadequate to define paternalism as "coercive beneficence."[36] In addition, not all paternalistic actions even involve interference with liberty of action. For example, deception is frequently paternalistic. In case #1, a nurse was instructed to act paternalistically by deceiving a woman who was injured in an automobile accident that killed her daughter. The woman wanted to know about her daughter's condition, but the physician ordered the nurse not to tell her the truth because it would upset her. While the woman was not coerced, and her liberty of action was not infringed, she was subjected to paternalistic deception. It is hardly adequate to hold that paternalistic deception is coercive because coercion would have to be used if deception did not work.[37] As this case indicates, in many instances of paternalism liberty of action is not at stake and coercion is not plausibly involved.

Many definitions identify paternalism with a single mode or means of nonacquiescence in a patient's wishes, choices, and actions, such as coercion. Attempts to recognize other modes or means of paternalism are frequently unsatisfactory. In a recent article, Allen Buchanan, a philosopher, incorporated into his definition misinformation or interference with freedom of information: "paternalism is interference with a person's freedom of action or freedom of information, or the deliberate dissemination of misinformation, where the alleged justification of interfering or misinforming is that it is for the good of the person who is interfered with or misinformed."[38] Although Buchanan's definition rightly includes more than interference with liberty of action, it *omits* a crucial element in paternalism: nonacquiescence in a person's wishes and choices. It has the odd implication that a physician acts paternalistically if *at the patient's request* he withholds information about the seriousness of the patient's condition. But if a professional acquieses in a patient's wishes, choices, and actions, he does not act paternalistically. Finally, even positive services can be paternalistic; for instance, providing food stamps or other in-kind goods instead of money when the recipients really want money.

The target of the benevolence is what distinguishes paternalism from other refusals to acquiesce in an individual's wishes, choices, and actions. By distinguishing some other relevant reasons for nonacquiescence, we can clarify the nature of paternalism. (At this point, I am considering types of reasons rather than their relative strength or weight.)

Perhaps the major reason for nonacquiescence is to protect other individuals or the society. A person's actions are legitimately restricted when they harm other parties without their consent. Mill defended this principle of the prevention of harm: "the only purpose for which power can be rightfully exercised over any member of a civilized community, against his will, is to prevent harm to others. His own good, either physical or moral, is not a sufficient warrant."[39] Mill's principle depends on a sharp and perhaps indefensible distinction between self-regarding and other-regarding conduct, which will be discussed in chapter VIII. When conduct harms, or imposes risks of harm on others, it may be prohibited or regulated. Examples in health care include some compulsory vaccinations to protect the society, forced treatment of adults in order to protect their minor children, and treatment of defective newborns against their parents' wishes.

A second reason for nonacquiescence invokes the principle of justice or fairness, which can sometimes but not always be restated in terms of the harm principle. For example, a person's actions might impose unfair burdens on others by requiring extensive resources to which members of the community have contributed (such as expensive rescue efforts). Thus, fairness not paternalism is one reason for providing medical care rather than money which people could spend as they chose. Because our society would have great difficulty in denying medical care to people who have spent all their money on goods other than insurance, we should provide medical care rather than money in order to avoid serious unfairness and inequities.

A third reason for nonacquiescence might be that a person's wishes, choices, and actions violate some moral principles other than nonmaleficence or justice. For example, some arguments for the legal prohibition of some sexual acts between consenting adults hold that such acts are wrong even if they do not harm others or violate principles of justice and fairness. Some arguments for the prohibition of contraception, sterilization, and abortion contend that they are inherently immoral. They urge the enforcement of morality as such.[40]

Sometimes physicians and other health care professionals appeal to their consciences to explain why they cannot undertake what a patient has requested, such as performing an abortion, or tying tubes, or aiding and abetting suicide. This sort of "conscientious objection" might appear to invoke a different reason than paternalism, moralism, justice, or protection of third parties. But conscientious objection is only the bottom line of an extended argument. Appeals to conscience presuppose other moral standards that shape and form conscience. For example, Eric Cassell's conscientious objection to performing a tubal ligation in case #19 is based on a judgment about E.S.'s welfare.[41] It is paternalistic. In practically all cases, conscientious objection can be restated in terms of the four major reasons for not acquiescing in a patient's wishes and choices. Conscience is usually invoked as a last resort to indicate the centrality of certain reasons in an agent's life: they cannot be violated without a loss of integrity or wholeness.[42] In most cases, but not always, a physician or other health care professional appeals to conscience to support passive nonacquiescence. He or she refuses to participate in or to be an agent in an activity that violates his or her moral principles.

Types of Paternalism

In contrast to other reasons, paternalism appeals to the welfare of the person (or group) whose wishes, choices, or actions are overridden. Rarely is the justification of an act, policy, or practice purely paternalistic. In contrast to *pure* paternalism, there is *impure* paternalism, mixed with other reasons such as prevention of harm to others. For example, in debates about legislation requiring motorcycle helmets some arguments are clearly paternalistic: legislation requiring helmets is designed to protect the motorcyclists themselves. Other arguments strain to show harm to others (such as hazards to passing vehicles) and unfair burdens for ambulance drivers, nurses, and neurosurgeons, as well as for the public. Yet another reason appears to be the conviction that the lifestyle of motorcyclists is immoral or at least unpatriotic.[43] Another example is involuntary sterilization (see case #22). Paternalism is often part of the argument that some mentally retarded persons should be sterilized; sterilization, it is argued, would be in their best interest. But other parts of the argument include prevention of harm to the offspring and to the society. Whether these reasons are sufficient to justify either involuntary sterilization or the requirement of motorcycle helmets is not at issue;

many of them are clearly inadequate (e.g., mistaken theories of the causes of mental retardation may be involved). Rather the relevance and mixture of different sorts of reasons is what is of interest.

A very important distinction regarding the scope of paternalism hinges on the patient's capacity to make his or her own decisions. This is the distinction between *limited* or *restricted* and *extended* paternalism, sometimes called *weak* and *strong* paternalism.[44] Limited or restricted paternalism overrides a person's wishes, choices, and actions for that person's own good because he or she suffers from some defect, encumbrance, or limitation in decision-making or acting. An example is overriding a patient's refusal of lifesaving medical treatment because he is not competent to make a decision as a result of long-term drug use. Few people deny that restricted paternalism is morally acceptable and even obligatory in some cases. It may, however, be an act of benefiting another that does not contravene and perhaps even expresses the principle of respect for persons. As a consequence, some philosophers insist that it is not even "paternalism," at least in any morally interesting sense. Thus, they can mount opposition to all paternalism because they deny that these morally acceptable acts are paternalistic.[45] In light of my definition, I will continue to count restricted paternalism as a genuine form of paternalism. For purposes of justification, it is difficult to determine both the *relevance* and *weight* of particular defects, encumbrances, and limitations in decision-making or acting. This task is complicated because extended paternalism sometimes masquerades as restricted paternalism, presenting value judgments as judgments about competency.

Extended or extreme paternalism protects the individual even though he or she does not suffer from severe defects, encumbrances, or limitations in decision-making. It overrides a person's wishes, choices, or actions because they are risky for that person. Examples are forcing a blood transfusion on a competent, adult Jehovah's Witness who insists that the transfusion will deprive her of everlasting life and withholding information about the risks of urography because it might cause needless anxiety (see case #6). While there is no dispute about whether extended paternalism is really "paternalism," there is great dispute about whether it can ever be justified.

Another distinction, to be amplified in the next chapter, is between promoting good and preventing or removing evil (all of which are in turn distinguishable from not doing evil). *Positive* paternalism involves

the promotion of good, while *negative* paternalism involves the prevention or removal of evil. Both may fall under the duty of beneficence,
as we will see, but it is important to distinguish them and to note that,
ceteris paribus, negative paternalism is easier to justify than positive
paternalism.[46]

If the values used in the assessment of harms and benefits belong to
the patient (i.e., the person acted upon even though he or she may not
be a patient in a medical sense), the paternalism is *soft*. By contrast,
hard paternalism imposes values that are alien to the patient, even
though they may be commonly accepted by the society or by the so-
called "reasonable person."[47] Soft paternalism is, *ceteris paribus*, easier
to justify than hard paternalism. For example, it may be possible to
appeal to a person's own values in deciding whether to seek a court
order for treatment against his wishes when he is incompetent to make
such a decision. It would be more difficult morally to justify treating him
by appealing to values that he had clearly rejected when he was competent.

Another important distinction is between *direct* and *indirect* paternalism. We will concentrate on direct paternalism, in which the person
whose benefit is intended is also the one whose wishes, choices, and
actions are directly overridden. A forced blood transfusion for a
Jehovah's Witness is an example. But indirect paternalism should
not be overlooked, even though examples may not be numerous. If we
ban a product such as cigarettes in order to prevent harm to users, we
restrict the actions of growers of tobacco and manufacturers of cigarettes not because they are harmed but because users are harmed. This
is indirect paternalism: A is restrained in order to protect P. As stated,
indirect paternalism might resemble the principle of preventing harm,
but there is one important difference: indirect paternalism concerns
harms that require what Gerald Dworkin calls "the active cooperation
of the victim" who could avoid the harm if he or she chose to do so.[48]
(In chapter VIII, I will consider whether this "cooperation" can be said
to be voluntary.) Actions that are restricted because they violate the
harm principle usually harm individuals against their will (e.g., drunken
driving, industrial pollution, and manufacture of faulty products).

I use the terms "direct" and "indirect" to characterize these two types
of paternalism because other terms such as "pure" and "impure" are
imprecise and ambiguous. Even Gerald Dworkin, whose use of "pure"
and "impure" gave these terms currency, used "pure" in two different

senses. He introduced "pure" for those interferences with liberty for which *only* paternalistic reasons are offered, but then he also used it for what I have called "indirect" interferences.[49] Paternalism is not "impure" when restraints are imposed on A in order to protect P who cooperates in the harm. Of interest is the *direction* of the efforts to protect P. Even if the efforts are indirect (e.g., restraint of A), they are a form of paternalism. When I use "paternalism" without a modifier, I shall mean direct paternalism.

The prevention of exploitation is somewhat similar to indirect paternalism but may, in fact, be another distinct, nonpaternalistic reason for nonacquiescence in a person's wishes, choices, and actions. Exploitation may be defined as taking unfair advantage of another person's situation in order to benefit oneself or others. Prevention of exploitation would seem to be an extension of prevention of harm and injustice to others. For example, even if we assume that prisoners can give voluntary consent to participate in research despite their environment (the prison considered as a total institution), we may nevertheless decide to prohibit or greatly to restrict their participation in research in order to reduce the possibility of exploitation. Prevention of exploitation is distinct from indirect paternalism, for in the latter the person protected is assumed to consent to his or her harm. In exploitation, however, the individual's situation may make refusal or resistance difficult if not impossible, and it may make consent difficult to monitor. In addition, the individual whose benefit is sought may have his or her freedom directly restricted; that is, P's liberty may be restricted to prevent A from exploiting P.[50]

While I will analyze different modes of nonacquiescence in more detail in chapter V, I now want to distinguish two basic forms of nonacquiescence: *active* and *passive*. In *active* nonacquiescence, a paternalist refuses to accept a patient's express wish or request that she not intervene. Active paternalism thus involves what Robert Nozick calls "border crossings,"[51] such as invasion of privacy, involuntary commitment, and coerced treatment. When claims to nonintervention in wishes, choices, and actions can be stated as negative rights, such as the right of privacy, health care professionals and others have correlative duties of nonintervention.[52]

In *passive* nonacquiescence, a paternalist refuses to carry out the wishes or choices of the patient or to assist the patient in his or her action. If a woman has a negative right to an abortion, no one can interfere with her choice and action. But if she has a positive right, she can claim others' assistance to provide support or perform the abortion. The Supreme Court, in the area of abortion, has recognized the first sort of legal right but not the second. In moral terms, if a woman wants to have an abortion, and a physician thinks that it is not in her best interest, he might engage in active nonacquiescence: he might try to stop her. But if she *wants him* to perform an abortion, and he thinks it is not in her best interest, he might engage in passive nonacquiescence. Most moral debates about paternalism focus on active rather than passive nonacquiescence, in part because the grounds of negative rights are firmer and more widely accepted in our society. But it would be a mistake to ignore positive wishes and passive nonacquiescence, for there are some affirmative duties such as disclosure of information in health care. While passive paternalism is, in general, easier to justify than active paternalism, the existence of such moral duties as disclosure of information in health care complicates matters, as I will argue in chapter VI, when I discuss the principle of veracity, which includes both the duty not to lie and the duty to disclose information. (When I use the term "paternalism," I mean *active* paternalism unless I specifically indicate that it is *passive* paternalism.)

An examination of case #19 should illustrate and illuminate the distinction between active and passive paternalism. E.S., a sexually active 26-year-old intern, requests a tubal ligation, insisting that she has thought about this matter for months, she doesn't like available contraceptives, she doesn't want children, and she understands that tubal ligation is irreversible. When the gynecologist suggests that she might sometime marry and that her future husband might want children, she responds that she would either find another husband or adopt children. She thinks that she is not likely to change her mind and wants the tubal ligation to make it impossible for her to reconsider. She has scheduled a vacation in two weeks and would like to have surgery then.

Eric Cassell has indicated that *he* would not sterilize E.S. as she requested but that his refusal would not be an instance of paternalism. According to his interpretation of paternalism, it is always active and coercive: "The medical response of times past was to assume control over the decision making as though the patient was incapable. That is what is called paternalism and it is justly condemned." Thus, he contends, his refusal to sterilize E.S. would not preempt her decision-making. She could, after all, locate another physician, and he might even have a duty to refer her to another physician. According to Cassell, "as long as mine is not the *final determinant* then it is simply not paternalism."[53] Refusing to carry out an action requested by a patient does not, of course, preclude the patient from securing the service elsewhere. But nonacquiescence can be paternalistic without necessarily eliminating a patient's choice altogether. As long as the physician justifies his refusal to perform the tubal ligation in terms of the patient's benefit, his action is paternalistic. Such passive paternalistic actions may be more easily justified than active paternalistic actions because the physician has no moral duty to satisfy the patient's desires if he finds them incompatible with acceptable medical practice. The physician's conscience merits protection too.

Finally, attempted paternalism should not be ignored. Paternalistic interventions may be attempted without being completed or succeeding. For example, physicians may seek a court order authorizing a blood transfusion for an adult Jehovah's Witness, but the court may reject the request. Or they may unsuccessfully try to have a patient civilly committed. Their actions are paternalistic even though they do not actually secure their object. Their intention makes them paternalistic; they are attempts to override a patient's wishes, choices, and actions for his or her own benefit. Likewise, it is not necessary that the benefit actually be obtained for the act to count as paternalistic. The fact that a court-ordered surgical procedure results in the patient's death does not make it less paternalistic. It is simply unsuccessful paternalism.

Some paternalistic acts may be justified, while others may not be. In order to determine which, if any, are justified, it is necessary to examine the principle(s) of beneficence offered in defense of paternalism. In chapter II, I will explore the meaning and deficiencies of beneficence in several traditions of health care, before turning in chapter III to the principle of respect for persons which constrains and limits (at least some) efforts to benefit patients.

Notes

1. I use the phrase "health care" to indicate the broad range of professionals, practices, policies, and activities under consideration. Interpretations of the phrase "health care" range from the narrow equation with *personal* medical care to the broad inclusion of various activities that may have an impact on health although they are not performed by health care professionals. I do not want to limit this discussion of

paternalism in health care to physicians, medicine, and medical care, although they will receive the most attention. Paternalism is also an important issue for nurses and other health care professionals as well as for health policy. For a good discussion of "parentalism" in nursing, see Martin Benjamin and Joy Curtis, *Ethics in Nursing* (New York: Oxford University Press, 1981), pp. 50–58.

2. *The Compact Edition of the Oxford English Dictionary* (New York: Oxford University Press, 1971). The concept of "paternalism" is common in discussions of political, social, and economic matters. See, for example, Gordon J. Schochet, *Patriarchalism in Political Thought: The Authoritarian Family and Political Speculation and Attitudes Especially in Seventeenth-Century England* (New York: Basic Books, 1975). He interprets Sir Robert Filmer's political theory in *Patriarchia*, against which John Locke developed his contract theory, as "explaining the political order in terms of familial symbols, which meant that political authority was identical with the rule of a father or patriarch over his family" (p. 7). "Parents, and especially fathers, were used as symbols for all persons vested with authority, including masters, teachers, and magistrates" (p. 15). Since the Ten Commandments include an admonition to "honor thy father and thy mother," political authority in a religious context benefitted from this filial duty of obedience. Other examples include Richard Sennett, *Authority* (New York: Alfred A. Knopf, 1980), especially chap. 2, "Paternalism, an Authority of False Love," which concentrates on the "high capitalism" of the 19th century, and John W. Bennett, "Paternalism," *International Encyclopedia of the Social Sciences*, ed. David Sills (New York: Macmillan and Free Press, 1968), Vol. 11, 472–77, which concentrates on economic paternalism in plantation and industrial contexts and on certain patron-client relations in local communities, both of which are often "modeled on roles and terminology of folk kinship systems."

3. David J. Rothman, "The State as Parent: Social Policy in the Progressive Era," in *Doing Good: The Limits of Benevolence*, Willard Gaylin, et al. (New York: Pantheon Books, 1978), p. 69.

4. David V. Erdman, "Coleridge as Editorial Writer," in *Power and Consciousness*, ed. Conor Cruise O'Brien and William Dean Vanech (New York: New York University Press, 1969), p. 197. See also Richard Sennett, *Authority*, pp. 51, 57, et passim.

5. Arthur Kopit, *Oh Dad, Poor Dad, Mamma's Hung You in the Closet and I'm Feeling So Sad* (New York: Hill and Wang, 1960), p. 40.

6. "When I die, my patients will bring neither apples nor tears to my house. Some of them will not even remember my name. 'Some big doctor did the operation,' they will say. But my father—how they loved him! And he loved them! They never knew—how could they?—how little he knew. And he, even he didn't know how little he knew. Not his fault, of course. He wouldn't believe it if he could come back and see what I am going to do to that young man tomorrow morning.

"So one pays for everything. We know more, we can do more; but we are not the fathers to the sick that my father was, and they do not love us." Belva Plain, *Random Winds* (New York: Delacorte Press, 1980), p. 495. I am indebted to Kenneth Crispell for this reference.

7. George Lakoff and Mark Johnson, *Metaphors We Live By* (Chicago: University of Chicago Press, 1980), p. 5. They contend that our conceptual system is largely metaphorical. Their book is one of the most exciting recent discussions of metaphor. See also the valuable essays in Andrew Ortony, ed., *Metaphor and Thought* (Cambridge: Cambridge University Press, 1979), especially Donald A. Schön, "Generative Metaphor: A Perspective on Problem-Setting in Social Policy."

8. Max Black, "Metaphor," *Models and Metaphors: Studies in Language and Philosophy* (Ithaca, N.Y.: Cornell University Press, 1962), pp. 25–47.

9. Paul Ricoeur, *The Rule of Metaphor* (Toronto: University of Toronto Press, 1977).

10. Black, *Models and Metaphors*, p. 40.

11. For structural metaphors, see Lakoff and Johnson, *Metaphors We Live By*.

12. James F. Childress, "Metaphors and Models of Health Care Relationships," unpublished paper. See also the discussion of some of these models by Robert Veatch, "Models for Ethical Medicine in a Revolutionary Age," *Hastings Center Report* 2 (June 1972): 5–7, and Childress, "A Response to Robert Veatch, 'Medical Ethics in a Revolutionary Age,'" *Journal of Current Social Issues* 12, no. 4 (Fall 1975): 20–25.

13. See, for example, Leon Kass, "Ethical Dilemmas in the Care of the Ill: 1. What is the Physician's Service?" *Journal of the American Medical Association* 244 (October 17, 1980): 1815. For a defense of the contractual model, see Robert M. Veatch, *A Theory of Medical Ethics* (New York: Basic Books, 1981), which appeared after this chapter was finished.

14. For a sensitive discussion of the tacit dimensions of judgments in health care, see Larry R. Churchill, "Tacit Components of Medical Ethics: Making Decisions in the Clinic," *Journal of Medical Ethics* 3 (1977): 129–32.

15. The notions of "reverberation" and "systematicity" appear in Lakoff and Johnson, *Metaphors We Live By*, which also uses the language of "highlighting" and "hiding."

16. For military metaphors in health care, see Samuel Vaisrub, *Medicine's Metaphors: Messages and Menaces* (Oradell, N.J.: Medical Economics Company, 1977), chap. 1. See also Susan Sontag, *Illness as Metaphor* (New York: Vintage Books, 1979). I am also indebted to Virginia Warren for suggestions about this theme.

17. This "principle of complete implication" is developed by N. Fotion, "Paternalism," *Ethics* 89 (January 1979): 191–98.

18. Lakoff and Johnson, *Metaphors We Live By*, pp. 54–55.

19. See Anne J. Davis and Mila A. Aroskar, *Ethical Dilemmas and Nursing Practice* (New York: Appleton-Century-Crofts, 1978), pp. 41–42, and Jo Ann Ashley, *Hospitals, Paternalism, and the Role of the Nurse* (New York: Teachers College Press, 1976).

20. For "parentalism," see Martin Benjamin and Joy Curtis, *Ethics in Nursing*, pp. 50–58.

21. Black, *Models and Metaphors*, p. 40.

22. Eliot Freidson, *Professional Dominance: The Social Structure of Medical Care* (New York: Atherton Press, 1970).

23. Brian Bird, *Talking with Patients*, 2nd ed. (Philadelphia: J. B. Lippincott, 1973), pp. 16–17, quoted in Bernard Barber, *Informed Consent in Medical Therapy and Research* (New Brunswick, N.J.: Rutgers University Press, 1980), p. 64. See also Franz J. Ingelfinger, "Arrogance," *New England Journal of Medicine* 303 (December 25, 1980): 1507–11.

24. Talcott Parsons, "Epilogue," in *The Doctor-Patient Relationship in the Changing Health Scene*, ed. Eugene B. Gallagher. Proceedings of an International Conference sponsored by the John E. Fogarty Center for Advanced Study in the Health Sciences, National Institutes of Health, April 26–28, 1976, DHEW Publication No.(NIH) 78–183 (Washington, D.C.: U.S. Government Printing Office, 1978), pp. 445–46.

25. This description of Parsons' position is drawn from one of his last discussions, "The Sick Role and the Role of Physician Reconsidered," *Millbank Memorial Fund Quarterly* 53 (Summer 1975): 257–78. See also Talcott Parsons, *The Social System* (New York: Free Press, 1951), pp. 428–79, and "Definitions of Health and Illness in the Light of American Values and Social Structure," in *Patients, Physicians and Illness*, ed. E. Gartley Jaco (New York: Free Press, 1958).

26. Parsons recognizes greater initiative and activity on the part of patients in chronic and rehabilitative care and in research involving human subjects, but his classic description of the sick role prevents him from being called a "collegialist" in his interpretation of the doctor-patient relationship, as Bernard Barber supposes (relying, incidentally, almost exclusively on Parsons' discussion of research involving human subjects). Barber, *Informed Consent in Medical Therapy and Research*, p. 54.

27. See Freidson, *Professional Dominance*. For a good analysis of Parsons' and Freidson's positions, see Samuel W. Bloom and Robert N. Wilson, "Patient-Practitioner Relationships," in *Handbook of Medical Sociology*, ed. Howard E. Freeman, Sol Levine, and Leo G. Reeder (Englewood Cliffs, N.J.: Prentice-Hall, Inc., 1972), pp. 315–39.

28. Barber, *Informed Consent in Medical Therapy and Research*, pp. 61–62.

29. This evidence is summarized in Robert M. Veatch and Ernest Tai, "Talking about Death: Patterns of Lay and Professional Change," *Annals of the American Academy of Political and Social Science* 447 (January 1980): 29–45. See also chapter VI below.

30. Not all metaphors are what Donald Schön calls "generative metaphors,"

that is, metaphors that set problems in a different way or generate new perceptions of problems. An example of "generative metaphor" appears in Schön's discussion of efforts to improve the performance of a new paintbrush made with synthetic bristles. This new brush applied the paint in a "gloppy" way. All efforts failed to make the artificial bristles work as well as natural bristles. But then someone observed, "You know, a paintbrush is a kind of pump!" Pressing a paintbrush against a surface forces paint through the spaces or "channels" between the bristles. When the researchers compared brushes with natural bristles and brushes with synthetic bristles, while viewing them as pumps, they saw things they had not seen and were able to improve the brushes with synthetic bristles. See Schön, "Generative Metaphor: A Perspective on Problem-Setting in Social Policy," pp. 257–58.

31. When this feature of paternalism is lost, the emphasis falls on decision-making for another person or group without attempting to benefit that person or group. David Roberts writes that "the essence of paternalism to the early Victorian was not benevolence as much as it was control, guidance, superintendence. . . ." *Paternalism in Early Victorian England* (New Brunswick, N.J.: Rutgers University Press, 1979), p. 275. Frequently paternalists in various areas of life (such as politics and economics) are criticized for being "exploitative," i.e., for serving their own interests rather than the interests of others. See John W. Bennett, "Paternalism," p. 472 and Richard Sennett, *Authority*, chap. 2. Later we will examine some of these criticisms in health care. But it is important to note that exploitative abuses of paternalism do not raise any important moral issues: they are to be morally condemned. Paternalism is morally significant in health care because it involves both features: altruistic beneficence (even when benevolence is not the exclusive motivation) and nonacquiescence in wishes, choices, and actions.

32. The terms "accept" and "acquiesce" are not fully satisfactory, for they may suggest that only a passive role is appropriate for the physician or health care professional. But active roles such as disclosing information to make sure that the patient knows what he or she is doing are certainly appropriate. I will examine several different modes of refusing to accept or acquiesce in a patient's wishes, choices, and actions.

33. See Thomas S. Szasz and Marc H. Hollender, "A Contribution to the Philosophy of Medicine: The Basic Models of the Doctor-Patient Relationship," *Archives of Internal Medicine* 97 (May 1956): 585–92; see also Thomas S. Szasz, William F. Knoff, and Marc H. Hollender, "The Doctor-Patient Relationship and Its Historical Context," *American Journal of Psychiatry* 115 (December 1958): 522–28.

34. John Stuart Mill, *On Liberty*, ed. Gertrude Himmelfarb (Harmondsworth, Eng.: Penguin Books, 1976).

35. Gerald Dworkin, "Paternalism," in *Morality and the Law*, ed. Richard A. Wasserstrom (Belmont, Calif.: Wadsworth Publishing Co., 1971), p. 108.

36. Daniel I. Wikler, "Persuasion and Coercion for Health: Ethical Issues in Government Efforts to Change Life-Styles," *Millbank Memorial Fund Quarterly/Health and Society* 56 (1978): 307.

37. Albert Weale, "Paternalism and Social Policy," *Journal of Social Policy* 7 (April 1978): 157–72.

38. Allen Buchanan, "Medical Paternalism," *Philosophy and Public Affairs* 7 (Summer 1978): 372. For an extended critique of another helpful but finally problematic definition of paternalism, see Appendix II, below, which examines the definition offered by Bernard Gert and Charles Culver.

39. Mill, *On Liberty*, p. 68.

40. For a defense of "perfectionism," see Vinit Haksar, *Equality, Liberty and Perfectionism* (New York: Oxford University Press, 1979).

41. See Eric Cassell, "The Refusal to Sterilize Elizabeth Stanley Is Not Paternalism," in *Rights and Responsibilities in Modern Medicine: The Second Volume in a Series on Ethics, Humanism, and Medicine*, ed. Marc D. Basson (New York: Alan R. Liss, 1981), pp. 146–52.

42. See James F. Childress, "Appeals to Conscience," *Ethics* 89 (July 1979): 315–35.

43. See Laurence H. Tribe, *American Constitutional Law* (Mineola, N.Y.: The Foundation Press, 1978), pp. 938–41.

44. See Joel Feinberg, "Legal Paternalism," *Canadian Journal of Philosophy* 1 (1974): 113–116; Feinberg, *Social Philosophy* (Englewood Cliffs, N.J.: Prentice-Hall, 1973); and Tom L. Beauchamp, "Paternalism and Biobehavioral Control," *The Monist* 60 (January 1977): 67 for the distinction between "strong" and "weak" paternalism.

45. Beauchamp, "Paternalism and Biobehavioral Control," pp. 62–80.

46. Joel Feinberg's distinction between "legal paternalism" (to prevent harm to self) and "extreme paternalism" (to benefit the self) is similar, but his categories are not useful since presumably one could use the law for either sort of paternalistic intervention. See Feinberg, *Social Philosophy*, p. 33. Michael Bayles distinguishes "promotive paternalism" and "preservative paternalism." See Bayles, *Principles of Legislation: The Uses of Political Authority* (Detroit: Wayne State University Press, 1978), p. 120.

47. See Rosemary Carter, "Justifying Paternalism," *Canadian Journal of Philosophy* 7 (March 1977): 133–45.

48. Dworkin, "Paternalism," p. 111.

49. *Ibid.*, pp. 108, 111. Henry Sidgwick argues for an "indirect method of paternal interference" because it can "reduce greatly the total amount of attempted coercion by punishing the trader rather than the consumer." Sidgwick, *The Elements of Politics* (London: Macmillan, 1908), p. 137.

50. Tom L. Beauchamp, who views cases of justified, restricted paternalism as extensions of Mill's harm principle and thus not really paternalistic at all, offers this reason for intervention: "There exist supportable grounds for believing that an individual or group or institution serving

the public interest has been or will be *injured* (wrongfully harmed) by the action or negligence of others. (Deliberately exploitative actions provide the strongest, though not the only grounds for injury claims. Informed consent only negatives injury, not harm; however one might give informed consent and still be injured if treated in a way not specifically consented to.)" On these grounds, then, we might refuse to allow a person to sell himself into slavery "because to do so would be to legalize an institution virtually certain to produce *unpoliceable* injuries." "Paternalism and Biobehavioral Control," pp. 71, 74.

The other expansion of Mill's harm principle that Beauchamp permits is to include physical or mental harm by some cause or condition "which is to that party not known or not within its control or both. . . ." (p. 71). But this second condition belongs under "restricted" or "weak paternalism," which Beauchamp insists is not paternalism in any interesting sense.

51. Robert Nozick, *Anarchy, State, and Utopia* (New York: Basic Books, 1974).

52. Not all wishes, choices, and actions are expressible in terms of negative rights (or positive rights). Even when they are not, they may raise moral questions; when they are, the moral burden on the justification of paternalism is even greater. Nevertheless, it is a mistake to suppose that all "paternalistic behavior" involves a violation of moral rights and duties or what Bernard Gert and Charles Culver call "moral rules." See their "Paternalistic Behavior," *Philosophy and Public Affairs* 6 (1976): 45–57, and my critique in Appendix II.

53. See Cassell, "The Refusal to Sterilize Elizabeth Stanley Is Not Paternalism." Contrast Tom L. Beauchamp's essay in the same volume.

II

Duties to Benefit Others

The Principle of Beneficence

In Alison Lurie's *The War between the Tates*, a character says, "I was less morally ambitious than you; I didn't aspire to do good. I only wanted not to do harm."[1] We commonly distinguish between doing good and not doing harm, the latter appearing to constitute the moral minimum in human interactions. Philosophers sometimes use "beneficence" to refer to doing good and "nonmaleficence" to refer to not doing harm.[2] Although not fully adequate, these terms are useful for shorthand purposes. Since paternalism is defined as benefiting others against their wishes, choices, and actions, it is necessary to try to clarify the principle of beneficence, which generates paternalism and provides its moral rationale. Although "beneficence" and "benevolence" are sometimes used interchangeably, I shall distinguish them, using "benevolence" to refer to the will or disposition to benefit others, and "beneficence" to refer to the act of benefiting, or attempting to benefit, others.

There are both broad and narrow definitions of beneficence, the broad definition encompassing nonmaleficence: doing good includes not doing harm. There is warrant for this broad definition because anyone who violates the duty of nonmaleficence cannot be said to have discharged the duty of beneficence. But unclarities remain, for the debate about "beneficent euthanasia" is precisely whether death is always a harm whose infliction is maleficent, and if it is a harm whether it can be outweighed by benefits such as the elimination of pain and suffering. One reason for distinguishing nonmaleficence and beneficence is that doing good sometimes seems to conflict with not doing harm in relation to the same person (e.g., euthanasia) or to different persons (e.g., nontherapeutic research). And in cases of conflict, the duty of nonmaleficence, *ceteris paribus*, has priority.

Offering a broad definition of beneficence, William Frankena distinguishes four elements: (1) One ought not to inflict evil or harm (what is bad), (2) One ought to prevent evil or harm, (3) One ought to remove evil, and (4) One ought to do or promote good.[3] Frankena has arranged these elements in order of priority: the first is more stringent than the second, and so on. And he admits that the fourth—one ought to do or promote good—may be an ideal rather than a duty. Even a broad definition has to encompass distinctions that are important for ordinary moral reflection; for example, the Hippocratic principle *primum non nocere* (first of all, or at least, do no harm) presupposes the distinction between not harming and doing good and gives the former priority over the latter (which it also recognizes in the principle of "benefiting the sick" that I will examine later in this chapter).

A more satisfactory approach is to recognize these distinctions at the outset in order to clarify the different weights of these two principles and their independence as well as the possibility that they may conflict. A major reason for the distinction between the duties of nonmaleficence and beneficence is that the former involves not doing, while the latter involves doing.[4] Beneficence involves positive, affirmative actions. Thus, using Frankena's categories, I would propose the following classification:

Nonmaleficence: 1. One ought not to inflict evil or harm (what is bad)

Beneficence: 2. One ought to prevent evil or harm
3. One ought to remove evil
4. One ought to do or promote good.

Some important features of the principle of beneficence can be explicated by analysis of a recent case. In 1978, Robert McFall, a 39-year-old, unmarried asbestos worker, was diagnosed as having aplastic anemia, which is usually fatal. While there is no cure, the victim's bone

marrow sometimes regenerates spontaneously. Drugs have been effica-
cious in some cases, as have transplants. According to McFall's physician, a bone marrow transplant from a genetically compatible donor
could increase McFall's chances of surviving a year from 25 percent
to 40–60 percent. The physician asked McFall's relatives to undergo
tests to determine their genetic compatibility. McFall's cousin, David
Shimp, was the only relative willing to undergo the tests. The first test—
the HLA test for tissue compatibility—indicated that he was a perfect
match. But then Shimp changed his mind and refused to undergo the
second test to measure genetic compatibility (the mixed lymphocyte
culture test). McFall sought to have Shimp legally compelled to undergo
the second test and to donate his bone marrow. But there is no duty to
rescue in Anglo-American common law. Even a good swimmer is not
legally bound to try to rescue a drowning child, unless he has taken on
the role of lifeguard, or has created the danger by pushing the child in
the water, or has told everyone else not to worry about the drowning
child because he will undertake the rescue. Exactly what was McFall's
lawyer's argument? It was widely reported as an argument about a
person's duty to rescue his cousin by donating part of his body. In fact,
McFall's lawyer used a different argument. He contended that Shimp had
led McFall to believe that he would help when he underwent the first
test. As a result, there was a "delay of critical proportions," prior to
Shimp's refusal. Thus, according to the legal argument, while Shimp had
no duty to intervene, he had a duty not to make the situation worse once
he had intervened. But Allegheny County Judge John P. Flaherty refused to order Shimp to undergo the second test and to donate bone
marrow because "in our law, there's no duty to rescue someone or save
someone's life." Nevertheless, he said, Shimp's refusal to help his cousin
was "morally indefensible."[5]

On what grounds could Shimp's refusal be considered "morally indefensible"? An examination of possible grounds will enable us to determine more precisely the distinction between nonmaleficence and
beneficence so that we can see more clearly what is involved in paternalism, which derives from the principle of beneficence in one of its several
forms.

First, Shimp clearly had a moral duty not to injure or harm McFall.
This duty could imply that any intervention, such as taking the first test,
should not worsen McFall's situation, perhaps by causing delays in seeking alternative treatments. But it is not clear that McFall had any other

options or that Shimp's intervention and subsequent withdrawal wors-
ened McFall's situation any more than an initial refusal would have.

Second, it might be argued that while Shimp had no duty to try to
rescue his cousin, his initial step created expectations that he should not
have breached. But whether his refusal was a morally unwarranted
breach of expectations would depend, in part, on what was conveyed
and even promised to McFall.

Third, if Shimp had been morally indebted to McFall, perhaps because of McFall's previous assistance, he would have had an obligation
to McFall. But it is important to distinguish having an obligation to a
person from having an obligation to do X for that person.[6] There is no
evidence of moral indebtedness in this case. But even if Shimp had an
obligation to McFall, it is not clear that he had an obligation to donate
bone marrow to McFall.

Fourth, apart from specific interactions, it is not clear that the relationship between cousins establishes special moral obligations of beneficence. Even in closer relationships, such as between parents and
children, an obligation to donate bone marrow may depend on prior
actions (such as the parents' explicit or implicit commitments to their
children in procreation).

Fifth, could Shimp have had a duty of beneficence to donate bone
marrow to McFall apart from their kinship and previous actions? Following a long tradition, John Stuart Mill noted that the duty of beneficence is an imperfect duty because we are free to practice it toward
various individuals; we have discretion in its application because no
other party has a correlative right to it.[7] Nevertheless, some philosophers have argued that there is an obligation of beneficence to specific
individuals under some conditions. A has a duty of beneficence to do X
for P: (1) When P is at risk of significant loss or damage (such as
severe injury or death), (2) when A's action is necessary to prevent this
loss or damage, (3) when A's action would probably prevent it, (4)
when the likely harms to A are minimal, and (5) when the benefit that
P will probably gain outweighs the likely harm to A.[8] These conditions
are sufficient to remove A's discretion about acting beneficently toward
P. In the McFall-Shimp case, the first two conditions were clearly met:
McFall was at risk of death, and Shimp's donation was necessary to
prevent it. The third condition was not as clearly satisfied, for the bone
marrow transplant would have given McFall a 40–60 percent chance
instead of a 25 percent chance of surviving a year. The risks to Shimp

were minimal. The necessary 100–150 punctures of the pelvic bone can be painlessly performed under anesthesia, and the major risk is a 1-in-10,000 risk of death from the anesthesia. Bone marrow regenerates itself. Shimp, however, believed that the risks were greater ("what if I become a cripple?") and that they outweighed the probability and magnitude of benefit to McFall, even though there was no medical evidence for his fears.

Finally, Shimp's refusal might be evaluated in terms of an ideal of beneficence, often expressed as love and emphasized by religious traditions. While an ideal of self-sacrifice or "going the second mile" would be morally optional from the standpoint of ordinary social morality, it might also be meritorious and praiseworthy.

As the McFall-Shimp case suggests, the principle of beneficence may operate on several different levels and with varying degrees of specificity and stringency. At its most general level, it is an ideal. Realizing or approximating it may bring praise, but falling short will not bring blame. At another level, there is a duty of beneficence, not only an ideal, but this duty is imperfect in that the agent has discretion about discharging it. Yet this duty may become specific in some circumstances: An individual may have a duty to perform a specific deed or provide a particular benefit.[9] Such specific duties of beneficence may derive from other moral principles and/or roles. For example, if I promise a friend to look after her child, my duty of beneficence toward that child is based in part on my promise.

Most often our duties of beneficence presuppose roles and relationships. Apart from a previously established relationship to a patient or a setting such as an emergency room, the physician is not legally bound to render emergency assistance even when no one else is available. Morally, however, the conditions that I described earlier for the duty of beneficence would create a specific duty. But in most situations, the physician's duty to "come for the benefit of the sick" (the Hippocratic Oath) flows from other duties such as fidelity to explicit or implicit promises, commitments, and contracts. If a health care professional enters into a relationship with a patient, he or she incurs strong duties to prevent and remove harm and to promote good. His or her failure to act beneficently would be a species of breach of faith or contract, injustice, and the like, and would be criticized in those terms. Nevertheless, I shall refer to these duties to benefit others that derive from roles and other moral principles as duties of beneficence for purposes of my analysis of paternalism. Their grounds may, however, be very relevant for determining the extent and content of beneficence.

So far I have asked mainly *toward whom* and *under what conditions* an agent may have a duty of beneficence. Another important question, already partially answered in the discussion of the conditions of the duty of beneficence, is "*who* has this duty?" This duty applies to the society as well as to particular individuals who also have a duty to work for institutions and policies that express benevolence. For example, the provision of health care falls under this duty (although it may also fall under other duties). Insofar as it is a matter of beneficence, the provision of health care by the society may not be as strictly required as some other acts and policies (such as those required by duties not to harm others). Nevertheless, it remains morally important even if it primarily derives from the duty of beneficence, does not involve rights, and is weaker than some other duties.[10]

A final critical question is *who* determines what counts as benefits to be produced and harms to be removed or prevented and how much particular benefits and harms are to count. Is this definitional and evaluative task in the hands of benefactor or beneficiary, of agent or recipient? Let me raise this question of paternalism through an example offered by Joel Feinberg:

> Suppose a stranger approaches me on a street corner and politely asks me for a match. Ought I give him one? I think most people would agree that I should, and that any reasonable man of good will would offer the stranger a match. Perhaps a truly virtuous man would do more than that. He would be friendly, reply with a cheerful smile, and might even volunteer to light the stranger's cigarette.[11]

Whether this moral "ought" is defined in terms of duty and obligation (which Feinberg rejects for this case) or in terms of ideals or virtue makes no real difference, for the central question is whether the stranger's *wishes* determine the content of my acts that fulfill the duty or approximate the ideal of beneficence. Suppose I am convinced by scientific evidence that the stranger's *needs*, in contrast to his wishes, would be served by my refusal to give him a match and by a stern lecture on the risks of cigarette smoking. When there is disagreement about harms and benefits, whose voice is authoritative? At the center of the controversy about paternalism, this question is raised by the application of the principle of beneficence in its various senses. Immanuel Kant held that the recipient should define beneficence: "I cannot do good to any-one according to my concept of happiness (except to young children and the insane), but only according to that of the one I intend to benefit; and I am not really being kind to someone if I force a gift on him."[12] But not all interpretations of beneficence are nonpaternalistic. Many focus on needs rather than desires and preferences. I now want to consider how selected traditions of beneficence—neighbor-love and the Hippo-cratic tradition of patient-benefit—tend to become paternalistic even though their interpreters sometimes recognize principles of constraint such as respect for persons.

The Principle of Neighbor-Love

The principle of love is frequently praised and even mandated within religious traditions. Both Jews and Christians, for example, recognize the duty to "love your neighbor as yourself." Nevertheless, it is inappro-priate to depict a "Judaeo-Christian ethic of love" as though there were a single, monolithic tradition. Against Downie's and Telfer's claim to "provide an analysis of the Judaeo-Christian concept of *agape*," it is sufficient to emphasize the important difference within (as well as be-tween) Judaism and Christianity.[13] Different religious viewpoints may determine (1) *who* counts as a neighbor (e.g., whether the fetus is a neighbor), (2) *which* neighbors are to be preferred in cases of conflict (e.g., near or remote neighbors, members of the religious community or others), and (3) *whether* and *to what extent* the agent should seek his/her own welfare (e.g., whether self-love is legitimate).

These questions have dominated both practical disputes and academic analysis. Very little attention has been devoted to love's tendency to become paternalistic: to meet the recipient's needs, as defined by the agent, at the expense of the recipient's wishes and choices. For example, the most important recent analysis of love, Gene Outka's *Agape*, con-centrates on the second and third questions, mentioning the first in passing.[14] Such an emphasis is not surprising, for if *agape*, active con-cern for the neighbor, transcends ordinary duties not to harm the neighbor, it may even demand self-sacrifice. Thus, it is important to determine the extent to which the agapist may legitimately protect his or her own interests. And if *agape* is universalistic and regards all neigh-bors as equally worthy of concern, how can the agapist distribute time, energy, and the like in situations of scarcity? In conflicts, how may the agapist legitimately use force or coercion (such as in war) against one neighbor on behalf of another neighbor? Can such preferential love be justified?

Obviously, these questions are important and even urgent for an ethic of *agape*. But the propensity of a love-ethic to become paternalistic has been overlooked, or only marginally considered, with unfortunate theoretical and practical consequences. In theoretical discussions, determination of the neighbor's welfare has been neglected: which of the neighbor's "goods" has priority is a particularly difficult question if they conflict in such a way that it is impossible to realize one good without sacrificing another or if the recipient favors one good rather than another. The principle of love becomes paternalistic when conjoined with certain values and beliefs about human nature, the soul, the body, life after death, and so forth. For example, if the agapist believes that suicide not only injures the self but breaks the relationship with God and costs the suicide eternal life, he/she is likely to intervene to prevent it. Thus, religious and other viewpoints may *qualify* morality by appealing to a different set of "facts" (such as life after death) or to a different interpretation and evaluation of the same facts (such as whether an action will lead to ill-health). Defenders of the same moral principle may dispute its application because of their divergent "evaluative descriptions" of the human condition and particular situations. "Evaluative descriptions" of human welfare give *agape* its content.[15]

Outka recognizes and briefly addresses this point: should the neighbor's generic characteristics be distinguished and ranked? Emphasizing that distinctions and priorities depend on more comprehensive doctrines about God and human nature, Outka identifies three characteristics that most commonly appear in Christian ethics: the God-relation, the neighbor's status as a creature including his or her "psycho-physical existence," and freedom including choices, decisions, and preferences.[16] Even these three generic characteristics require further analysis. For example, the second includes physical interests such as health and survival and psychological interests such as affection and self-respect, which may also come into conflict:

> if a person is injured physically or mentally there is often a tendency for friends to help too much; it is often easier to do something for

people than to wait patiently and encourage while they do it for themselves, and this ease and convenience can assume the guise of kindness.
But this may well be a subtle way of eroding an individual's nature as a
person.[17]

Obviously disputes about what love requires will hinge on distinguishing
and ranking various human interests. Perhaps more importantly, they
will hinge on *who* should determine what counts as human interests and
how much different interests should count. Does the agapistic agent or
the recipient have the privileged position for determining which interests
are relevant to human well-being and how much weight they should
have in actions and policies?

Such matters are rarely illuminated in contemporary religious ethics.
In bilateral relations—the self and another—the emphasis is on how
much self-interest is legitimate, and in multilateral relations—the self
and several others whose claims conflict—the emphasis is on which
neighbor(s), if any, the agent should prefer. Such questions emerge in
biomedical ethics as well as in other areas. For example, many health
care professionals have to determine how much self-interest, such as
security, they should sacrifice in order to meet the needs of others. And
sometimes they may have to choose between the needs of different
neighbors—when they distribute a scarce lifesaving medical resource
such as kidney dialysis in the 1960s and early 1970s, or when they
balance the interests of a defective newborn (survival) against the interests of the family (emotional and financial resources). These dilemmas
have received more attention within religious ethics than the conflict
between the health care professional and the patient over the patient's
best interests. As a consequence the constraints upon paternalism within
a love-ethic are not secure and strong.

It is easier for a love-ethic to appreciate the importance and even the
necessity of *justice* in conflicts among the interests of the agapist and
others or among the interests of different people to whom the agapist
responds. *Agape* should not fall below justice toward neighbor, and the
agapist perhaps should sacrifice his own claims of justice in order to
meet the needs of others. When, however, the agapist is not concerned
with his/her own welfare but is directed solely toward the neighbor's
welfare, he or she may not perceive the persistent claims of justice in the
form of various rights that the recipient may assert (such as the right of
self-determination). For example, early in the 20th century, many pro-

gressives and supporters of the social gospel (the latter often a religious version of the former) urged and secured various "reforms" designed to benefit the citizenry. It is difficult to dispute their worthy motives, often expressed as love or benevolence, but their reforms focused on "needs" rather than "rights" and conceived the state as a parent who could meet those needs. In this "parent-child" relation between the state and the citizen, a motivation of benevolence was considered more important than procedural protections and guaranties. One example will suffice: the reform of the juvenile justice system. This reform, undertaken by the "child-savers," appealed to the social gospel for its moral framework. Stressing benevolence and love, it was demonstrably paternalistic. It was more concerned with the "needs" of youthful offenders than with their "rights." In the process it stripped youthful offenders and their families of various procedural protections for their own best interests.[18]

The difficulties that plague a love-ethic also plague related conceptions such as care, compassion, kindness, and mercy, sometimes used interchangeably with but sometimes distinguished from love. The concept of care can serve as an example. It appears in both religious and humanistic contexts, particularly in regard to health care, medical care, and the caring professions. Some theologians even substitute "care" for "love."[19] The interchangeability of the terms can be seen in the parable of the Good Samaritan (Luke 10:29–37), which Jesus uses in response to a lawyer's question "who is my neighbor?" The lawyer's question follows a discussion of a summary of the law: "You shall love the Lord your God . . . and your neighbor as yourself." A man going from Jerusalem to Jericho was beaten by robbers who left him "half-dead." After two other travellers passed him by, failing to render help,

> a Samaritan, as he journeyed, came to where he was; and when he saw him, he had compassion, and went to him and bound up his wounds, pouring on oil and wine; then he set him on his own beast and brought him to an inn, and took care of him. And the next day he took out two denarii (about forty cents) and gave them to the innkeeper, saying, "Take care of him; and whatever more you spend, I will repay you when I come back."

Jesus asked the lawyer which one of these three travellers proved to be a neighbor to the wounded man, and he answered, "The one who showed mercy on him." For our purposes the language of the English translation

(Revised Standard Version) is more significant than the original Greek, for the terms chosen to render the translation reflect contemporary conceptions.

First, as an explication of the duty to love one's neighbor, the Good Samaritan is described as "having compassion" and "showing mercy." In short, he expressed the attitude and discharged the duty of *caring for* the neighbor, both attitudes and actions being required by the principle of neighbor-love. Second, the Good Samaritan "took care of him" and also asked the innkeeper to "take care of him." It is important to distinguish "caring for" (or "caring about") from "taking care of," though the former often is the foundation of the latter. For example, I may "take care of" my neighbor's cat, while she is on vacation without "caring for" either the neighbor or her cat. Perhaps I am merely repaying a favor. And while the Good Samaritan displayed compassion and mercy, the innkeeper may have lacked both and responded instead to the Samaritan's business contract with him.[20]

"Taking care of" others involves skills. The Samaritan and the innkeeper rendered care in various ways, from feeding the injured man to binding his wounds. Because they were not health care professionals, their skills may have been inadequate to take care of the injuries. While there may be a minimum (moral or legal) standard of care that applies to anyone (e.g., "carelessness," however defined, would be excluded), certainly health care professionals, who offer themselves as having certain knowledge and skills, must render "due care," defined in the contemporary context as the degree of care exercised by ordinary professionals in the community.[21]

It is important then to distinguish three notions of care: (1) Caring for others—which involves discharging the duty to care and expressing the attitude of care. (2) Taking care of others—which involves specific acts that provide care and perhaps express care. (3) "Due care"—which, for our purposes, primarily refers to *how* caring for and taking care of others are carried out. We are expected to "take care" and to act "with care" or "carefully" even as we care for and take care of others.

"Care" is thus ambiguous. As Hauerwas notes, "care" is a context-dependent term, whose meaning is indefinite until specified within a particular context, often provided by principles, roles, and institutions.[22] Whether there is a general duty of care, or only role-dependent duties, parallels questions asked about beneficence and love. In both cases, the content of the duty or duties will depend either on general perspectives about human needs and interests or on institutional settings.

An ethic of love or care is basically oriented toward benefiting the neighbor. It is, at least in part, teleological or consequentialist. It considers both the aim and the effects of actions. But some interpreters of biomedical ethics, such as Paul Ramsey and Charles Fried, emphasize that love or care can or must be expressed in, or controlled by, various duties and rights.[23] They contend that moral principles and rules, which may be either independent of or derived from love/care, also determine what should be done. Often they define personal care in medicine in order to defend the interests or claims of individual patients over against the interests and claims of society (such as in clinical research). But several rights or duties, which they recognize, also have implications for personal care when attention is directed solely at the welfare of the individual patient, apart from any conflict with the welfare of others. Whether rights are built into the conception of personal care, or supplement and even constrain it, may not be decisive. Either perspective may be satisfactory, but it is clearer and more helpful to view care as benefit-oriented (both for material benefits and personal gestures) and rights based on respect for persons as indicating the channels of that care.

The Hippocratic Tradition: Patient-Benefit

The Hippocratic tradition is clearly benefit-oriented. It is necessary, of course, to distinguish *motivating* reasons and *justifying* reasons without implying that they may not be identical in many instances.[24] For example, while the justifying reason for an action may be that it accords with the principle of benefiting the sick, the motivating reason may be desire for honor and respect or fear of blame and punishment. Of course, agents may (and should) take justifying reasons as their motivating reasons too. With this distinction, we can better consider the language and theme of benefiting patients in the Hippocratic Oath, which was originally associated with the religio-scientific cult of Pythagoreanism. The "benefit of the sick" serves as the justifying reason for the Hippocratic physician's conduct:

> I will apply dietetic measures for the *benefit of the sick according to my ability and judgment*; I will keep them from harm and injustice. I will neither give a deadly drug to anybody if asked for it, nor will I make a suggestion to this effect. Similarly I will not give to a woman an abortive remedy. . . . Whatever houses I may visit, I will come for the *benefit*

of the sick, remaining free of all intentional injustice, of all mischief and in particular of sexual relations with both female and male persons, be they free or slaves. (emphasis added)

Another summary of Hippocratic morality is: "As to diseases, make a habit of two things—to help, or at least to do no harm."[25]

Paternalism is implied by this benefit-oriented ethic. If we ask "who should decide?," the answer is clear and emphatic: the Hippocratic physician promises to act for the benefit of the sick "according to my ability and judgment."[26] In addition, the promise to keep the sick "from harm and injustice" is also paternalistic. Examining both the text and the context, Ludwig Edelstein concludes that the physician

promises to guard his patients against the evil which they may suffer through themselves. That men by nature are liable to inflict upon themselves injustice and mischief and that this tendency becomes apparent in all matters concerned with their regiment, this is indeed an axiom of Pythagorean dietetics. . . . The physician must protect his patient from the mischief and injustice which he may inflict upon himself if his diet is not properly chosen.[27]

Thus, if Edelstein is correct, the Hippocratic physician has a duty to protect the patient from himself/herself. Paternalism also emerges elsewhere in this short oath. As Konold notes,

The paternalism implicit in the Oath's instruction that the physician refuse his patient's requests in some cases and judge what confidences to keep is an important element of its legacy. . . . This tradition honors the individuality of the doctor-patient relationship, professional secrecy, and the physician's duty to promote the patient's welfare. In these and other matters, ethical formulations by physicians have been paternalistic, making the physician the dominant part in determining what action will best advance both the doctor's and the patient's interests.[28]

Both the form and content of codes of medical ethics deserve attention. First, medical codes emphasize the professional's duties and obligations. While such an emphasis is not surprising or unwarranted, it contrasts sharply with recent developments such as the emphasis on patients' *rights* in "A Patient's Bill of Rights" of the American Hospital Association.[29] Even if rights and duties are, for the most part, correlative, emphasis on one or the other will certainly affect the tone of the code, particularly because the language of rights arms patients and strengthens their agency. Second, while medical codes emphasize certain principles and rules, or duties, such as benefiting and not harming the patient, they rarely include other principles and rules, or duties, such as truthfulness and respect for autonomous choices.[30]

Thus, both the language of physicians' duties, in contrast to patients' rights, and the content of those duties tend to be paternalistic, for they appear to allow and even to require the professional to determine the relevance and weights of benefits and harms to the patient. For example, since, according to the codes, the physician has a duty to benefit (or at least not to harm) the patient and no duty of truthfulness, he may and even should consider carefully whether to tell a terminal cancer patient the truth, especially if the truth might undermine hope and create anxiety and despair.

In accord with the Hippocratic tradition, the Principles of Medical Ethics (1957) of the American Medical Association (AMA) identify benefit of the sick as the main objective of medicine, but they add a clause that could constrain paternalism: "The principal objective of the medical profession is to render service to humanity with full respect for the dignity of man. Physicians should merit the confidence of patients entrusted to their care, rendering to each a full measure of service and devotion." The objective "to render service to humanity," a benefit-oriented approach, may be constrained by "full respect for the dignity of man." While the former can warrant paternalism, the latter can limit it.

The Principles of Medical Ethics (1957) offer an explicit example of "justified" paternalism. Breaches of confidentiality are held to be justified under three sorts of circumstances: "A physician may not reveal the confidences entrusted to him in the course of medical attendance, or the deficiencies he may observe in the character of patients, unless he is required to do so by law or unless it becomes necessary in order to protect the welfare of the individual or of the community." Thus these three exceptions are invoked to justify some violations of confidentiality: legal duties (e.g., to report gunshot wounds, venereal disease, and child abuse), duties to protect the welfare of the community (e.g., to prevent patients from imposing serious risks on other individuals or on the community, perhaps by threats of violence or by health conditions that might lead to accidents involving others), and duties to protect the individual patient. Perhaps the most controversial is the last: the paternalistic breach of confidentiality (e.g., telling a patient's wife that he has some health problem in order to ensure his compliance with treatment). In the 1980 revision of the Principles of Medical Ethics, a new statement on confidentiality no longer makes the physician the judge of "the welfare of the individual or of the community." It holds that the law should determine when the physician should break confidences: "A physician shall respect the rights of patients, of colleagues, and of other health professionals, and shall safeguard patient confidences within the constraints of law" (Principle IV).

This standard of respect for the rights of patients is novel as is also the demand for honesty in physicians' dealing with patients and colleagues (see Principle II). Both depart from the tradition of paternalism. More generally, the first report of the committee established by the AMA to revise its Principles of Medical Ethics appeared to repudiate paternalism: "The medical profession is no longer perceived as the sole guardian of the public health, and consequently the traditional paternalism of the profession is in conflict with society." The shift in tone and substance is striking and may be attributed to numerous factors, including the emphasis on patients' rights in the society, the altered legal situation including the spectre of malpractice, and the increased significance of other health professionals some of whom now define their responsibilities in terms of patients rather than physicians. Whether the code mainly reflects or also directs medical practice, it is too early to determine the significance of these changes in language and substance.[31]

Rarely are we philanthropists, pure and simple. While our duties of beneficence often derive from other principles and duties, codes of medical ethics tend to view them as instances of philanthropy, almost gratuitous in nature. These codes have traditionally distinguished physicians' duties to their patients from their obligations to their teachers and colleagues. For example, according to the Hippocratic Oath, the physician's duties to his patients represent philanthropy and service, while his obligations to his teachers represent debts he has incurred in becoming a physician. Another way to state this distinction is to describe the former as a "code" and the latter as a "covenant."[32] "Covenant" suggests a reciprocal relationship in which there is receiving and giving. But it is not reducible to a contract with a specific quid pro quo, for it also contains an element of the gratuitous which cannot be specified.

As William May stresses, codes of medical ethics tend to view the professional as independent and self-sufficient when in fact in the contemporary world he or she is greatly indebted to the society (for education and privileges) and to patients, past and present (for research and "practice"). Because of this indebtedness, the medical profession's duty of beneficence cannot be construed as mere philanthropy. It is rooted in the "reciprocity of giving and receiving."[33]

This perspective has implications for several areas of biomedical ethics, such as debates about a right to health care. If beneficence is located in a covenant of receiving and giving, if it is a matter of response as well as of initiative, the physician's attitude may and should be significantly different than in philanthropy. This perspective should loosen the professional's grip on the definition of the content of beneficence, that is, on the benefits sought for the patient.[34]

Deficiencies of Beneficence

Beneficence in its various forms provides the justification for paternalistic acts and practices. But it has several deficiencies, particularly in application, that are distinct from limits set by other principles such as respect for persons.

One common argument against paternalistic practices is that their alleged benevolence or beneficence really masks self-interest. Critics frequently claim that paternalism is "an authority of false love" because paternalistic agents seek the other's welfare only insofar as it is in their interest to do so. And it is often in the paternalist's interest as long as the recipient is grateful, subservient, and passive.[35] An even stronger criticism is sometimes heard. Asking whose claim of benevolence toward diseased people should be believed, Robert Burt holds that no one's claim should be wholly believed or disbelieved. He continues,

> Rules governing doctor-patient relations must rest on the premise that anyone's wish to help a desperate, pained, apparently helpless person is intertwined with a wish to hurt that person, to obliterate him from sight. It is not accidental that the injunction to "take care of" someone has a two-edged meaning in popular speech.[36]

While there is little warrant for this strong psychological claim about the paternalist's desire to hurt patients, there is reason to suspect that the paternalist's motives and intentions are not always purely benevolent. But such a conclusion about the motives and intentions of any group, profession, or person should not be surprising. Financial considerations, prestige, and status are no doubt important, as are the concern to save time and energy by cutting corners in explanations and the desire to avoid inconveniences. It is not necessary to accept strong theories of socio-economic determinism, rationalization, or "bad faith" in order to appreciate the importance of these motives. As we have seen, motivating reasons may diverge from justifying reasons. But even when motives are mixed, and even when one motive for beneficence is self-interest, there is no reason to doubt the sincerity of many paternalists: they believe that they act in the patient's best interests, whatever the patient may think. Although it is important to be aware of self-interested reasons for putative beneficence, it is more important to examine other reasons to suspect even sincere beneficence.

The principle of beneficence is both teleological and consequentialist. It is teleological because it involves pursuing goods for others. It is consequentialist because it considers the effects of actions on the welfare of others. A major difficulty in its application is the necessity for prediction and assessment of outcomes, and this difficulty tends to undermine paternalism on its own grounds without appeal to other principles of morality. At any rate, it makes the model of paternalism less plausible. If it is difficult to predict outcomes and if prediction as well as assessment depends on values that are not shared in our society, then paternalism as applied beneficence is perhaps indefensible on its own terms.[37]

Because it is difficult in most situations to produce benefits without some risks, it is necessary to balance risks and benefits, that is, to balance the probability and magnitude of harm and the probability and magnitude of benefit. Application of the principle of beneficence requires judgments about balance; it requires appeal to proportionality. Application is even more complicated, for it is not sufficient for an action to have a favorable risk-benefit ratio and therefore to be expected to produce a net benefit. The action should also have a more favorable risk-benefit ratio than alternative courses of action or inaction. For example, if both X and Y have favorable risk-benefit ratios, they may not be equally acceptable if Y's ratio is more favorable.

It might appear that prediction of consequences such as harm is within the province of medicine, and that the professional's capacity to predict and to control consequences supports a claim of paternalism. But consider two sorts of predictions of harm that paternalistic professionals have to make. In one situation, a paternalist predicts that telling a patient about his terminal cancer would lead to anxiety and even to suicide. But the tendency to over-predict dangerousness is well-known, and the evidence for such a prediction is frequently inadequate. Such predictions depend on insight into persons that is not necessarily a matter of medical expertise or even of psychiatric expertise (which most physicians lack anyway). Samuel Johnson once insisted, "I deny the lawfulness of telling a lie to a sick man for fear of alarming him. You have no business with consequences; you are to tell the truth. Besides, you are not sure what effects your telling him that he is in danger may have."[38]

In another situation, a paternalist predicts that a Jehovah's Witness will lose her life without a blood transfusion or that an elderly woman will die without amputation of her gangrenous foot. These predictions would appear to be medical judgments, based on experiences with similar diseases or injuries. But they may not be sufficient to justify medical paternalism. Not only are medical judgments fallible,[39] but value considerations "dictate the manner in which uncertainty as to the potential adverse consequences will be resolved."[40] To some persons, the absence of evidence that harm will result is taken as evidence that the harm will not result.

In addition, the categories of "harm" and "benefit" are not clinical. Some philosophers argue that most, if not all, of our language of health and disease is value-laden.[41] Even diagnostic and prognostic judgments presuppose values that are rarely articulated much less defended. Szasz and Hollender offer an example:

> This question is often posed: Is surgical, medical or psychiatric treatment the "best" for peptic ulcer? Unless we specify conditions, goals, and the "price" we are willing to pay (in the largest sense of the word), the question is meaningless. In the case of peptic ulcer, it is immediately apparent that each therapeutic approach implies a different conception of "disease" and correspondingly divergent notions of "cure."[42]

It is not necessary to argue that all categories of disease, diagnosis, and prognosis are equally value-laden. Values pervade enough categories and judgments to make us cautious about simply accepting clinical judgments as final, because they may presuppose values that are not articulated or defended and that would be opposed if stated.

Even though we lack a value consensus in our pluralistic society, much medical practice operates on a presumed consensus. To be sure, there is a moral presumption in favor of patient choice at many points (such as the importance of informed consent at various stages in treatment and research). But because of a presumed value consensus, medical practice is often paternalistic until questions are raised. As Wendy Carlton notes,

> Unless one of the parties to a clinical decision makes explicit the lack of value consensus, as when the patient asserts religious beliefs, the illusion of consensus will be assumed and maintained. In particular, the physician's judgment of what is in the best interest of the patient will be offered and accepted, unless the patient or the hospital administrator [or some other agent] is prepared to challenge the physician.[43]

If there were no disagreements about values and ends, decisions would be technical because they would involve only reasoning about means to ends; perhaps then they could be delegated to experts. But expertise in instrumental rationality does not ensure expertise in substantive rationality, and the latter is often at stake in paternalism and at dispute in a pluralistic society.

Paternalism is widespread in health care not simply because beneficence tends to become paternalistic or because professionals desire power. To a great extent, health care professionals are paternalistic in response to social expectations. Paternalism is not merely assumed, it is assigned. Yet social expectations are complex and perhaps even contradictory. As Carlton observes, our society wants to expand and to contract medical responsibility and authority at the same time.[44]

On the one hand, our society tends to urge professional concern with the "whole person" and to "medicalize" more and more areas of life. Among the many indications of this tendency is the World Health Organization definition of health as "complete physical, mental and social well-being."[45] If such a definition were taken seriously, medical responsibility and authority would be greatly expanded. Another indication is the eagerness of many to transform such problems as alcoholism into medical problems, subject to medical management. Many segments of society also call for medical and health care professionals to exercise greater and greater social responsibility.

On the other hand, our society tends to limit medical power and authority. For example, it reduces medical discretion by various moral and legal rules, particularly by requiring informed consent, granting patients more power in decision-making, and ensuring greater liberty and equality on the part of patients. From this standpoint, problems of biomedical ethics are not only problems about, but mainly problems of, patients, who should be making their own choices. Patients would then become final interpreters of beneficence. In its extreme version, this tendency would make the physician only a technician.

Whereas children usually have little choice, at least up to a certain age, about subjection to parental authority, patients have more options. Paternalism in health care depends to a great extent on patient acceptance. If it is effective, paternalism presupposes trust, which involves putting oneself in the hands of others. Trust cannot exist where there is total control over others. Of course, because of the complexity of human interactions, many acts are mixtures of trust and control; but insofar as control is present, trust is to that extent impossible. Trust requires the possibility of betrayal. Attempts to impose controls often stem from distrust. For example, one aim of the contract model is to substitute control for trust in medical relationships.[46]

While trust presupposes the absence of control, it is, nevertheless, an attitude of expectation about the other's actions. Trust involves confidence in and reliance upon the other to act in certain ways. Although "trust" sometimes refers to expectations that another's behavior will be consistent with his public face, it has a narrower meaning: it is confidence in and reliance upon others to act morally. But morality has several different rules and principles, including beneficence and respect for persons. I am concentrating on beneficence, the rationale for paternalism, before turning to the principle of respect for persons. The question is whether trust in health care professionals to act as paternalists, that is, as beneficent decision-makers on our behalf, is warranted.

The decline of trust in medical relationships has been widely noted and deplored. The increase in medical malpractice suits is only one indication.[47] Such a decline in trust does not necessarily imply that physicians and other health care professionals are no longer committed to the moral principles that form the basis for trust. Several reasons for withholding or withdrawing trust from another person do not impugn his or her commitment to moral principles. For example, we may attribute the best intentions to a physician but refuse to trust him because we think he lacks the skills, intelligence, or imagination to fulfill the trust. Or we may express only partial trust by offering precise instructions and by viewing the interaction in contractual terms.

Several developments have lessened trust in the professional's interpretation and application of the principle of beneficence. The first
change—pluralism in values—has already been mentioned. In a pluralistic society, it is not possible to establish clear and universal standards
of benefit and harm. Thus, the likelihood and the rationality of trust are
diminished. Encounters with health care professionals have been characterized as encounters among strangers because of the absence of shared
values. As Alasdair MacIntyre notes,

> Where a community of moral and metaphysical beliefs is lacking, trust
> between strangers becomes much more questionable than when we
> can safely assume such a community. Nobody can rely on anyone
> else's judgments on his or her behalf until he or she knows what the
> other person believes. It follows that nobody can accept the moral
> authority of another in virtue simply of his professional position. We
> are thrust back by our social condition into a form of moral autonomy.[48]

A second change is the decline of close, intimate contact over time
among professionals and patients and their families. Third is the decline
of contact with the "whole person," who is now parcelled out to various
specialists. Fourth is the growth of large, impersonal, and bureaucrati-
cally structured institutions of care. In these institutions there is discontinuity of care (the patient may not see the same professionals on
subsequent visits).[49] In a more traditional community, bound by shared
values, close ties, and intimate contacts over time, some of the conditions for the model of paternalism, or even the model of friendship, may
be present. But these conditions are no longer met in our society (if they
ever really were).

Even where there is estrangement, trust may still be possible. It may
have a different content, and it may be combined with increased control.
As reconceived in a pluralistic setting, trust may be confidence in and
reliance upon health care professionals to respect persons and their
rights. These rights within health care, as distinct from rights to health
care, may limit and constrain the professional's actions even when they
are directed at the patient's welfare.

Even "strangers" may be "friendly." They may be strangers because
of differences regarding values; they may be friendly because they accept
common rules and procedures. If consensus exists in a pluralistic society, it is primarily about rules and procedures. When agents disagree
about primary virtues, which concern the "what" of action, or when

their agreement cannot be presumed or known, interactions often depend on secondary virtues, which concern the "how" of action.[50] In such a setting, trust may presuppose commitment to secondary virtues and to procedures (such as not declaring a person dead unless certain conditions are met). It may involve respect more than care. Trust may express itself as confidence in and reliance upon others to adhere to moral limits that derive from respect for persons and their rights. The principle of respect for persons is not simply one value among others in a world of conflicting values. It limits the pursuit of any value even for another person. It thus constrains even beneficence, love, and care.

Notes

1. Alison Lurie, *The War Between the Tates* (New York: Warner Books, 1975), p. 271.
2. See W. D. Ross, *The Right and the Good* (Oxford: Clarendon Press, 1930), pp. 21–23.
3. William K. Frankena, *Ethics*, 2nd ed. (Englewood Cliffs, N.J.: Prentice-Hall, 1973), p. 47. The National Commission for the Protection of Human Subjects of Biomedical and Behavioral Research articulated three principles—respect for persons, beneficence, and justice. See *The Belmont Report: Ethical Principles and Guidelines for the Protection of Human Subjects of Research*, DHEW No. (OS) 78-0012, 1978. For a defense of a broader range of moral principles, as well as the distinction between nonmaleficence and beneficence, see Tom L. Beauchamp and James F. Childress, *Principles of Biomedical Ethics* (New York: Oxford University Press, 1979).
4. For debate about these matters, see Bonnie Steinbock, ed., *Killing and Letting Die* (Englewood Cliffs, N.J.: Prentice-Hall, 1980), especially Philippa Foot, "The Problem of Abortion and the Doctrine of the Double Effect" and Nancy Davis, "The Priority of Avoiding Harm."
5. The case is *McFall* v. *Shimp*, No. 78-17711 In Equity (C.P. Allegheny Country, Penn., July 26, 1978). My discussion draws upon the *International Herald Tribune*, August 12–13, 1978; "Court Upholds Refusal to be Medical Good Samaritan," *Science* 201 (August 18, 1978): 596–97; and Alan Meisel and Loren H. Roth, "Must a Man Be His Cousin's Keeper?" *Hastings Center Report* 6 (October 1976): 5–6.
6. See A. I. Melden, *Rights and Right Conduct* (Oxford: Basil Blackwell, 1959).
7. John Stuart Mill, *Utilitarianism*, in *Utilitarianism and Other Writings*, ed. Mary Warnock (New York: New American Library, 1974), pp. 304–06. See also Immanuel Kant, *Groundwork of the Metaphysic of Morals*, trans. H. J. Paton (New York: Harper and Row, 1964), pp. 90–91.

8. Except for one major modification, this list is drawn from Eric D'Arcy, *Human Acts: An Essay in their Moral Evaluation* (Oxford: Clarendon Press, 1963), pp. 56–57. The major modification is the addition of the fourth condition, which is necessary because otherwise one might have an obligation to yield one's life in order to save two lives. Such an obligation would be too extreme even though it would satisfy D'Arcy's conditions of risk-benefit analysis.

9. John Stuart Mill and others contend that omissions can count as *causes* of harm. Mill writes, "A person may cause evil to others not only by his actions but by his inaction, and in either case he is justly accountable to them for the injury." *On Liberty*, ed. Gertrude Himmelfarb (Harmonds-worth: Penguin, 1976), pp. 136–37. From this perspective one could claim that while Shimp did not actively violate the duty of nonmale-ficence, he nevertheless caused harm to McFall by his omission—his failure to act—and thus violated the duty of nonmaleficence. This line of argument sometimes appears in Marxist interpretations of violence. See John Harris, "The Marxist Conception of Violence," *Philosophy and Public Affairs* 3 (Winter 1974) and John Kleinig, "Good Samaritanism," *Philosophy and Public Affairs* 5 (Summer 1976). A good rejoinder to both articles can be found in Eric Mack, "Bad Samaritanism and the Causation of Harm," *Philosophy and Public Affairs* 9 (Spring 1980): 230–59.

10. See James F. Childress, "A Right to Health Care?" *Journal of Medicine and Philosophy* 4 (June, 1979): 131–47.

11. Joel Feinberg, "Supererogation and Rules," in *Ethics*, ed. Judith J. Thomson and Gerald Dworkin (New York: Harper and Row, 1968), p. 392.

12. Immanual Kant, *The Doctrine of Virtue: Part II of the Metaphysic of Morals*, trans. Mary J. Gregor (New York: Harper and Row, 1964), p. 122.

13. See R. S. Downie and Elizabeth Telfer, *Respect for Persons* (New York: Schocken Books, 1970), p. 10. For various interpretations of *Agape* within Christian ethics, mainly since 1930, see Gene Outka, *Agape: An Ethical Analysis* (New Haven: Yale University Press, 1972). Jewish positions are represented in *Contemporary Jewish Ethics*, ed. Menachem Marc Kellner, (New York: Sanhedrin Press, 1978), esp. chaps. 9 and 10.

14. See Outka, *Agape*, p. 268. For a discussion that focuses on whether *agape* as altruistic beneficence invalidates or yields the "ordinary moral network" of rights and duties, see John P. Reeder, Jr., "Assenting to Agape," *The Journal of Religion* 60 (January 1980): 17–31.

15. For a discussion of religion *qualifying* morality, see James M. Gustafson, *Can Ethics Be Christian?* (Chicago: University of Chicago Press, 1975).

16. Outka, *Agape*, pp. 263–67.

17. Downie and Telfer, *Respect for Persons*, p. 21.

18. Anthony Platt, "The Triumph of Benevolence: The Origins of the Juvenile Justice System in the United States," in *Criminal Justice in*

America, ed. Richard Quinney (Boston: Little, Brown, 1974) pp. 356–88 and Steven L. Schlossman, *Love and the American Delinquent: The Theory and Practice of "Progressive" Juvenile Justice, 1825–1920* (Chicago: University of Chicago Press, 1977), pp. 191–92. See also David J. Rothman, "The State as Parent: Social Policy in the Progressive Era," in Willard Gaylin, et al. *Doing Good: The Limits of Benevolence* (New York: Pantheon Books, 1978), pp. 67–96.

19. For example, in *On Human Care: An Introduction to Ethics* (New York: Abingdon Press, 1977), Arthur J. Dyck discusses love rather than care, apparently viewing them as identical. For a phenomenological interpretation of care, see Milton Mayeroff, *On Caring* (New York: Harper and Row, 1971).

20. I do not contend that "taking care of" and "caring for" are always used in just the ways I have indicated, for our language does not always demarcate such differences. A recent book on law in doctor-patient relations is entitled *Taking Care of Strangers: The Rule of Law in Doctor-Patient Relations* by Robert A. Burt (New York: Free Press, 1979). Burt's thesis is expressed in the double-edged meaning of the injunction to "take care of" someone, which may not mean to render care but to hurt and even kill; for example, in popular literature, a criminal may threaten to "take care of" someone.

21. Charles Fried explicates the notion of negligence: "In general, one acts negligently in failing to abide by the standard of due care. The concept of due care is compounded of two elements. First, in requiring that a person act reasonably the law invites an inquiry into the purposes of his action. If an actor's goal is sufficiently important and urgent, then he may be justified in imposing a corresponding level of risk of those who are in his way. Second, due care refers also to the way in which the (let us assume) proper goal is pursued. It may be quite proper to exceed the speed limit when driving an ill person to the hospital for emergency treatment, but one is still obliged to use due care as one drives, by keeping a lookout, sounding the horn and so on." *Medical Experimentation: Personal Integrity and Social Policy* (New York: American Elsevier Publishing Co., 1974), pp. 16–17. See also William L. Prosser, *Handbook of the Law of Torts*, fourth ed. (St. Paul, Minn.: West Publishing Company, 1971), chap. 5, "Negligence: Standard of Conduct."

22. Stanley Hauerwas, "Care," *The Encyclopedia of Bioethics*, ed. Warren T. Reich (New York: Free Press, 1978), Vol. I, p. 145.

23. See Paul Ramsey, "Conceptual Foundations for an Ethics of Medical Care: A Response," in *Ethics and Health Policy*, ed. Robert M. Veatch and Roy Branson (Cambridge, Mass.: Ballinger Publishing Co., 1976), esp. pp. 47 and 51, and *The Patient as Person: Explorations in Medical Ethics* (New Haven: Yale University Press, 1970). Charles Fried writes: "In developing my ideas regarding this concept of personal care I have been greatly aided by P. Ramsey, *The Patient as Person* (1970), where very similar notions are developed." Fried, *Medical Experimentation*,

p. 67, fn. 27. There are important differences. For example, Fried uses the language of rights, while Ramsey tends to avoid it because it is too individualistic. Instead, Ramsey uses the language of duties. Whereas Fried emphasizes autonomy, Ramsey pays little attention to it, perhaps in part because of his emphasis on objective goods such as the sanctity of life. See also Ramsey, *Ethics at the Edges of Life: Medical and Legal Intersections* (New Haven: Yale University Press, 1978) and James F. Childress, "Ethical Issues in Death and Dying," *Religious Studies Review* 4 (July 1978): 180–88.

24. See William K. Frankena, "Obligation and Motivation in Recent Moral Philosophy," in *Essays in Moral Philosophy*, ed. A. I. Melden (Seattle: University of Washington Press, 1958), pp. 40–81, esp. 44–45.

25. Hippocrates, "Epidemics" 1: 11, in *Hippocrates*, ed. W. H. S. Jones (Cambridge: Harvard University Press, 1923), Vol. I, p. 165.

26. Although this statement occurs in the context of a pledge regarding dietetic medicine, its significance is more general. Also, while the Pythagorean physician practiced dietetics and pharmacology, he did not practice surgery, not because he opposed it but because he reserved it for others. See Ludwig Edelstein, "The Hippocratic Oath: Text, Translation, and Interpretation," in *Ancient Medicine: Selected Papers of Ludwig Edelstein*, ed. Owsei Temkin and C. Lillian Temkin (Baltimore: The Johns Hopkins University Press, 1967).

27. *Ibid.*, pp. 23 and 25.

28. Donold Konold, "Codes of Medical Ethics: History," *The Encyclopedia of Bioethics*, Vol. I, pp. 164 and 170. See also Robert M. Veatch, "Codes of Medical Ethics: Ethical Analysis," *The Encyclopedia of Bioethics*, I, pp. 172–79 for further discussion of paternalism in medical codes. Veatch has a longer and fuller analysis in "The Hippocratic Ethic: Consequentialism, Individualism, and Paternalism," in *No Rush to Judgment: Essays on Medical Ethics*, ed. David H. Smith and Linda M. Bernstein (Bloomington: The Poynter Center, Indiana University, 1978), pp. 238–64.

29. American Hospital Association, "A Patient's Bill of Rights," reprinted in Beauchamp and Childress, *Principles of Biomedical Ethics*, Appendix II. See also George J. Annas, *The Rights of Hospital Patients: The Basic ACLU Guide to a Hospital Patient's Rights* (New York: Avon Books, 1975).

30. See Sissela Bok, "The Tools of Bioethics," in *Ethics in Medicine: Historical Perspectives and Contemporary Concerns*, ed. Stanley Joel Reiser, Arthur J. Dyck, and William J. Curran (Cambridge: The MIT Press, 1977), pp. 137–41.

31. See Robert M. Veatch, "Professional Ethics: New Principles for Physicians," *Hastings Center Report* 10 (June 1980): 16–19.

32. This distinction was suggested but not developed by Edelstein, "The Hippocratic Oath." It has been developed with elegance and insight by William F. May, "Code and Covenant or Philanthropy and Contract?"

in *Ethics in Medicine*, ed. Reiser, Dyck, and Curran, pp. 65–76, which has greatly influenced these paragraphs.

33. See May, "Code and Covenant. . . ." Although the terms "duty" and "obligation" are frequently used interchangeably, they are sometimes distinguished: "duty" depends on status and "obligation" on voluntary acts such as accepting benefits. Such a distinction is embedded in the tradition of medical ethics in the West, but I will continue to use the terms interchangeably in this book.

34. For a failure to recognize these matters, or perception through a glass darkly, see Carleton B. Chapman, "On the Definition and Teaching of the Medical Ethics," and, especially, H. Thomas Ballantine, Jr., "Annual Discourse—The Crisis in Ethics, Anno Domini 1979," *New England Journal of Medicine* 301 (September 20, 1979): 630–34 and 634–638. The latter stresses the physician's position of *noblesse oblige* but recognizes the privileges that society has bestowed on the medical profession. The tension between these points is never identified much less resolved.

35. See Richard Sennett, *Authority* (New York: Alfred A. Knopf, 1980) and Rothman, "The State as Parent."

36. Burt, *Taking Care of Strangers*, vi.

37. A good attack on medical paternalism on its own grounds appears in Allen Buchanan, "Medical Paternalism," *Philosophy and Public Affairs* 7 (1978): 370–90.

38. Boswell, *Life of Johnson*, as quoted in Alan Donagan, *Theory of Morality* (Chicago: University of Chicago Press, 1978), p. 89.

39. See Samuel Gorovitz and Alasdair MacIntyre, "Toward a Theory of Medical Fallibility," *Hastings Center Report* 5 (December 1975): 13–23.

40. Harold P. Green, "The Risk-Benefit Calculus in Safety Determinations," *George Washington Law Review* 43 (1975): 799.

41. For this debate, see *Concepts of Health and Disease: Interdisciplinary Perspectives*, ed. Arthur J. Caplan, H. Tristram Engelhardt, Jr., and James J. McCartney (Reading, Mass.: Addison Wesley, 1981).

42. Thomas S. Szasz and Marc H. Hollender, "A Contribution to the Philosophy of Medicine: The Basic Models of the Doctor-Patient Relationship," *Archives of Internal Medicine* 97 (May 1956): 589–91.

43. Wendy Carlton, *"In Our Professional Opinion. . . ." The Primacy of Clinical Judgment over Moral Choice* (Notre Dame, Ind.: University of Notre Dame Press, 1978), pp. 5–6.

44. *Ibid.*, pp. 6, 178–79, et passim.

45. See "Constitution of the World Health Organization," reprinted in Beauchamp and Childress, *Principles of Biomedical Ethics*, pp. 284–85; for an extended discussion, see Daniel Callahan, "The WHO Definition of Health," *Hastings Center Studies* 1, no. 3 (1973): 77–87. It should also be noted that arguments about allocation of resources for health care needs and desires sometimes spill over into debates about paternalism. For example, a strong defense of the *discontinuity* between health

care needs and other needs or desires might be used to support increased resources for health care. But if there is such a discontinuity, it tends to support overriding a person's desires in order to meet his or her health needs. Nevertheless, it is one matter to hold that we are giving X a scarce drug because she needs it and because she has as much right to it as anyone else. It is another to hold that we are giving X a drug because she needs it although she doesn't want it and even refuses it. On discontinuity and continuity among needs and desires, see Childress, "A Right to Health Care?"

46. For a fuller analysis of trust, see James F. Childress, "Nonviolent Resistance: Trust and Risk-taking," *Journal of Religious Ethics* 1 (1973): 87–112.

47. Although I do not deal with mutual trust within the physician-patient interaction, this is an important matter. Perhaps physicians feel that they have to practice defensive medicine in part because they can no longer trust patients who are prone to file malpractice suits.

48. Alasdair MacIntyre, "Patients as Agents," in *Philosophical Medical Ethics: Its Nature and Significance*, ed. Stuart F. Spicker and H. Tristram Engelhardt, Jr. (Boston: D. Reidel Publishing Co., 1977).

49. On the conditions of the decline of trust, see Michael Jellinek, "Erosion of Patient Trust in Large Medical Centers," *Hastings Center Report* 6 (June 1976): 16–19.

50. This distinction is drawn by Alasdair MacIntyre in *Secularization and Moral Change* (London: Oxford University Press, 1971), p. 24. See also John Rawls, *A Theory of Justice* (Cambridge: Harvard University Press, 1971), p. 519. As Thomas Hobbes noted, "form is power, because, being a promise of good, it recommends men to the favor of women and strangers." *Leviathan*, Parts I and II (Indianapolis: Bobbs-Merrill, 1958), p. 79.

III

Respect for Persons

Respect, Love, and Benevolence

Several philosophers contend that the principle or attitude of respect for persons is the same as, or at least an explication of, the principle or attitude of neighbor-love (*agape*).[1] Such an identification or explication is problematic for several reasons.

First, we can love a person without respecting him and respect him without loving him. This point may appear to apply mainly to love as a feeling or as liking a person, but it also applies to love as an active determination of the will toward the welfare of the neighbor and also to active benevolence or beneficence. Seeking a neighbor's welfare is not identical to respecting him even if we include freedom and respect among the goods that we seek for him. Indeed, the provision of goods essential to welfare out of love or benevolence frequently displays disrespect and leads to the recipient's loss of self-respect. Thus, as Kant suggested, "we shall recognize an obligation to help a poor man; but since our favour humbles him by making his welfare dependent on our generosity, it is our duty to behave as if our help is either what is merely due to him or but a slight service of love, and so to spare him humiliation and maintain his self-respect."[2]

Second, the principle of respect for persons presupposes and even maintains *distance* between persons. It recognizes their separateness, or at least their distinctiveness, and their independence. It thus tends to be noninterventionist. Neighbor-love, however, is more likely to cross the borders that mark independent persons and to intervene, particularly if it is based on objective criteria of human well-being rather than subjective preferences of recipients.

Third, love or beneficence requires *positive* action on behalf of the neighbor, whether in promoting good or preventing and removing evil. Respect for persons need not, however, involve positive action; it appears primarily in negative duties (such as the duty not to treat persons merely as means to ends), in negative rights and liberties (such as the right to noninterference), and in constraints and limits.

Fourth, the *range* of the principle of respect for persons is more restricted than the range of the principle of love or beneficence, for the latter may apply to all sentient creatures and to all human beings, even those who lack certain capacities as persons (such as rationality). It is possible that some constraints of the principle of respect for persons do not apply in interactions with persons of seriously diminished autonomy and that in such cases our conduct should be determined by the principle of beneficence. Thus, weak paternalism may be more easily justified because it may not violate the principle of respect for persons.

Insofar as love or beneficence is directed toward persons, I will argue that it needs to be limited and constrained by the principle of respect for persons. In part, this means identification with the projects of others who are ends in themselves. It is not even sufficient to state, as Kant does, that love is the "duty of making others' *ends* my own (in so far as these ends are only not immoral)."[3] For respect for persons is not only a matter of pursuing and promoting ends, but of respecting whatever choices a person makes, at least within the limits set by moral principles and rules. Perhaps it is better to say not that we should respect his *ends*, but that we should respect them as *his* ends, i.e., as his representation of his values, purposes, and choices.

Whatever the case with the principle of beneficence, the principle of respect for persons may encompass the principle of nonmaleficence (the noninfliction of harm) so that any violation of the latter would also be a violation of the former. Surely the unjustified infliction of harm on persons displays disrespect toward them. Whether the principle of respect for persons transcends the principle of nonmaleficence (such as by proscribing offensive and insulting conduct) depends on the breadth of the definition of harm. The object of harm is always an interest, and persons have various interests that may be harmed, such as health, property, reputation, dignity, privacy, and liberty. If we take a broad definition of harm to include all personal interests, then the duty of nonmaleficence would include most, if not all, of the content of respect for persons. If we take a narrow definition of harm and concentrate on physical and mental harms in contrast to other interests, then the duty of respect for persons would prohibit harms to interests in dignity and the like.

As we have seen, responding to persons and respecting them is not identical with meeting their needs. It is possible to meet their needs without responding to and respecting them as persons. The distinction between persons and roles is also necessary: to respect persons is to refrain from reducing them to roles and functions and to refrain from seeing them only from certain limited points of view. Bernard Williams stresses the distinction "between regarding a man's life, actions or character from an aesthetic or technical point of view, and regarding them from a point of view which is concerned primarily with what it is *for him* to live that life and do those actions in that character."[4] This would imply, for instance, that a sick person is never to be regarded merely as a holder of the sick role, as a patient, or as the object of technological power. Even if, by and large, we do not encounter persons except through roles, they are still persons in and through those roles and should be respected as such. Thus, as Williams elaborates, "each man is owed an effort at identification: that he should not be regarded as the surface to which a certain label can be applied, but one should try to see the world (including the label) from his point of view."

Persons have intentions and purposes and regard themselves and their world in certain ways. They have both beliefs and values that inform their choices and actions. At the risk of excessive rationalization of personal life, we can say, in Charles Fried's language, that persons have "life plans" and "risk budgets." Each person has at least an inchoate life plan that comprises values and ends. It also includes a risk budget, for people are willing to accept some risks to health and survival in order to express and realize certain values and ends.[5] As required by the prin-

ciple of respect for persons, identification involves considering situations
from others' standpoints, including their beliefs about the world, their
life plans, and their risk budgets.

But, as Williams notes, it may not be sufficient to see how victims
view what appears to be their state of oppression, exploitation, or
degradation; for sometimes they will view themselves just as their masters view them.[6] This is true, for example, in some forms of slavery.
Therefore, it is not sufficient simply to point to a person's "consent" to a
situation if there is reason to think that it may have been manufactured
by the situation. The principle of respect for persons requires that we
sometimes look beyond what people say and do to the determinative
conditions.

Without necessarily accepting all of Kant's framework, we can view
the Kantian injunction to "treat persons as ends in themselves, and
never as a means only" as a requirement of the principle of respect for
persons.[7] Like the principle of respect for persons generally, this injunction is clearer in its negative than in its positive import. What it
proscribes is clearer than what it prescribes. At the very least it proscribes *using* persons merely as means or tools to accomplish one's own
or others' ends. Thus, exploitation is ruled out. An example of such
exploitation would be using persons as subjects in nontherapeutic research without their voluntary, informed consent. Most often we think
of exploitation as using a person for someone else's benefit, but the
principle of respect for persons also implies that we should not treat
persons merely as *means* to *their* own benefit, for example, to fail to
disclose relevant information to a patient for that patient's own benefit.
In case #6 a radiologist did not warn his patients of the risk of a fatal
reaction to urography because, he said, it would do no good and would
cause needless anxiety. He also insisted that, as radiologists, "our responsibility is to our patients and to do what is best for our patients
medically. Informing patients of risks and possible death from urography may not be in the best interest of the patient and . . . it may be
dangerous." Although this is not exploitation in any customary sense, it
views the person only as a means through which medical benefits can be
realized for the patient, and that is treating a person merely as a means
to his or her own ends. The rights that apply and express the principle of
respect for persons "block" or "trump" appeals to the good consequences of disregarding or overriding them, whether those good
consequences are for others or for the one whose rights are disregarded

or overridden.[8] And, as we will see later, there are special reasons for the strength or force of rights against appeals to good consequences for the patient.

Autonomy

One aspect of respecting persons is respecting their *autonomy*; this is an implication of respecting persons as independent ends in themselves. Etymologically, "autonomy" is compounded of *autos* (self) and *nomos* (law or rule). *Autonomia* originally was used to indicate the independence of Greek city-states from outside control, perhaps from a conqueror, and their determination of their own laws. The notions of independence, self-rule, and self-determination recur in explications of "autonomy," and their analysis is essential if we are to understand "what is essentially a metaphor."[9]

It is customary to contrast "autonomy" and "heteronomy," "autonomy" referring to self-rule and "heteronomy" referring to rule by other objects or persons. Heteronomous persons, for example, might have surrendered their judgment-making and decision-making to the state or to the church; their actions would be heteronomous because they would be determined by what the state or the church dictates. But although such persons may fall short of the ideal of autonomy (which will be discussed later), they may have exercised and even continued to exercise autonomy in the choice of the state or the church as the source of their judgments and decisions. Thus, there is an important distinction between *first-order* and *second-order* autonomy.[10] Persons who are subservient to state or church would lack first-order autonomy, i.e., self-determination regarding the content of decisions and choices, because of their exercise of second-order autonomy, i.e., selection of the institution to which they are subordinate. In other situations, first-order choices and actions such as the use of some drugs may appear to be under inner compulsion or addiction. But these agents retain some *second-order* autonomy: when they are made aware of their condition, they may choose to seek help or to remain under compulsion or addiction because they want to. As Gerald Dworkin contends, a person who is a drug addict and cannot break his physiological dependence on the drug, and yet who wants to be under this compulsion, is autonomous at least in this second-order sense, for he identifies with *his* addiction.[11]

Autonomy does not imply that an individual's life plan is his or her own creation and that it excludes interest in others. The first implication focuses on the *source*, the second on the *object* of autonomy.[12] Neither implication holds. Autonomy simply means that a person chooses and acts freely and rationally out of her own life plan, however ill-defined. That this life plan is *her own* does not imply that she created it *de novo* or that it was not decisively influenced by various factors such as family and friends. Some existentialists who use the language of autonomy suggest that if an individual does not create his own life plan, or at least an independent series of choices, he is guilty of "bad faith." Recall Jean-Paul Sartre's advice to the young man who was trying to decide whether to join the Free French Forces or to remain to help his mother: "You're free, choose, that is, invent."[13] More satisfactory interpretations of autonomy recognize that it may be rooted in both society and history. The source of an individual's life plan may well be, for example, a religious tradition with which he identifies and which he appropriates. An example is a Jehovah's Witness' life plan which gives everlasting life priority over earthly life if the latter can be maintained only by blood transfusions. Thus, personal autonomy does not imply an asocial or ahistorical approach to life plans. It only means that whatever the life plan, and whatever its source, an individual takes it as his own.

Likewise, the *object* of autonomous life plans and choices is not limited to the individual himself or herself but may include various principles and values such as altruistic beneficence. Autonomy does not presuppose that the individual is uninterested in the positive or negative impact on others. For example, some discussions of autonomous suicide seem to suppose that the agent is acting autonomously only if she is uninterested in an impact on others. But the agent may view the act of suicide primarily as expression and communication. This was certainly true of Jo Roman, who committed suicide in order to create "on [her] own terms the final stroke of [her] life's canvas" (see case #8). A 62-year-old artist, she had originally planned to commit suicide on her 75th birthday but acted earlier because of her breast cancer. In addition, she carefully staged her suicide in order to have a public impact, particularly to convince others that "life can be transformed into art."[14] Her desire for expression and communication did not, however, make her act less autonomous. It is a distortion of autonomy to limit the object to the agent's own self. Both points can be summarized: in terms of input and output, autonomy is not asocial or ahistorical. Both communication and influence occur both ways.

Does this analysis of autonomy imply the "separateness of persons," a conception that undergirds several recent critiques of utilitarianism? According to these criticisms, utiltarianism tends to view separate individuals as having only instrumental, not intrinsic, value as either depositors or depositories of good. Against utilitarianism, they emphasize either the separateness of agents or the separateness of recipients or patients (i.e., those acted upon). In the former, the emphasis will be on the agent's projects and commitments; in the latter, it will be on the patient's rights.[15] But because the separateness of persons tends to suggest an atomistic individualism, it is better to focus on the *distinctiveness* of persons, while recognizing that both their sources and their objects may be social.

Respect for persons who are autonomous may differ from respect for persons who are not autonomous. Formal equality, sometimes referred to as the formal principle of justice, demands that similar cases be treated similarly and that equals be treated equally. But because it does not specify relevant similarities or dissimilarities, it is formal and thus empty until it receives material content from other sources. My interpretation of the principle of respect for persons identifies autonomy as one relevant similarity. When persons are autonomous, respect for them requires (or prohibits) certain actions that may not be required (or prohibited) in relation to nonautonomous persons. Several principles, particularly nonmaleficence, may establish minimum standards of conduct, such as noninfliction of harm in relation to all persons whatever their degree of autonomy. But what the principle of respect requires (and prohibits) in relation to autonomous persons will differ. Thus, Kant excluded children and the insane from his discussion of the principle of respect for persons and Mill applied his discussion of liberty only to those who are in "the maturity of their faculties."[16] I will examine some aspects or criteria of autonomy before considering some specific requirements of respect for autonomous persons.

Two essential features of autonomy are (1) acting freely and (2) deliberating rationally. I will provide only a brief statement of these features which will be discussed in more detail in subsequent chapters. First, what is the relationship between *competence* and these two features of autonomy? Logically competence might be viewed as a precondition of deliberating rationally and acting freely or as a summary term for these two (and perhaps other) conditions. A person suffering from mental defects, for example, that would preclude either acting freely or deliberating rationally would be incompetent to make decisions. Competence is not an all or nothing matter. It may vary over time and from situation to situation. A person may be competent part of the time but incompetent the rest of the time; this will be called *intermittent* competence. And a person may be competent to act in X (e.g., to drive a car) but not in Y (e.g., to make decisions in a large family-operated business); this will be called *limited* competence.[17] One difficult question that will occupy our attention in later chapters is which way to err in borderline cases of competence.

(1) *Acting freely*. To act freely is, in part, to be outside the control of others. This point is implied by independence, and it excludes coercion, duress, undue influence, and manipulation. If a person is coerced —"your money or your life"—she is not acting freely even though she is deliberating rationally and acting intentionally. But, as we have seen, a person may exercise second-order autonomy by freely choosing to become dependent on a religious community for moral guidance. For example, a woman may decide not to have an abortion to save her life because she freely accepts the authority of the Catholic Church. To act freely also involves the absence of certain internal constraints such as compulsion and drug addiction. A person's action can be so seriously encumbered or limited by either internal or external constraints that he or she cannot be said to be autonomous.

Indeed, internal constraints, for example, may be so severe that we do not hold the agent responsible for what he does. In some cases, although the agent was casually responsible for what occurred, we do not hold him morally or legally responsible because he lacked the capacity for responsibility. Nonetheless, a general use of the language of disease to discount responsibility for wrongful conduct is a sign of disrespect for persons:

> A *total* reinterpretation of wrong doing in terms of disease amounts to a denial of personal responsibility altogether. It *insults* the wrongdoer under the guise of *safeguarding* his interests. It treats him as though he were *not* a person, and falls foul accordingly of the very principle of respect to which it appeals. This is the element of vital truth in the doctrine which to many has seemed merely a bad joke, that a man has a *right* to be punished.[18]

(2) *Deliberating rationally*. Deliberation is "an imaginative rehearsal of various courses of action."[19] It can be encumbered or limited in

various ways, particularly by a person's inability to reason because of mental illness or to reason fully because of inadequate or incomplete information about various courses of action and their consequences. It is possible in some cases to judge that a person's deliberation is irrational without calling into question the life plans, values, and ends on which the deliberation is based and without calling into question the weighting of the alternatives and their consequences. For example, a person may seek incompatible ends (such as preservation of his life and preservation of a gangrenous leg) or choose ineffective means to his ends.[20] Suppose two patients refuse amputations of gangrenous feet, one because she wants to die and the other because she does not believe that the condition is fatal. In the latter case there may be grounds for holding that the patient is not deliberating rationally and thus is not autonomous (see case #15). Nevertheless, as Bruce Miller reminds us, it is not always possible to separate factual and evaluative errors in nonrational deliberation.

> A patient may refuse treatment because of its pain and inconvenience, e.g. kidney dialysis, and choose to run the risk of serious illness and death. To say that such a patient has the relevant knowledge, if all other alternatives and their likely consequences have been explained, but that a non-rational assignment of priorities has been made is much too simple. A good accurate characterization may be that the patient misappreciates certain aspects of the alternatives. The patient may be cognitively aware of the pain and inconvenience of the treatment, but because he or she has not experienced them, the assessment of their severity may be too great. If the patient has begun dialysis, assessment of the pain and inconvenience may not take into account the possibilities that the patient will adapt to them or that they may be reduced by adjustments in the treatment. Misappreciating the consequences of treatment in this way is not a lack of knowledge, nor is it simply a non-rational weighting; it involves matters of fact and value.[21]

In addition, even when it is possible to identify errors in factual beliefs, it may be difficult to determine that the person is not autonomous. In case #16 a woman refused a hysterectomy for cancer because she felt quite well and insisted that "anyone knows that people with cancer are sick, feel bad and lose weight."[22]

Several philosophers have used the notion of authenticity to explicate autonomy. For example, Gerald Dworkin views autonomy as authenticity plus independence, while Bruce Miller identifies four aspects of autonomy as free action, authenticity, effective deliberation, and moral reflection. For Dworkin, authenticity is a person's identification with the determinants of his behavior so that they become *his* own. For Miller, it means that "an action is consistent with the attitudes, values, dispositions and life plans of the person."[23] The intuitive idea of authenticity is "acting in character." We wonder whether actions are autonomous if they are not consistent with what we know about a person (e.g., a sudden and unexpected decision to discontinue dialysis by a man who had displayed considerable courage and zest for life despite his years of disability). If they are in character (e.g., a Jehovah's Witness' refusal of a blood transfusion), we are less likely to suspect that they do not represent genuine autonomy. In addition, the notion of authenticity captures our sense that selves develop over time with persistent and enduring patterns; they are not simply collections of choices and acts. And yet it would be a mistake to make authenticity a criterion of autonomy. At most authenticity alerts us to relevant questions. If it is not satisfied, if the choice or action (such as refusal of treatment) is inconsistent with what we know of the person and his character, then we should seek justifications or explanations, some of which may indicate that the action is not autonomous (perhaps because it was under inner compulsion). We should also consider whether the person has experienced a change or even conversion in basic values and life plan and even whether we really knew the person as well as we previously thought. Actions apparently out of character and inauthentic can be caution flags that alert others to press for justifications and explanations in order to determine whether the actions are autonomous. By contrast, actions that are not free cannot count as autonomous.

An important distinction, drawn from Robert Nozick, may help to clarify the meaning of the principle of respect for persons: (1) autonomy as an end state or goal and (2) autonomy as a side constraint.[24] Frequently debates about paternalism are confused because all parties appeal to autonomy to justify their proposals without attending to differences that result from viewing autonomy as an end state as opposed to a side constraint. If autonomy is a *side constraint*, it limits the pursuit of goals such as health and survival; it even limits the pursuit of the goal of the preservation and restoration of autonomy itself. In pursuing goals for ourselves or for others we are not permitted to violate others' autonomy. Because what we do and not merely what happens is morally important, our nonviolation of autonomy is required. Whether autonomy is an absolute limit would depend on the moral theory; perhaps it could be violated in order to prevent a catastrophe. In contrast, when autonomy is viewed as an *end state* to be realized, its function in moral argument is very different. Autonomy is a condition, not a constraint, and the goal might be to minimize damage to autonomy whether that damage results from nature, disease, or other persons. In this view, some violations of autonomy (such as some decisions to reject patients' refusals of treatment) might be justified because overall more autonomy would result, and that is the desirable end state.

Eric Cassell, a strong proponent of autonomy, views it mainly as an end state rather than as a side constraint. He contends that autonomy (for which he uses Gerald Dworkin's formula, autonomy = authenticity + independence) is seriously compromised by illness, "the most important thief of autonomy," and that the primary function of medicine is to preserve, to repair, and to restore the patient's autonomy. When we are sick, our autonomy is greatly diminished because we are not "ourselves," our freedom of choice is limited, our knowledge is incomplete, and our reason is impaired. Although Cassell emphasizes the importance of relationships with family, friends, and physicians, he affirms that the best way to restore autonomy is "to cure the patient of the disease that impairs autonomy and return him to his normal life."[25]

To be sure, autonomy is an important end state of health care that professionals should pursue for their patients in order to benefit them. But it is an end state that individuals may autonomously choose not to pursue. By expanding the notion of autonomy to include freedom from the effects of disease,[26] and by conceiving it as a goal rather than as a right, Cassell fails to address the most important and difficult question: Can autonomy as a goal override autonomy as a right? Or does autonomy as a side constraint preclude its violation even to achieve the end state of restored or increased autonomy? The principle of respect for persons requires that autonomy be conceived as a side constraint and as a right, rather than as an end state, even if it does not establish an absolute limit (an issue that I will consider later). Pursuit of another's autonomy as an end state may be an important goal of altruistic beneficence, but the patient, rather than the agent, should determine how important it is.

The *ideal* of autonomy, especially moral autonomy, is neither a presupposition nor an implication of the principle of respect for persons, however much we admire persons who realize or approximate this ideal, so widely praised in the tradition of Western individualism. Recognition of this ideal and praise for the "autonomous person" would require additional premises that are not required for a defense of autonomy as a side constraint. Indeed, it is possible to emphasize autonomy as a side constraint without denying the burden of autonomy for individuals and the importance of community and tradition. Gerald Dworkin argues that the ideal of moral autonomy

> represents a particular conception of morality—one that, among other features, places a heavy emphasis on rules and principles rather than virtues and practices. Considered purely internally there are conceptual, moral, and empirical difficulties in defining and elaborating a conception of autonomy which is coherent and provides us with an ideal worthy of pursuit. It is only through a more adequate understanding of notions such as tradition, authority, commitment, and loyalty, and of the forms of human community in which these have their roots, that we shall be able to develop a conception of autonomy free from paradox and worthy of admiration.[27]

My argument is that the principle of respect for persons requires that we construe autonomy as a constraint upon our pursuit of goals for ourselves or for others. It does not require that we view autonomy as a goal or as an ideal, although these two views have often been associated with recognition of autonomy as a side constraint. It is possible to respect others' wishes, choices, and actions in that they constrain and limit our pursuit of goals, whether these goals are for them, for others, or for ourselves, without committing ourselves to the goal of promoting autonomy or to the ideal of autonomous existence.

Equality, Liberty, and Insult

To respect persons is to treat them as *equals* in the respects in which they are equals. Thus, it may be legitimate to treat autonomous and nonautonomous persons and their choices and actions in different ways (at least within limits). Both liberty and equality are thought to have special relations to the principle of respect for persons. Because liberty and equality are commonly understood to be competing values, moral, social, and political theories are often classified by how much weight they give to these values as well as others such as order. For example, Reinhold Niebuhr has insisted that liberty and equality are regulative principles of justice because they cannot be realized simultaneously without compromise and limitation.[28] Whether one is a liberal or a conservative or a socialist is often held to turn on whether one emphasizes liberty or equality. For instance, one recent classification of health care systems identifies four types that vary according to the weights they assign to liberty and equality. They can be viewed on a spectrum from pure liberty to pure equality: laissez-faire, liberal humanitarian, liberal socialist, and pure socialist.[29] While such classifications may be useful and illuminating in some contexts, they may mislead in others because, as Ronald Dworkin has emphasized, they operate with a conception of liberty as such or liberty as license to do what one wants to do without obstacles and barriers.[30] To value liberty as such or liberty as license is to view every social regulation as a restraint on liberty. Such a perspective may conceive liberty in terms of amounts and degrees, holding, for instance, that it is necessary to sacrifice X amount of liberty for the sake of greater equality or order or some other value. In its absolute form, it may repudiate political authority for anarchism in the name of an autonomy that can brook no social restraints.[31] In most forms, it will sacrifice some liberty in order to prevent individuals from being harmed by other individuals.

Nevertheless, as Ronald Dworkin argues, this view of liberty may cast its nets too broadly. If taken as a right, liberty in this sense would encompass acts that we think people have no right to perform and would imply that every interference with a person's wishes, choices, and actions involves a conflict between liberty and some other value or right such as equality. Significantly, liberty as license can lead us to condemn some policies without having to determine exactly what is wrong with them. This conception, then, is too easy and even superficial. For example, it clearly offers a prima facie reason for holding that paternalistic interventions are wrong. But if we stop at this point, we may miss what is particularly wrong about paternalism in light of the principle of respect for persons.

In addition to liberty as license, there is what Dworkin calls liberty as independence. This conception of liberty focuses on "the status of a person as independent and equal rather than subservient."[32] Liberty as license is indiscriminate; it does not distinguish liberties. Liberty is liberty, and each liberty is on the same level as any other (e.g., economic liberty is on the same level as civil liberty). Liberty as independence, by contrast, is discriminate; it distinguishes and even ranks various liberties according to their importance. Although Dworkin does not offer a list of basic liberties and their rank, such a list would depend on his general principle of equal concern and respect. Indeed, this principle embodies the right to treatment as an equal. Particularly problematic from his standpoint are paternalistic interventions, not only because of the basic liberties they sometimes violate but because of their rationale. As Dworkin interprets John Stuart Mill, "laws that constrain one man, on the sole ground that he is incompetent to decide what is right for himself, are profoundly insulting to him. They make him intellectually and morally subservient to the conformists who form the majority, and deny him the independence to which he is entitled."[33] Thus, personality, dignity, and insult are important moral concepts for many political and other matters.

Much of this analysis can be transferred from general social-political-legal relationships to health care, especially to relationships between health care professionals and patients. These narrower relationships, like the more general ones, involve power and control: Who may do what to whom? There appears to be little difficulty in determining that a person's liberty (as license) in health care matters may be curtailed to prevent harm to others, or that liberty (as independence) does not include the right to harm others and thus is not violated by some restrictions on choices and actions. Therefore, whether one holds that liberty as license or liberty as independence is involved, one arrives at the same point: the justified restriction of liberty under some conditions.

Either approach can provide a strong argument against paternalism. The ground offered by liberty as license is clear enough: any curtailment of liberty, any interference with wishes, choices, and actions, is at least prima facie wrong and requires justification. That justification usually involves prevention of harm or injustice to others or to the society. What ground is offered by liberty as independence? When a refusal to accept or to acquiesce in a person's wishes, choices, and actions is based on protecting others, that person is not insulted or treated with indignity. That person is insulted, however, when what is involved is only his conception of the good life and when his wishes, choices, or actions are rejected solely on the grounds that he is not competent to have a conception of good, or is ignorant, or has the "wrong" values. In short, a professional's refusal to acquiesce in a person's wishes, choices, and actions, where no one else is harmed, and merely because the professional disagrees with the values of the patient's life plan and risk budget, is a profound affront to dignity and independence. It makes one person subservient to another person's conception of the good. The patient loses his or her independence and status as an equal. Paternalism is insulting because it treats the patient as a child, that is, as one who has not yet freely and competently, and with adequate information, formed a conception of good and evil, of benefits and harms, or is not able to act on that conception in these circumstances. It is morally suspect because of its *reason* for interference with a person's wishes, choices, and actions.

Some argue that it does not insult people to treat them as they would want to be treated if they were fully rational, wise, and good, regardless of how they say they want to be treated. Indeed, they contend, it is a form of respect to treat them this way, for we ascribe to them the highest purposes and aspirations. Both equality and liberty have been interpreted to include this idea of respect for persons. Thus, it has been argued, we display respect when we treat all people as *equally* concerned for and capable of the highest ideals of life and restrict their pursuit of other values. Likewise, proponents of "positive liberty," as interpreted by Isaiah Berlin, hold that *freedom* is not freedom to do what is irrational, stupid, or bad; it is not the negative freedom of noninterference with what one "wants" to do. Rather freedom is realized when a person's *higher or true self* is master over his or her wishes, choices, and actions. To enable or even to force a person to live up to this higher or true self is either (a) justified coercion for that person's own benefit or (b) not even coercion at all because it is what the higher or true self really wants.[34]

Such "positive" conceptions of respect, equality, and liberty are misguided and dangerous. In the absence of widely shared and compelling pictures of the fully rational, wise, and good person, the state and professionals should be neutral. This does not mean, however, that they should become mere technicians to help people realize whatever life plans they have. Their own life plans would prevent them from entering certain kinds of relationships (e.g., a physician may feel that he cannot perform an abortion), and the principle of respect for persons requires that society grant them this autonomy. In addition, they may even interpret and justify their conceptions of the rational, wise, and good to their patients. But they may not curtail patients' basic liberties in the name of their own (or what they take to be society's) conception when others are not threatened. Such a curtailment insults persons by depriving them of rights and liberties that belong to them as persons.

According to Alasdair MacIntyre, autonomy may be a matter of *last resort* in a pluralistic society where we cannot rely on each other to act in certain ways because we lack a common system of beliefs, values, and principles. We lack authority because we lack common traditions. On the one hand, in such a situation, as MacIntyre puts it, our "truthfulness and integrity both demand that we allow nobody else to make our own decisions for us."[35] Problems of medical ethics thus become everyone's problems in a society which cannot ascribe authority to the physician because there is no moral consensus. Patients have to become agents. On the other hand, in such a situation the principle of respect for persons requires that we respect autonomy, whatever might be (or have been) the case in a society with a substantive moral consensus.

Even inequalities in technical information and skills and in the capacity to predict and understand consequences do not necessarily warrant overriding personal life plans and risk budgets. Robert Veatch, a strong proponent of liberties, grounds them in a social egalitarianism that does not deny such inequalities. For example, his proposal to extend patients' control of decisions affecting their death and dying rests, in part, on a metaethical thesis about the equality of decision makers: no one by acquiring expertise in any area can claim to be a moral expert and, therefore, to make decisions for others. Everywhere he opposes what he calls "the fallacy of the generalization of expertise."[36]

There is a value attached to a person's freedom to make certain choices such as consent to or refusal of medical treatment. This value does not depend on the likelihood that a person will be able to make better choices than anyone else. It is intrinsic, not only instrumental. But even more significantly, the principle of respect for persons mandates that certain freedoms or liberties be recognized as *rights*. A right is a justified claim, and a moral right is a morally justified claim, that is, a claim justified by moral principles and rules. For the most part, rights and duties are correlative so that one implies the other. Exceptions may be found in certain positive duties (such as charity) for which there may be no correlative right. The language of rights, exploding so loudly in our society, has a special function: It arms individuals with a powerful weapon. It makes agents of patients and gives them a sense of control. The language of rights stresses the individual's justified claim rather than the duty or virtue of the party refraining from interference or providing certain goods. As a symbolic expression of the principle of respect for persons, it blocks appeals to good consequences.

Many rights that derive from the principle of respect for persons are *negative* just as the principle itself serves as a side constraint. Joel Feinberg distinguishes negative rights from positive rights: "A *positive* right is a right to other persons' positive actions; a *negative* right is a right to other persons' omissions or forebearances. For every positive right I have, someone else has a duty to *do* something; for every negative right I have, someone else has a duty to *refrain* from doing something."[37] Negative rights identify, define, and protect the person's status as independent and equal.

Instead of trying to offer a comprehensive list of the rights that are justified by the principle of respect for persons, I shall simply identify a few and discuss their significance in later chapters in relation to specific problems:[38] (1) Noninterference with autonomous choices through force, coercion, manipulation and the like. This negative right does not, of course, preclude efforts at persuasion and conversion, for such efforts operate through the agent's autonomy. (2) Nondeception. This negative right not to be deceived and lied to is supplemented by the positive right to the disclosure of information within certain relationships such as fiduciary relationships between lawyer and client and between health care professional and patient. The positive right as expressed in the rule of informed consent emerges from the application of principles of respect for persons to these relationships. (3) Noninvasion of privacy. Although there is considerable debate about whether anything significant is captured by the idea of privacy that is not already and better expressed in other rights, it plays an important role in current debates about sexuality, abortion, and refusal of medical treatment, where it often resembles the first right identified above.[39] In a narrower sense, it refers to the control over access to information about oneself and can also generate a rule of confidentiality.

Principles, Conflicts, and Coherence

In chapter II, I analyzed and defended a principle of beneficence, and in this chapter I analyzed and defended a principle of respect for persons. In each case I also indicated certain limits (e.g., boundaries of the concepts) and limitations (e.g., in application of the principle). But it is

also necessary to consider further whether the conflict between beneficence and respect is inevitable and whether they might actually be
reduced to a single principle.

While some theologians hold that *agape* or altruistic beneficence is the
fundamental principle of ethics from which all other principles and rules
can be derived, some philosophers hold that respect for persons is such a
principle. For example, according to Downie and Telfer, the principle of
respect for persons can "sum up or characterize what all the other
specific requirements have in common—they will all be ways or modes
of respecting persons."[40] Thus, it is the supreme regulative principle.
The advantages of such an approach are obvious: it provides coherence
to morality by grounding all principles and rules on one basic principle
and by providing an ultimate source of appeal in cases of conflict among
principles and rules. But coherence and harmony are purchased at a
very high price, and a different perspective can better interpret and guide
moral experience.

First, some one-party and two-party moral conflicts are not reducible
to a single moral principle and its implications. Such conflicts are better
interpreted and resolved, if resolution is possible, in terms of a framework that recognizes the plurality and independence of principles. While
we need not suppose that the moral life is dominated by dilemmas and
quandaries, they sometimes emerge.

Second, some theories avoid conflicts of principle by offering an ultimate principle that is susceptible to different interpretations because it is
so vague and general. Ronald Dworkin's ultimate principle of political
morality operates in this way. He holds that the ultimate justificatory
principle of *equal concern and respect* is accepted by both liberals and
conservatives; they interpret it differently rather than invoking different
principles such as equality and liberty. It is the source of collective
justifications and of the rights that trump them.[41] But this principle can
be affirmed as ultimate only because of its generality and vagueness, and
it also embodies its own internal conflicts. For example, "concern" is
close to beneficence, "respect" is close to respect for persons, and
"equal" is close to justice. It is more plausible and helpful to recognize
several basic principles.

Third, while a search for coherence and harmony may be desirable, it
may be conducted more successfully elsewhere than in a final principle.
G. J. Warnock distinguishes a thesis that all moral principles are ultimately reducible to a single principle from a thesis that all moral prin-

ciples have a single rationale. He goes on to argue that the single rationale for classifying various principles as *moral* principles is that "their voluntary recognition would tend to counteract the maleficent liabilities of [our] limited sympathies, and in *that* way to work towards amelioration of the human predicament."[42] Whether his own constructive argument about the rationale of moral principles and of morality is acceptable, his distinction is a sound one, and we can possibly find a single rationale when we cannot find a single principle.

Instead of a single principle, then, it is preferable to think in terms of both a principle of beneficence, in both its general and its role-specific forms, and a principle of respect for persons that sometimes limits and constrains beneficence. A person should not be treated merely as a means to an end even when that end is one that the person accepts. To treat an autonomous person, who is able to act freely and to deliberate rationally, as nonautonomous is an insult and an affront to that person's dignity. It violates the principle of respect and of treating equals as equals as well as basic liberties and rights. A fundamental question is what to do when these principles of beneficence and respect for persons come into conflict. That is, we need to determine how strong the side constraint of respect for persons really is. Is it absolute? Or is it only prima facie binding so that it can be overridden by another principle in a conflict? As we determine its strength we also need to determine its range or its meaning in more precise terms. Sometimes apparent conflicts can be avoided or eliminated by a clearer definition of the principles, as I proposed in specifying the meaning of the principle of respect for persons in terms of autonomous and nonautonomous persons. It is often very difficult to determine what the principle of respect for persons requires because people give conflicting signals, especially over time. Thus, in the next chapter, I want to consider how autonomy as expressed in past, present, and future consent relates to paternalism. When health care providers override a person's current wishes in order to respect his past wishes or his probable future wishes, are their actions paternalistic and are they justified?

Notes

1. For example, see R. S. Downie and Elizabeth Telfer, *Respect for Persons* (New York: Schocken Books 1970), p. 10: "For we provide an analysis of the Judaeo-Christian concept of *agape*, and in general present in secular or humanistic terms a view of morality which is characteristically expounded by Judaeo-Christian thinkers." See also W. G. Mac-

lagan, "Respect for Persons as a Moral Principle," *Philosophy* 35 (July and October 1960): 193–217, 289–305. Maclagan suggests "that respect for persons and Agape are identical as regards their objective significance, their practical or directive import, but that they are subjectively different; or perhaps rather that in speaking of 'respect for persons' we abstract altogether from the subjective, emotional quality of the attitude" (pp. 216–17). For a useful discussion of principles of respect for person, see Carl Cranor, "Toward a Theory of Respect for Persons," *American Philosophical Quarterly* 12 (October 1975): 309–19.

2. Immanuel Kant, *The Doctrine of Virtue: Part II of the Metaphysic of Morals*, trans. Mary J. Gregor (New York: Harper and Row, 1964), pp. 115–16 (447).

3. *Ibid.*, p. 117.

4. Bernard Williams, "The Idea of Equality," in *Philosophy, Politics and Society*, 2nd Series, ed. Peter Laslett and W. G. Runciman (Oxford: Basil Blackwell, 1967), pp. 116–17.

5. See Charles Fried, *An Anatomy of Values: Problems of Personal and Social Choice* (Cambridge: Harvard University Press, 1970), pp. 224f.

6. Williams, "The Idea of Equality," pp. 117–18.

7. See Kant, *Groundwork of the Metaphysic of Morals*, trans. H. J. Paton (New York: Harper and Row, 1964), p. 96, 429: "Act in such a way that you always treat humanity, whether in your own person or in the person of any other, never simply as a means, but always at the same time as an end."

8. The conception of rights as "trumps" appears in Ronald Dworkin, *Taking Rights Seriously* (Cambridge: Harvard University Press, 1977).

9. Gerald Dworkin, "Autonomy and Behavior Control," *Hastings Center Report* 6 (February 1976): 23.

10. *Ibid.* For an important discussion, see Harry G. Frankfurt, "Freedom of the Will and the Concept of a Person," *Journal of Philosophy* 58 (January 14, 1971): 5–20. Frankfurt argues that "it is having second-order volitions [when one wants a certain desire to be his will], and not having second-order desires generally, that I regard as essential to being a person" (p. 10). Yet reason is presupposed because it is "only in virtue of his rational capacities that a person is capable of becoming critically aware of his own will and of forming volitions of the second order" (p. 12).

11. Dworkin, "Autonomy and Behavior Control," p. 25.

12. For use of this distinction between *source* and *object* in relation to ethical individualism, see Steven Lukes, *Individualism* (New York: Harper and Row, 1973), chap. 15.

13. Jean-Paul Sartre, "Existentialism," in *Existentialism and Human Emotions* (New York: Philosophical Library, 1957), pp. 24f.

14. See " 'Rational Suicide'?" *Newsweek*, July 2, 1979, p. 87; Laurie Johnston, "Artist Ends Her Life. . . ." *The New York Times*, June 17, 1979; and *Choosing Suicide*, a Documentary on PBS, June 16, 1980.

15. As a matter of emphasis, Bernard Williams represents the former, while Robert Nozick represents the latter. Also, see the illuminating discussion of the debate about the separateness of persons by H. L. A. Hart, "Between Utility and Rights," in *The Idea of Freedom: Essays in Honour of Isaiah Berlin*, ed. Alan Ryan (Oxford: Oxford University Press, 1979), pp. 77–98.

16. See Kant, *The Doctrine of Virtue*, p. 122, and Mill, *On Liberty*, ed. Gertrude Himmelfarb (Harmondsworth, Eng.: Penguin, 1976). For an argument that paternalistic treatment is not necessarily incompatible with a concern to respect moral autonomy, see Douglas N. Husak, "Paternalism and Autonomy," *Philosophy and Public Affairs* 10 (Winter 1981): 27–46.

17. For a fuller discussion of competence, including these terms, see Tom L. Beauchamp and James F. Childress, *Principles of Biomedical Ethics* (New York: Oxford University Press, 1979), chap. 3. I do not treat competence as merely or primarily a legal matter, although the law has much to say about it.

18. Maclagan, "Respect for Persons as a Moral Principle," p. 301.

19. John Dewey, *Theory of the Moral Life* (New York: Holt, Rinehart and Winston, 1960), p. 135.

20. J. B. Mabbott, "Reason and Desire," *Philosophy* 28 (1953): 113–23.

21. Miller, "Autonomy and the Refusal of Life-Saving Treatment," *Hastings Center Report* 11 (August 1981): 22–28.

22. See Ruth Faden and Alan Faden, "False Belief and the Refusal of Medical Treatment," *Journal of Medical Ethics* 3 (1977): 133.

23. Dworkin, "Autonomy and Behavior Control," and Miller, "Autonomy and the Refusal of Life-Saving Treatment."

24. This distinction is developed by Robert Nozick, *Anarchy, State, and Utopia* (New York: Basic Books, 1974), pp. 28–35. I use it for analytical purposes without accepting his normative theory.

25. I have drawn this statement of Cassell's position from his article "The Function of Medicine," *Hastings Center Report* 7 (December 1977): 16–19. See also his *The Healer's Art: A New Approach to the Doctor-Patient Relationship* (Philadelphia: J. B. Lippincott, 1976). Elsewhere he also considers cases of chronic care: "Naturally, autonomy is best served by a return to health. Increasingly, however, success in medicine does not mean a return to normalcy as it did with the infectious diseases. Rather, we are successful when patients requiring continuing care are able to function and live their lives with the least possible interference from their diseases or their medical care." Cassell, "Autonomy and Ethics in Action," *New England Journal of Medicine* 297 (August 11, 1977): 333–34. His discussion of cases sometimes expresses appreciation of autonomy as a side constraint, which is usually absent from his more theoretical statements.

26. This sort of expansion shifts the argument away from human interactions to conditions and goals: people are less autonomous when they are

sick. While it is true that people are affected in various ways when they are sick, including having their options more severely limited, they can still be self-determining within these conditions. That is the important point, sometimes obscured by Cassell's contention that a sick person is not simply a person with a disease added on but a "sick person." See *The Healer's Art*.

27. Gerald Dworkin, "Moral Autonomy," in *Morals, Science and Sociality, Vol. III* of *The Foundations of Ethics and Its Relationship to Science*, ed. H. Tristram Engelhardt, Jr. and Daniel Callahan (Hastings-on-Hudson, N.Y.: The Hastings Center, 1978), p. 170.

28. Reinhold Niebuhr, *On Politics*, ed. Harry R. Davis and Robert C. Good (New York: Charles Scribner's Sons, 1960), pp. 174–79.

29. Elizabeth Telfer, "Justice, Welfare and Health Care," *Journal of Medical Ethics* 2 (September 1976): 107–11.

30. Ronald Dworkin, *Taking Rights Seriously*, chap. 10.

31. See Robert Paul Wolff, *In Defense of Anarchism* (New York: Harper and Row, 1970) and "On Violence," *The Journal of Philosophy* 66 (October 2, 1969).

32. Dworkin, *Taking Rights Seriously*, p. 262.

33. *Ibid.*, p. 263.

34. See Isaiah Berlin, "Two Concepts of Liberty," in *Four Essays on Liberty* (New York: Oxford University Press, 1969), chap. 3; for a discussion of the conservative interpretation of equal respect, see Ronald Dworkin, "Liberalism," in *Public and Private Morality*, ed. Stuart Hampshire (Cambridge: Cambridge University Press, 1978), pp. 136f.

35. Alasdair MacIntyre, "Patients as Agents," in *Philosophical Medical Ethics: Its Nature and Significance*, ed. Stuart F. Spicker and H. Tristram Engelhardt, Jr. (Boston: Reidel Publishing Co., 1977), p. 210.

36. Robert Veatch, *Death, Dying and the Biological Revolution* (New Haven: Yale University Press, 1976) and "Generalization of Expertise," *Hastings Center Studies* 1, no. 2 (1973): 29–40.

37. Joel Feinberg, *Social Philosophy* (Englewood Cliffs, N.J.: Prentice-Hall, 1973), p. 59.

38. I do not here include the negative rights that would correlate with the duty of nonmaleficence because I want to emphasize those that correlate with the duty to respect persons.

39. See Judith Jarvis Thomson, "The Right to Privacy," Thomas Scanlon, "Thomson on Privacy," and James Rachels, "Why Privacy Is Important," *Philosophy and Public Affairs* 4 (Summer 1975).

40. Downie and Telfer, *Respect for Persons*, p. 15. As Maclagan puts it, because of the principle of respect for persons, we have more than "a mere heap of unrelated duties." "Respect for Persons as a Moral Principle," p. 299.

41. Dworkin, "Liberalism," pp. 123–25 and *Taking Rights Seriously*, esp. xv.

42. G. J. Warnock, *The Object of Morality* (London: Methuen, 1973), p. 87.

IV

Consents

The Nature and Importance of Consent

The principle of respect for persons generates several rights. These justified claims against others express the principle of respect for persons. A person may assign or transfer her rights to others in various ways. For example, I may accord John Doe the right to use my property for five years for a certain fee. Many rights are shifted through contracts and promises which deliberately alter the structure of rights and obligations. But we may also create rights in others by actions that are not intended to create rights. For example, if I accept the benefits of a practice, I may have an obligation to contribute when my turn comes, and others within that practice may have a right to my contribution. This obligation-right rests on the principle of fair play. As a result of voluntary actions, rights and obligations can be redistributed.[1]

Among the voluntary actions that deliberately change the structure of rights and obligations is consent. However benevolent a health care professional is, a special transaction is usually required before he or she can try to meet the needs of another person. This special transaction involves the patient's voluntary and informed consent. What are consent's important characteristics? First, consent that creates a right in another person is distinguishable from an attitude of approval. For instance, although I may approve of a particular research protocol involving human subjects, I may refuse to participate in it. However much I may approve of that research, without my consent no researcher can morally enroll me as a subject. My consent, as distinguished from my approval, is a necessary condition for the research to go forward with me as a subject. (I exclude proxy permission for the present.) Consent that creates or transfers rights is more than approval.

Second, consent is an intentional act. A person cannot consent to or authorize the actions of another person without doing so intentionally. For example, a person cannot accidentally consent to some action by another. Consent as an intentional action requires awareness, knowledge, and understanding. Even if a patient signs a consent form to have an operation or to participate in a research project, he does not give valid consent and thus does not create a right on the part of the physician or researcher if he does not understand what is going on. (I will deal with the duty to disclose information in chapter VI.)

Third, consent must be voluntary. If, for example, a person consents to an action under duress, it does not count as consent and thus does not change the structure of rights and obligations. If a woman "consents" to sexual intercourse under the threat of blackmail, her "consent" does not permit the man to proceed with impunity.

Fourth, consent need not involve oral or written statements. Although there are good reasons to require that consent forms be signed by patients and subjects, such forms are not indispensable. For example, in case #10 a Jehovah's Witness who was dying from uncontrolled bleeding after delivering a child needed a blood transfusion. Although she was conscious, she could not speak because of a tube in her windpipe; she could only communicate by blinking her eyes. She blinked her eyes twice to refuse the blood transfusion. Such actions and gestures can count as consent or refusal.

Consent is one ground for special rights among other grounds, such as making promises and contracts and accepting benefits. These rights are largely independent of their content, for their ground is a voluntary transaction rather than their moral characteristics or qualities. Yet they are not completely independent of their content. Various moral principles and rules may set limits and boundaries for the sorts of actions to which one may consent. Even voluntary and informed consent does not always create rights; it cannot create rights involving matters prohibited by moral principles and rules (e.g., a right to have someone commit murder or rob a bank). Although moral principles and rules may set limits and boundaries and thus prevent some consents from creating rights in others, the ground of these special rights is the voluntary transaction, not the moral quality of the action to which one consents.[2]

Volenti non fit injuria—to one who consents there is no injury. This maxim from Roman law is ambiguous because "injury" may be taken in two different senses. If "injury" means *harm* to one's interests, obviously an injury may be inflicted even though the "victim" consents. But if "injury" means *wrongful* action, the "victim's" consent cancels the injury even though harm occurs. In law, however, consent is not always a sufficient grounds for allowing an action. Appeal to the victim's consent will not, for example, remove a charge of mayhem or a charge of murder even if a person suffering from terminal cancer begs for death. These legal limits on the operation of consent may emerge because it is difficult to determine the voluntariness of consent (e.g., if a person has requested to be killed because of terminal cancer) or to avoid exploitation if a practice is allowed (e.g., selling oneself into slavery).[3]

Consent is one possible ground for special rights that are created, or transferred, by transactions between parties. These rights are special because they depend on relationships and thus do not belong to all people.[4] If a patient consents to medical treatment, she grants the health care professional a right that the latter did not have prior to the transaction. And for most rights there are correlative obligations. There exists what David Braybrooke calls "a firm but untidy correlativity" between obligations and rights, both of which are justified by appeals to principles and rules: if X has a right, then Y has a duty or obligation.[5] Rights imply obligations, and vice versa.

This rough correlation holds for both general and special rights. Our general right as persons to noninterference holds against all people, who thus have an obligation not to interfere in our affairs. If we alter the structure of rights and obligations by consent, we assign rights to others and assume obligations. Indeed, in a medical relationship, each party transfers some rights and assumes some obligations. But can it be said that a patient through consenting to medical treatment incurs an obligation correlative to the physician's right to treat him? If so, what sort of obligation is this? Hart writes, "If I consent to your taking precautions for my health or happiness or authorize you to look after my interests, then you have a right which others have not, and I cannot complain of your interference if it is within the sphere of your authority. This is what is meant by a person surrendering his rights to another. . . ."[6]

But then Hart seems to suggest that a distinguishing feature of special rights and their correlative obligations is that they are not revocable at will by the consenter: "Cases where *rights*, not liberties, are accorded to manage or interfere with another person's affairs are those where the license is not revocable at will by the person according the right."[7] Surely, however, apart from very special circumstances, the patient retains a moral and legal right to revoke the right assigned to a health care professional and hence the correlative obligation he assumed. And yet what the health care professional can claim until he or the patient revokes the relationship is stronger than a mere liberty. He has a *right* even though it is not as strong as the rights that Hart wrongly ascribes to the medical relationship. It is a right to proceed within limits set by the patient and until the patient or the professional terminates the relationship. Hart appears to confuse two matters: an obligation not to complain about the interference as long as it follows accepted limits and an obligation not to revoke the relationship. The latter is not an obligation for patients. As federal guidelines for research involving human subjects indicate, the information to be disclosed to a prospective subject before he gives consent includes "[a]n instruction that the person is free to withdraw his consent and to discontinue participation in the project or activity at any time without prejudice to the subject."[8]

Varieties of Consent

In medical relationships, the paradigm case of consent creating rights is *express consent*. For example, a patient expressly consents to medical treatment, thereby creating rights on the part of health care professionals. But there are other varieties of consent, some of which are invoked in health care to override a patient's express wishes and choices. Among these varieties are tacit consent, implied consent, and presumed consent. In addition, both past consent and future consent, which may take one of these forms, need to be analyzed.

Tacit consent is a favorite tool of political theorists in the contract tradition. If the basis of political obligation is consent, then it is important to determine if and when individuals consent to obey the government. Because it is difficult to find express consent by many individuals, theorists such as John Locke have resorted to tacit consent. Although tacit consent is distinguished from express or explicit consent, it is not unexpressed. It is rather expressed silently or passively by omissions and by failures to indicate or signify dissent.[9] In tort law, according to William Prosser, "silence and inaction may manifest consent where a reasonable person would speak if he objected."[10] If a woman does not protest verbally or in other ways when a man proposes to kiss her, he has her tacit consent. Or, to take another example, when students in a class are asked if they object to a change in the time of the final examination, their failure to object constitutes tacit consent under certain conditions. John Simmons identifies several conditions of tacit consent: the potential consenter must be aware of what is going on and that consent or refusal is appropriate, must have a reasonable period of time for objection, and must understand that expressions of dissent will not be allowed after the period ends; he must understand the acceptable means for expressing dissent; these means must be reasonable and not too difficult to perform; and, finally, "the consequences of dissent cannot be extremely detrimental to the potential consenter" (for example, if there is a threat of imprisonment for dissent, the absence of dissent cannot count as tacit consent).[11] Some of these conditions ensure understanding, others ensure voluntariness. If these conditions are met, the potential consenter's silence may be construed as tacit consent to a course of action. The consent is not implied, it is tacitly given or expressed. Obviously it is sometimes difficult to determine whether these conditions are met, for silence may indicate a lack of understanding of the means of consent or dissent as well as of the proposed course of action.

As many critics have recognized, theories of political obligation that appeal to tacit consent often claim too much. John Locke, for example, held that "every man that hath any possession or enjoyment of any part of the dominions of any government doth thereby give his tacit consent, and is as far forth obliged to obedience to the laws of that government."[12] On this view, the agent may not will or even be aware of her tacit consent. Her acts are not consensual in a full or personal sense. Yet tacit consent, as Simmons notes, is signified consent. It involves various signs that are silent or inactive, but they are appropriate signs (as determined by the context and agent's understanding) of his or her intention to consent and thus to create a special right for another party. The acts emphasized by Locke do not have this quality. But even if these acts fail to pass the test of tacit consent, they may, as Simmons suggests, engender obligations on other grounds (such as fair play and gratitude) and they may even *imply* consent (as distinct from *signifying* consent).[13]

Whereas tacit consent is expressed through failures to dissent, *implied* or implicit consent is not expressed at all. It is inferred from actions. First, consent to a specific action may be implied by general consent to an authority. If a person goes to the doctor's office for a physical examination, his visit implies consent to customary tests even though he may not expressly consent to them. Second, consent to a specific action may be implied by consent to other specific actions. For example, if a patient consents to an operation to remove a cancerous tumor in order to save her life and during the operation the surgeon discovers another life-threatening condition that could easily be removed without increased risk, it might be argued that the surgeon has her implied consent. Third, actions that do not involve either general consent to an authority or consent to some specific action may nevertheless imply consent. They may express attitudes or values that imply that the agent would consent if he could consent or if he were asked to consent. Suppose, before falling unconscious, a man who has just been shot by an intruder dials the 911 number, indicates an emergency, and pleads for help. Such a person implicitly consents to medical treatment; his actions imply that he would consent if he could consent. Indeed, his actions only make sense if he is willing to consent. (If he is unconscious when taken to the hospital, his treatment will probably be justified in terms of *presumed consent*, which I will examine below.)

Case #4 indicates some difficulties of implied consent. A 65-year-old retired army officer voluntarily entered a psychiatric ward because of chronic abdominal pain, loss of weight, and social withdrawal. He relied on six daily self-administered injections of Talwin (Pentazocine) which he thought was essential to control his pain, but he had trouble finding injection sites because of tissue and muscle damage. The program of this psychiatric ward was designed to develop self-control of pain. When the patient refused to allow direct modification of his Talwin dosage levels, the therapists decided to withdraw the Talwin over time, without the patient's knowledge, by diluting it with increasing proportions of normal saline. This placebo worked, and within six weeks he could control his pain more effectively with the self-control techniques than previously with Talwin. The therapists' major justification for this deceptive use of a placebo was its probable effectiveness in realizing a goal that the patient also affirmed. Later we will consider this case in terms of future consent, or ratification, since the patient subsequently ratified the therapists' decision on his behalf, but now it is important to ask whether the patient *implicitly* consented to the modification in medication although he continued *explicitly* to refuse it. Did he implicitly consent when he voluntarily admitted himself to a ward where adjustment in medication was a clear expectation and when he accepted the goals of therapy—"to get more out of life in spite of pain"? It might be argued that his recognition of his difficulties and the importance of other means to control pain, as expressed in his willingness to enter the ward, implied consent. But this argument will not do. It might succeed if we had no other information about his wishes. But we do have other information— he expressly refused to allow direct modification of his medication. We cannot appeal to implied consent to override express refusal unless we can show that the patient has some defect, encumbrance, or limitation in decision-making. But these flaws in decision-making might also invalidate implied consent.

The doctrine of implied consent does not offer a firm moral or legal foundation for medical interventions because implied consent is not really consent. It does not depend on a person's intention to consent. Its appeal is that it appears to involve consent and thus to respect persons. But rarely does it create rights, especially rights to override a person's express will. It does not offer a way around paternalism. At most it alerts us to the need to discern a person's will by considering various actions, not merely his or her express consent or refusal. People are more complex than their express consents and refusals.

Closely related to, and often confused with, implied consent is *presumed consent*. It presumes what a person would consent to if he or she could consent or were asked to consent. If consent is presumed on the basis of what we know about a person, his or her actions and values, it is identical to implied consent. But if it is presumed on the basis of a theory of human goods, values, and interests or a rational will, it is very different. In their own distinctive ways, express consent, tacit consent, and implied consent refer to an individual's own actions and inactions, while presumed consent need not refer to them at all.

Consider two settings in which presumed consent operates. First are emergencies in which people desperately need medical treatment. This treatment may be given without an individual's informed consent if he is unable to consent because of his condition or if the process of disclosing information and securing consent would consume too much time and thus endanger him. William Prosser summarizes the tort law:

> in an emergency which threatens death or serious bodily harm, as where the patient is bleeding to death and it is necessary to amputate his foot to save his life, it is generally recognized that these requirements [of obtaining informed consent] must be waived, and the surgeon must be free to operate without delaying to obtain consent. It is said in these cases that the consent is "implied" under the circumstances. This is obviously a fiction, since consent does not exist, and there is no act which indicates it. It is probably more accurate here, and perhaps likewise in many other cases of so-called "implied" consent, to say that the defendant is privileged because he is reasonably entitled to assume that, if the patient were competent and understood the situation, he would consent, and therefore to act as if it had been given.[14]

Of course, it is important to define emergency in a rigorous way—a task beyond this study—so that it cannot be used as a cloak for convenience. Even so, there will be borderline cases.[15]

Second, presumed consent is also invoked for incompetent patients. Obviously, incompetent patients may be involved in emergencies, but presumed consent for them also applies to nonemergency situations. Thus, it may be assumed that a child would consent to medical treatment if she could, or that a mentally retarded or mentally ill patient would consent if he could. Who should provide proxy consent or permission for incompetents is a matter of debate. (See my discussion of "Procedures" in chapter V.)

It is one matter to appeal to presumed consent when a person's will cannot be known because of that person's condition or because it would require too much time and would endanger him. It is another matter to appeal to presumed consent *against* his express will. As I will argue in the next chapter, the latter approach is morally warranted only where his decision-making, willing, or acting is defective and where he is at risk of harm. It may, however, take one of two different forms. On the one hand, it may appeal to the hypothetical unencumbered will of the patient, that is, to what the patient, given his values, *would* will if he could.[16] This approach, of course, presupposes some knowledge of the patient, his actions, values, and so forth. Thus, it may approximate implied consent. On the other hand, presumed consent may appeal to the "rational will," to what fully rational people would want, to a theory of "primary goods," or to objective values built into human nature.[17] Such an appeal may be unavoidable when the individual's biography cannot be known. It does not, however, justify strong or extended paternalism that would override a patient's express wishes, choices, and actions for his own good merely because they are based on values that would not be accepted by the "rational will."

Because consent is so important an implication of the principle of respect for persons, we resort to fictions such as presumed consent. We extend the meaning of consent and the principle of respect for persons in order to avoid conflicts with our other moral principles such as beneficence. Yet we should resort to fictions such as presumed consent only with the greatest care and caution, for under the guise of "consent" they may imply a more extensive paternalism than is warranted.[18]

Either we define "consent" very broadly or we recognize that we are more than our consents and dissents. The political theorist Michael Walzer defines "consent" and "consenting acts" broadly to encompass almost any commitment:

> Our moral biographies are constituted in large part by trains of consents —consents of many different sorts, to many different people. Consent itself is sometimes signified not by a single act but by a series of acts, and the determining sign is always preceded, I think, by something less than determining; a succession of words, motions, involvements that might well be analyzed as tentatives of or experiments in consent. In fact, we commit ourselves very often by degrees, and then the expectations that others form as to our conduct are or ought to be similarly graded.[19]

Extended too far, the notion of consent becomes vacuous. But if we take a narrower definition of consent, we are more than our "trains of consents" (and dissents), even those proffered tentatively and experimentally. Within either the broad or narrow interpretation, sometimes only the most sensitive and extensive process of communication can disclose (on the broad view) a person's tentative and experimental as well as his final consents and dissents, or (on the narrow view) his "real will" which is not clearly expressed in consents and dissents.

Appeals to a patient's real will, as distinct from his consents and dissents, are notoriously uncertain and even dangerous. But they cannot always be avoided, for we cannot be content with a simplistic interpretation of human will that equates it with overt expressions. Just as we may approve of something or even wish it without consenting to it, so we may consent to something without truly wishing it. For example, a person may say to a guest, "Please stay and join us for dinner," when he really wishes that the guest would leave. What manifests or signifies a person's consent may not express his true wishes. While our rights and responsibilities usually hinge on people's consents and dissents, in many settings, perhaps especially in health care, it is essential to consider what the patient really says and what he really wants. But, as we have seen, we should not confuse interpretations of his "real will," based on his actions and values, with the "rational will" of some abstract being.

In a well-known and widely discussed case (#12), Mr. C., a 27-year-old former athlete (football and rodeo) and jet pilot in the military, was severely burned in an accident that killed his father. After almost ten months of treatment, including several operations, he refused to consent to further surgery and asked to be allowed to die. All along he had indicated that he wanted to die, but he had continued to accept treatment until this time. In a videotaped conversation with the psychiatrist, Robert B. White,[20] he appeared to be competent, rational, lucid, and determined to die with good reasons in view of his own values and prospects: "I do not want to go on as a blind and crippled person." But once his right to die was finally acknowledged, he chose not to exercise it and continued what proved to be a somewhat successful course of rehabilitation. Perhaps his earlier demand to be allowed to die was mainly a protest against fate, against the loss of control over his destiny, against his dependence, or against what he perceived as depersonalized and even incompetent care. At any rate, if he had intended to die, he changed his mind; but clearly he wanted the right to make that decision for himself—to gain at least this much control.

It was morally mandatory (and legally mandatory also) to acknowledge and to accede to his right to decide for himself, for he did not suffer from the defects, limitations, and encumbrances of decision-making that could justify a paternalistic refusal. But other responses were also morally important. As Robert Burt argues, if we ignored "the emotional context" of Mr. C.'s invocation of the principle of self-determination, "we would find ourselves purporting to obey the wishes of a caricature." Mr. C.'s dependence led him to inquire about the wishes of others, not only to express his own wishes. His plea, Burt notes, was perhaps "more a question to others about their wishes toward him" because his means of death would involve their collaboration.[21] In this setting, it was morally important as an expression of beneficence for physicians and other health care professionals as well as the family to extend care so as to affirm his existence. Such care might also have required altering some features of his environment, e.g., reduction of pain and gestures of concern. These responses do not override the right to self-determination, but they structure the context, particularly the emotional context, in which the patient makes his choices. They pay attention to what patient is "really" saying.

The process of communication is exceedingly complex and requires time as well as attention to various verbal and nonverbal signs. Consent itself is given and withdrawn over time, and a patient's present statements should not always be taken at face value. In addition to determining whether a patient meets the conditions for self-determination, it is necessary to put the patient's present consents and dissents in a broad temporal context that includes both past and future.

Past Consent

Not only does consent take different forms. It also occurs at different times. A patient may consent to an operation one day, but refuse it the next day. Which expression of will is binding on others? In determining whether an act is paternalistic and whether it can be justified even if it is paternalistic, it is important to consider the temporal process. Too often ethical analyses focus on a narrow span of time, usually the present that is arbitrarily cut off from the past and future. A notorious difficulty for "situation ethics" is determining exactly what counts as a "situation" in terms of relationships, space, and time. And consequentialist theories of morality encounter effects that ripple through time. But time also raises questions for moral theories that emphasize respect for persons. If we are bound to respect people's wishes, it is necessary to determine *which* of their wishes, choices, and actions to respect. Not only does a person have several different and perhaps even contradictory wishes and choices at one time, but also these wishes and choices may vary from time to time. Which wishes, choices, and actions should we respect? If the changes are dramatic, we may ask which "person" we should respect. In particular, if we override a patient's present wishes, choices, and actions in the name of her *past* consent or her probable *future* consent, do we act paternalistically? And is our action justified?

The issue of past consent usually surfaces when a person has previously accepted a course of action that he now repudiates. Should the

past consent or the present repudiation determine our rights and responsibilities toward that person? Rosemary Carter presents the following case:

> Bill has resolved to refrain from buying cigarettes, but knowing that
> once tempted, he will probably break his resolve, he informs Jim that
> he would appreciate being prevented from making such a purchase. Sub-
> sequently, Jim does interfere in the envisaged circumstances. Normally,
> this would constitute a violation of Bill's right to freedom of action, but
> because Bill has given prior consent to such interference, thereby alienat-
> ing his right to non-interference in the specified circumstances, Jim's
> action is justified. This will be true regardless of Bill's protestations at
> the time. (Obviously there are moral limits on what Jim can do to pre-
> vent the purchase. Bill still has the right to be treated humanely, as well
> as any number of other rights which might be relevant.)[22]

While some philosophers hold that past consent removes the label of
paternalism from actions, Carter holds that Jim's interference with Bill's
freedom of action in the present is paternalistic but is justified because
of Bill's prior consent.[23] I agree that overriding a person's express will
in the present may be paternalistic, even if we have his or her prior
consent, but whether that prior consent justifies the paternalistic intervention is a more difficult question.

The story of Odysseus and the Sirens is a paradigm case of an agent's
consent to a course of action that he expects to repudiate under certain
pressures. It involves what Gerald Dworkin calls a "social insurance
policy."[24] Before Odysseus and his men sailed by the island of the
enchanting Sirens, who used beautiful music to lure sailors to their
deaths, he ordered his companions to stuff their ears with wax so that
they could not be tempted. He also ordered them to bind him to the
mast and to swear not to release him whatever he said: "you are to tie
me up, tight as a splint, erect along the mast, lashed to the mast, and if I
shout and beg to be untied, take more turns of the rope to muffle me."[25]
Hearing the music of the Sirens, Odysseus demanded his release, but his
companions obeyed his earlier orders. Although they had his past consent for what they did, their actions were paternalistic for they acted
against his express commands at that time. (What the sailors did was
impure paternalism, because Odysseus' actions also put them at grave
risk.)

This story exemplifies what John Elster calls imperfect rationality:
Odysseus "was not fully rational, for a rational creature would not

have to resort to this device; nor was he simply the passive and irrational vehicle for his changing wants and desires, for he was capable of achieving by indirect means the same end as a rational person could have realised in a direct manner. His predicament—being weak and knowing it—points to the need for a theory of *imperfect rationality* that has been all but neglected by philosophers and social scientists."[26] Elster argues that binding oneself, or precommitment, is a privileged way to resolve the problem of weakness of will; it is the major indirect way to achieve rationality. It is indirect because the agent operates on the environment to try to guarantee her choices and actions in the future instead of directly altering herself. Such indirect techniques are common, for example, in efforts to control cigarette smoking or obesity, but they also appear elsewhere. Suppose a woman knows that she will ask to have her dialysis discontinued when her uremia worsens. She might instruct the physician to ignore what she says under those conditions because her statements are simply "her uremia talking."[27]

In case #11, 28-year-old James McIntyre decided to terminate chronic renal dialysis which required trips to the Medical Center three times a week. He had diabetes, was legally blind, and could not walk because of progressive neuropathy. He was upset because of his restricted lifestyle and the burdens on his family, particularly their finances. He worked out an agreement with his family and physicians: He would stop his dialysis and insulin, and his physician, Dr. Robert Lincoln, would give him morphine sulfate to relieve his pain while he died. Both Dr. Lincoln and Mrs. McIntyre also acceded to Mr. McIntyre's request that he not be returned to dialysis even if he requested it under the influence of uremia, morphine sulfate, and ketoacidosis (the last resulting from the cessation of insulin). While dying, Mr. McIntyre awoke complaining of pain and asked Dr. Lincoln to put him back on dialysis. Dr. Lincoln and Mrs. McIntyre decided to act on Mr. McIntyre's original request that he be allowed to die, and Dr. Lincoln gave him another injection of morphine sulfate. Mr. McIntyre died four hours later. The physician and the family probably should have put Mr. McIntyre back on dialysis to make sure that he had not knowingly rescinded his earlier request. If Mr. McIntyre had then reaffirmed his earlier decision, dialysis could have been stopped again.

While imperfect rationality is a rich topic, the most important aspect for paternalism is that the agent exercises control over her future wishes, choices, and actions by requesting or consenting to actions by others that will probably contradict what she will want in the future. As Elster suggests, the agent controls the controller in order to control herself.[28] She exercises second-order autonomy. But such a situation raises difficult empirical, conceptual, and moral questions.

First, it may be difficult to determine the validity of a person's past consent: has she actually bound herself and others to a course of action? The fact that the consent occurred in the past does not obviate the need to determine whether it was voluntary and informed. Prior consent is invalid if the agent did not understand and voluntarily consent to control.

Second, it may be difficult to determine when a person revokes prior consent. When are a person's current wishes, choices, and actions not only inconsistent with, but also an informed and voluntary revocation of, prior consent? Recall Rosemary Carter's example of Bill asking Jim to prevent him from buying cigarettes if he should be tempted to do so in the future. She holds that Jim's interference, within limits, will be justified "regardless of Bill's protestations at the time." Her claim is unwarranted, because Bill may have changed his mind and decided to smoke for reasons that he would have accepted earlier if he had foreseen the consequences of not smoking, such as his nervousness and patterns of compensation. Thus, it is necessary to continue to assess a person's competence, his level of understanding, and the voluntariness of his choices in order to determine whether prior consent remains in effect. Odysseus' prior consent remained in effect because his repudiation of it was obviously under compulsion. An agent can bind himself and others over time, but he can also release himself and others as long as he meets such conditions of competence, understanding, and voluntariness. The principle of respect for persons requires that we attend to both his prior consent and his present revocation but that his present revocation take priority if it is informed and voluntary.

Prior consent is not sufficient to justify paternalistic interventions in most situations of interest in health care, that is, when an individual's current refusal contradicts his prior consent. Suppose that a patient voluntarily enters a psychiatric hospital because of severe problems. He has given consent to psychiatric treatment. But after several weeks, he changes his mind and decides to leave. The staff, however, refuses to discharge him because he is mentally ill and dangerous to himself. Their paternalistic action is not justified by his past consent but by the conditions that I will defend in the next chapter. And his prior consent, by itself, would not be sufficient to detain him if these conditions were not met.

Prior consent is sufficient to justify a professional's current actions on behalf of a patient, as long as the patient does not now refuse them. If the patient reaffirms, even by silence, his past consent, the professional does not act paternalistically because, after all, he acts in accord with (not against) the patient's express wishes. But prior consent does not justify paternalistic intervention when the patient's present wishes, choices, or actions contradict his past consent. In such a conflict, prior consent may be useful in identifying the patient's values so that "soft" paternalism can be undertaken if the patient, now at risk, suffers from some defect in deciding, willing, or acting.

Prior consent is also unnecessary to justify paternalism, for, as we will see, other conditions are sufficient. Odysseus' men would have been justified in restraining him for his own good as they passed the Island of the Sirens even without his prior consent since his attempt to go to the Island was under compulsion and put him at grave risk.

Although prior consent is neither necessary nor sufficient to justify paternalism, it is not unimportant. First, it identifies agents who have a right to intervene on one's behalf. For example, if Bill does not actually revoke his consent to Jim to prevent him from buying cigarettes, his consent authorizes Jim to act in ways that others may not. This point follows from the idea of special rights created by transactions: Jim has a right that no one else has unless Bill has also granted it to them. At the very least, prior consent establishes a relationship that authorizes an agent to look after one's welfare in ways specified by the consent. This agent has the right, and perhaps the duty, to continue to assess the other's capacities and the likelihood of harm.

Second, as I have suggested, prior consent may be useful in determining a patient's values over time so that paternalistic intervention against his current express wishes may actually be in accord with his long-term preferences. Such an intervention would be a form of "soft" paternalism, which is easier to justify than "hard" paternalism. In addition, authenticity of a patient's decisions is important. Their consistency or inconsistency with his life plan and risk budget may help to indicate whether their repudiation is genuine. Nevertheless, the possibility of a transformation of values over time cannot be ignored.

If the self changes greatly over time, authenticity may not be a helpful

criterion. At stake is the solidity and plasticity of the self. Derek Parfit
has emphasized what would result if we thought in terms of successive
selves, selves changing so dramatically that they could be said not to
exist any longer. Consider his example of the problem with later selves:

> Let us take a nineteenth-century Russian who, in several years, should
> inherit vast estates. Because he has socialist ideals, he intends, now, to
> give the land to the peasants. But he knows that in time his ideals may
> fade. To guard against this possibility, he does two things. He first signs
> a legal document, which will automatically give away the land, and
> which can only be revoked with his wife's consent. He then says to his
> wife, "If I ever change my mind, and ask you to revoke the document,
> promise me that you will not consent." He might add, "I regard my
> ideals as essential to me. If I lose these ideals, I want you to think that
> *I* cease to exist. I want you to regard your husband, then, not as me,
> the man who asks you for this promise, but only as his later self.
> Promise me that you would not do what he asks."[29]

It is plausible, Parfit suggests, to hold that the wife can "never be
released from her commitment. For the self to whom she is committed
would, in trying to release her, cease to exist." Parfit's example can be
restated to highlight issues in health care. Suppose that an adult Jehovah's Witness is deeply committed to the beliefs and ideals of that
religion, including its prohibition of blood transfusions. Indeed, his identity is tied up with his activities in this movement. Nevertheless, he is
aware that he deeply loves life and that his commitment might waver
under circumstances that might require a blood transfusion. Consequently, he asks his wife and his sympathetic physician *not* to view any
subsequent indication of a willingness to receive a blood transfusion as
his expressions. If "he" makes such statements, he will have ceased to
exist. Thus, he says, those statements should be disregarded. But both
his wife and his physician have to determine whether a subsequent
indication of a willingness to receive a blood transfusion indicates a
change in self and which self, the earlier or later, should be listened
to.[30] From both legal and moral standpoints, the *competent* patient
should be treated as he or she indicates at the time of need.

Future Consent or Ratification

Parents often justify overriding their children's present wishes, choices,
and actions by appealing to their future consent: "Someday you'll be

glad I made you eat your food and brush your teeth!" Education and other activities that children may not accept and may even resist at the moment are allegedly justified by their future consent, their retrospective acceptance of actions on their behalf. As Gerald Dworkin describes "future-oriented consent,"

> parental paternalism may be thought of as a wager by the parent on the child's subsequent recognition of the wisdom of the restrictions. There is an emphasis on what could be called future-oriented consent— on what the child will come to welcome, rather than on what he does welcome.[31]

It is important to determine what this model of future consent implies for paternalism in health care.

I will also refer to "future consent" as "ratification," because the patient ratifies, confirms, or approves the action on his or her behalf. Because the intervention has already occurred (or at least begun), it may be misleading to describe the patient's subsequent approval as "consent," as though it creates rights in the same way as past or present consent. Even though I will continue to use the language of "future consent" in accord with the literature, "ratification" is a more appropriate term.

Bernard Gert and Charles Culver distinguish "immediately forthcoming consent" and "future consent," the former occurring immediately after the intervention.[32] To take John Stuart Mill's example, if I forcibly stop a person from crossing a dangerous bridge, I may think that he will approve of my action once I explain the danger to him. In such a situation, Gert and Culver argue, my intervention is not paternalistic, for consent that is given immediately after an intervention removes the label of paternalism just as effectively as present consent. In contrast, while future consent may justify a paternalistic act, it cannot nullify the paternalism.

Where is the line between immediately forthcoming consent and future consent? Gert and Culver hold that stopping persons from committing suicide because of their temporary depression is paternalistic even though we expect them to thank us when they recover.[33] In case #1, a physician ordered a nurse to lie to an injured woman about the condition of her daughter until the woman's husband can be brought to the hospital the next day. In this case, the woman was upset when she learned of the deception, but suppose she had ratified the decision on her behalf immediately upon hearing about it: "Thank you for not telling me until my husband could be with me." It is not clear whether Gert and Culver would hold that this retrospective consent *nullifies* or *justifies* the paternalism. The deception lasted several hours, but the patient ratified it immediately upon disclosure. Probably they would hold that nullifying consent must be given immediately after an intervention, rather than immediately after the disclosure or explanation of an intervention that occurred over time.

A more plausible interpretation is that future consent, whether immediate or forthcoming, affects the justification of paternalism rather than the application of the concept. We act paternalistically in stopping a person who unwittingly starts to cross a dangerous bridge whether he ratifies our act immediately or in the future. Intervening in his action, which we think may not be in accord with his own wishes, is a form of soft and limited paternalism, whatever his future response. But his subsequent ratification may affect the justification of our paternalistic intervention.

In case #4, which we have already examined from the standpoint of implied past consent, a patient felt that he could not control his pain without medication, and his therapists substituted a placebo. Through this deception, they were able to get him to use self-control techniques for pain. Three weeks later, they explained what they had done. At first he was incredulous and angry, but he then asked to stop the placebo and to continue the self-control techniques. He ratified their decision by his words and actions even though he did not explicitly consent.[34]

To take another example, resistance to difficult and painful rehabilitation programs is not uncommon. After her stroke, Patricia Neal, the actress, was not sure that she wanted to embark on and then to continue a rehabilitation program because of what it involved. Subsequently she wrote,

> Oh, what a mess I was. I wanted to give up. I was tired. I felt certain I was as good as I would ever be. But Roald, that slave-driving husband of mine, said no. And today I cannot thank him enough. That is why it is so important for a stroke victim to have someone around who cares enough to force him into doing whatever must be done, regardless of how cruel it may seem at the time. When a person has had a stroke, he doesn't feel like doing anything. I know from experience, that had it been left up to me I would still be the idiot I was after that terrible ordeal in California.[35]

In both cases, patients subsequently ratified actions on their behalf—actions that they had previously resisted.

Many of the difficulties that plague discussions of informed consent in the present also apply to future consent. Which words and actions will count as consent or ratification? Is the consent or ratification informed and voluntary? As we have already noted, rarely are questions raised about a patient's competence to consent when her decision agrees with what the professional proposes. But the patient may be incompetent to consent even though she accepts the professional's recommendations now or later.

It is also important to distinguish *actual* ratification from *predicted* ratification. Although some of the same difficulties arise for both, each has its own special difficulties that merit attention as we consider whether future consent is necessary and/or sufficient to justify paternalistic interventions.

Although some theorists have apparently held that future consent, either actual or predicted, is sufficient to justify paternalistic interventions,[36] this position is not defensible, because other conditions are necessary to justify paternalism. Suppose, for example, that we could force medical treatment on Christian Scientists or blood transfusions on Jehovah's Witnesses and at the same time use some psychological processes to change their religious beliefs so that they would later ratify our actions. Their ratification would not justify our actions. The paternalistic intervention, considered as a whole process, must not itself create its own ratification.[37]

But even when the actual or predicted consent is not created by the intervention itself, justified paternalism hinges on factors I will discuss in the next chapter: the patient's defects, encumbrances, and limitations in decision-making or acting, and the probable net harm of nonintervention to the patient. Actual or predicted consent is not sufficient, even though it may be useful in determining that these criteria have been met.

While few theorists deny that *both* future consent and other considerations such as the criteria I mentioned are morally important, they dispute which is primary in justification. Some insist that future consent is primary and even sufficient in justification, but also concede that other considerations are useful in determining the *probability* of a person's future consent. These other considerations are important, according to Rosemary Carter, "because they provide grounds for assessing the likelihood that the interference will be justified by subsequent consent, and thus grounds for deciding whether one ought to interfere."[38] For other theorists, including myself, other criteria such as those identified above are primary in *justification* of paternalism, while the patient's probable future consent may provide *evidence* that these criteria have been satisfied.[39]

If actual or predicted ratification is not sufficient, is it *necessary* to justify paternalism? To make justification hinge on *actual* ratification is unsatisfactory. Many patients never gain or regain the capacity to ratify decisions and actions of others. Furthermore, an intervention's justification would be held in abeyance until the resistant patient died and thereby exhausted all his possibilities to "consent"; then it would be declared "unjustified," if actual ratification were necessary for justification. Thus, at most the paternalist's action is a "wager" that the patient will concur in the future if he gains or regains his capacity.[40]

John Rawls holds that *predicted* ratification, in contrast to actual ratification, is a necessary condition for justified paternalism: "We must be able to argue that with the development or the recovery of his rational powers the individual in question will accept our decision on his behalf and agree with us that we did the best thing for him."[41] But this criterion is both redundant and too restrictive. It is redundant, for ratification is predicted *because* other criteria are met. If the patient is incompetent and at risk of harm, especially as defined by his own values, we can hope and perhaps even expect that he will ratify our decision and action in the future, if and when he becomes competent. The ground of the justification of our paternalism is the patient's incompetence and his risk of harm; the probability of his ratification of our intervention is marginal evidence of the rightness of our judgment.

The criterion of predicted ratification is also too restrictive, for some paternalistic interventions may be justified even when it can be reliably predicted that the patient will never ratify them. Perhaps no patients pose this problem more dramatically than some Jehovah's Witnesses who refuse blood transfusions. Jehovah's Witnesses believe that the biblical admonition to "abstain from blood" applies to blood transfusions, which can never be justified even to save life. They do not, however, want to die. Some Witnesses, perhaps representing the mainstream of the tradition, affirm a doctrine of strict liability. The blood transfusion itself defiles the recipient even when he or she is unconscious, deceived, or coerced. Other Witnesses appear to hold that what is prohibited is past, present, and future *consent* to blood transfusions. They imply that a court-ordered transfusion would not be their responsibility and would not deprive them of everlasting life. Some courts have authorized transfusions against the express wishes of adult Witnesses, sometimes offering impure paternalistic reasons (e.g., to protect both the patient and her children) and sometimes offering pure paternalistic reasons.[42] In such cases, the Witness' future consent is highly unlikely, because, at the very least, his or her religious doctrines prohibit consent at any time.[43]

In conclusion, the principle of respect for persons generates the requirement of patient consent in medical relationships. Through consent, a patient transfers, assigns, or creates rights. Because there are many different varieties of consent, I analyzed express, tacit, implied, and presumed consents in order to determine which of them can create rights on the part of health care professionals. Furthermore, it was necessary to situate a person's present consents and dissents in the context of both past and future consents and dissents. Thus, respecting a person may require that health care professionals consider which current wishes—which may or may not be expressed—and which wishes—past, present, or future—to respect. The process of communication may be long, complex, and difficult. Nevertheless, there is a presumption in favor of acquiescing in present, express wishes. Where, however, the patient appears to be incompetent and where his or her express wishes put him or her at considerable risk, paternalistic interventions may be justified. In the next chapter, I will analyze the conditions of justified paternalism, indicating that past or prior consent may identify legitimate agents of intervention and provide the values for "soft" paternalism and that future consent may provide evidence of justification. But neither past consent nor future consent is necessary or sufficient for justified paternalism.

Notes

1. See H. L. A. Hart, "Are There Any Natural Rights?" *Philosophical Review* 64 (1955): 175–91. See also my discussion in *Civil Disobedience and Political Obligation: A Study in Christian Social Ethics* (New Haven: Yale University Press, 1971).
2. This paragraph is greatly influenced by Hart, "Are There Any Natural Rights?" and A. John Simmons, "Tacit Consent and Political Obligation," *Philosophy and Public Affairs* 5 (Spring 1976): 274–91, esp. 283–86.

3. William L. Prosser summarizes the relevant tort law: "The consent of the person damaged will ordinarily avoid liability for intentional interference with person or property. It is not, strictly speaking, a privilege, or even a defense, but goes to negative the existence of any tort in the first instance. It is a fundamental principle of the common law that *volenti non fit injuria*—to one who is willing, no wrong is done. The attitude of the courts has not, in general, been one of paternalism." *Handbook of the Law of Torts*, 4th ed. (St. Paul, Minn.: West Publishing Company, 1971), p. 101. There might be good nonpaternalistic (or partially non-paternalistic) reasons for not permitting people to sell one of their paired organs such as a kidney.

4. Hart, "Are There Any Natural Rights?"

5. David Braybrooke, "The Firm but Untidy Correlativity of Rights and Obligations," *Canadian Journal of Philosophy* 1 (March 1972): 351–63. See also Joel Feinberg, *Social Philosophy* (Englewood Cliffs, N.J.: Prentice-Hall, 1973), p. 61, where this logical thesis is distinguished from a moral thesis which holds that if X has rights, X also has certain obligations. I will return to this moral thesis in chapter VIII.

6. Hart, "Are There Any Natural Rights?," p. 176.

7. *Ibid.*, p. 182.

8. Department of Health, Education, and Welfare Regulations on the Protection of Human Subjects, Code of Federal Regulations, Title 45, U.S. Code, Part 46, revised as of January 11, 1978. Probably the emphasis in the philosophical literature on the consenter's obligation stems from its concentration on political obligation.

9. My analysis of "tacit consent" is deeply indebted to Simmons, "Tacit Consent and Political Obligation," pp. 274–91. See also his *Moral Principles and Political Obligations* (Princeton: Princeton University Press, 1979).

10. Prosser, *Handbook of the Law of Torts*, p. 102.

11. Simmons, "Tacit Consent and Political Obligation," pp. 278–81.

12. John Locke, *Treatise of Civil Government*, ed. Charles L. Sherman (New York: Appleton-Century-Crofts, 1937), pp. 78–79, #119.

13. Simmons distinguishes acts that are "signs of consent" and acts that "imply consent." See "Tacit Consent and Political Obligation," p. 286.

14. Prosser, *Handbook of the Law of Torts*, p. 103.

15. For example, there has been considerable debate in recent years about the participation of severely burned patients, for whom survival is unprecedented, in decisions about their medical care. See case #13 and the discussion in chapter V.

16. John Hodson's principle of paternalism appeals to "what the individual's empirical will *would be* if it were unencumbered. The individual's empirical will is overridden, but in favor of that same individual's empirical will as it would be in more favorable circumstances." John D. Hodson, "The Principle of Paternalism," *American Philosophical Quarterly* 14 (January 1977): 67. In some cases it is possible empirically to verify

this will, e.g., by providing information to the patient and then listening to his response; in other cases, it is not.

17. See, for example, Richard A. McCormick, S.J., "Proxy Consent in the Experimentation Situation," *Perspectives in Biology and Medicine* 18 (Autumn 1974): 2–20.

18. One of the dangerous fictions is "surrogate consent." Contrast Norman Fost, "A Surrogate System for Informed Consent," *Journal of the American Medical Association* 233 (August 18, 1975): 800–803. For a proposal of consent to deceptive research by a group of mock subjects, see Robert Veatch, "Ethical Principles in Medical Experimentation," *Ethical and Legal Issues of Social Experimentation*, ed. A. M. Rivlin and P. M. Timpane (Washington, D.C.: The Brookings Institution, 1975). For criticism of this proposal, see Alan Soble, "Deception in Social Science Research: Is Informed Consent Possible?" *Hastings Center Report* 8 (October 1978): 43–44.

19. Michael Walzer, *Obligations: Essays on Disobedience, War, and Citizenship* (Cambridge: Harvard University Press, 1970), p. xiii.

20. This videotape, *Please Let Me Die*, is available for rental or purchase from Robert B. White, M.D., Department of Psychiatry, University of Texas Medical Branch, Galveston, Texas. The transcript is available in Robert A. Burt, *Taking Care of Strangers: The Rule of Law in Doctor-Patient Relations* (New York: The Free Press, 1979), where it is also analyzed with great care and sensitivity in chap. 1. See also the discussion of this case by Robert B. White and Tristram H. Engelhardt, Jr., "A Demand to Die," *Hastings Center Report* 5 (June 1975): 9–10, 47.

21. Burt, *Taking Care of Strangers*, pp. 6, 10–11.

22. Rosemary Carter, "Justifying Paternalism," *Canadian Journal of Philosophy* 7 (March 1977): 134–35.

23. Bernard Gert and Charles Culver argue that past consent removes an act from the class of paternalistic acts. See their "Paternalistic Behavior," *Philosophy and Public Affairs* 6 (1976): 53.

24. Gerald Dworkin, "Paternalism," *Morality and the Law*, ed. Richard A. Wasserstrom (Belmont, Calif.: Wadsworth Publishing Company, 1971), p. 120.

25. Homer, *The Odyssey*, trans. Robert Fitzgerald (Garden City, N.Y.: Doubleday, 1963), Book 12, pp. 214–16.

26. John Elster, *Ulysses and the Sirens: Studies in Rationality and Irrationality* (Cambridge: Cambridge University Press, 1979), p. 36.

27. I read about a similar case several years ago, but I do not have the citation.

28. Elster, *Ulysses and the Sirens*, p. 43. In case #9 a woman requested a tubal ligation in part to ensure that she could not change her mind about not having children.

29. Derek Parfit, "Later Selves and Moral Principles," *Philosophy and Personal Relations*, ed. A. Montefiore (London: Routledge and Kegan Paul, 1973), p. 145. See also Donald H. Regan, "Justifications for Pa-

ternalism," in *The Limits of Law, Nomos* XV, ed. J. Roland Pennock and John W. Chapman (New York: Lieber-Atherton, 1974). Regan argues that "paternalism" can be subsumed under the principle of preventing harm to others because "persons may, despite bodily continuity, become different persons *for some purposes* as they change over time" (p. 206).

30. It is not even clear, of course, that these matters should be conceived in terms of successive selves. Another possibility, as Elster suggests, is "a situation where several selves coexist simultaneously and hierarchically, representing the lowest, the intermediate and the highest forms of ethical life. . . . The question is how other persons can pick out the authorized spokesman for the hierarchy; how they can decide whether the revocation of an order is issued by the lowest or the highest self. Other individuals have no direct access to our bright lines. Parfit seems to think that one should never give in, say, to a person begging me to give him the cigarettes he has begged me to withhold from him, but this is to beg the very question raised by Ainslie and James, which is that *sometimes I may have good reasons for asking to be released, in the sense of reasons that I would have accepted before I asked to be bound.*" Elster, *Ulysses and the Sirens*, pp. 109–10, emphasis added. This is why it is important to determine whether the prior consent was really voluntary and informed (i.e., whether the agent really had access to all the relevant reasons), but even then his appreciation of their weight may change with experience.

31. Dworkin, "Paternalism," p. 119.

32. Gert and Culver, "Paternalistic Behavior," pp. 51–52.

33. *Ibid.*

34. For purposes of argument I will construe this case as one of subsequent ratification, but the patient may not have approved of their deceptive use of a placebo even though he did not subsequently want to reverse the good effects.

35. Quoted in Miriam Siegler and Humphry Osmond, *Patienthood: The Art of Being a Responsible Patient* (New York: Macmillan, 1979), p. 165.

36. Gert and Culver in "Paternalistic Behavior" write, "Future consent, though it may justify A's act, does not make the action nonpaternalistic" (p. 53). They do not follow up on this suggestion about the sufficiency of future consent for justification. See Gert and Culver, "The Justification of Paternalism," *Ethics* 89 (January, 1972): 199–210. Rosemary Carter has argued "that consent plays the central role in justifying paternalism, and indeed that no other concepts are relevant." Either prior consent or subsequent consent is necessary and sufficient. She concentrates on subsequent consent, which voluntarily "alienates" the prima facie right to noninterference and thus justifies paternalistic interventions. See Carter, "Justifying Paternalism," pp. 133–45.

37. This point is made by John Rawls, *A Theory of Justice* (Cambridge: Harvard University Press, 1971), pp. 249–50 and Jeffrie Murphy, "Incompetence and Paternalism," *Archiv für Rechts- und Sozialphilosophie*

60 (1974). Stanley Milgram has defended the deception used in his famous studies of the phenomenon of obedience by appealing to retro-active consent: "The central moral justification for allowing a procedure of the sort used in my experiments is that it is judged acceptable by those who have taken part in it." See Milgram, *Obedience to Authority* (New York: Harper & Row, 1974), pp. 198–99 and "Subject Reaction: The Neglected Factor in the Ethics of Experimentation," *Hastings Center Report* 7 (August 1977): 21. But, as Alan Soble notes, it is difficult to believe that retroactive subject approval was independent: "for both obedient and defiant subjects the nature of the experiment provides powerful psychological reasons (self-respect, exculpation, self-righteous-ness) for giving approval afterwards." Soble, "Deception in Social Science Research: Is Informed Consent Possible?" p. 43.

38. See Carter, "Justifying Paternalism," p. 139.

39. Murphy, "Incompetence and Paternalism," p. 483: "future consent can at most serve as *evidence* that . . . the genuine criterion . . . has been satisfied. Future-consent cannot itself be the criterion."

40. Because many individuals who are subject to paternalistic interventions will never gain or regain their capacity to consent, ratification often takes a hypothetical form: what individuals *would* consent to if they could consent. Their consent is presumed even though it may not be implied by their actions. See my discussion of presumed consent earlier in this chapter.

41. Rawls, *A Theory of Justice*, p. 249.

42. *Application of the President and Directors of Georgetown College*, 331 F 2d 1000 (D.C. Cir.), certiorari denied, 377 U.S. 978 (1964); see also *United States* v. *George*, 239 F. Supp. 752 (D. Conn. 1965); *Powell* v. *Columbia Presbyterian Medical Center*, 267 N.Y.S. 2d. 450 (Sup. Ct. 1965); and *Charles W. Folker, Melvin Casberg and Coleta Valley Com-munity Hospital* v. *Arlen Knight and Florence Knight*, Court of Appeal, CA., 2nd Appellate District, Div. 1 (1976). This last case is discussed in John J. Paris, S.J., "Compulsory Medical Treatment and Religious Freedom: Whose Law Shall Prevail?" *University of San Francisco Law Review* (Summer 1975): 2–5. Contrast *In Re Osborne*, 294 A. 2d 372 (D.C. App. 1972).

43. For a fuller analysis of moral issues in the Jehovah's Witness refusal of blood transfusions, see James F. Childress, "Moral Responsibility and Blood Transfusion: Ethical Issues in the Treatment of Jehovah's Wit-nesses," *Journal of Religion*, forthcoming. For a very different analysis, see Ruth Macklin, "Consent, Coercion and Conflicts of Rights," *Perspec-tives in Biology and Medicine* 20 (Spring 1977): 360–71.

V
Justified Paternalism

Conditions for Justified Paternalism:
The Principle of Limited Paternalism

Parents sometime override their children's wishes in order to protect them. Such parental actions are often justified because of children's incompetence and risk of harm or loss of some good. This example from familial relations yields two conditions that are frequently invoked to justify medical paternalism: (1) the defects, encumbrances, and limitations of a person's decision-making and acting, and (2) the probability of harm to that person unless there is intervention.[1]

If the second condition—probable harm—is held to be sufficient to justify paternalism, apart from the person's incapacity for decision-making, we have extended or strong paternalism. According to this position, paternalistic interventions can be justified when a patient's risk-benefit analysis is unreasonable even though he is competent and his wishes, choices, or actions are informed and voluntary. If, however, the first set of conditions is held to be necessary, we have limited or weak paternalism, which allows paternalistic interventions only when a person's wishes, choices, or actions are defective because of incompetence, ignorance, or some internal or external constraint.[2]

Both conditions, yet to be explained and amplified, are jointly necessary to justify active paternalism. (I will consider only *active* paternalism for most of this chapter). To intervene merely because a person suffers some defect, encumbrance, or limitation in decision-making or in acting is unwarranted. It would be intervention for the sake of intervention. As "paternalism" implies, intervention requires justification in terms of the patient's interests as well as in terms of the patient's defects in deciding or acting. If the patient is not at risk, intervention is not warranted, however much his or her capacity to make decisions is reduced. Even a person with diminished capacity for decision-making should be free except when he or she is at risk. This is an implication of holding that both conditions are jointly necessary.

If these two conditions are jointly necessary for justified active paternalism, and if only limited paternalism is justified, we are able to express both the principle of beneficence and the principle of respect for persons. In limited paternalism, agents meet the needs of other persons without insulting them. For example, if another person is incompetent to make decisions and is also at risk, interventions even against that person's express wishes do not signify disrespect or constitute an indignity. Not to intervene might even violate the principle of respect for persons; certainly, it would violate the principle of beneficence in some circumstances.

Since both of these conditions are necessary to justify paternalistic acts, it is possible to start with either one. An apparent reason to start with prevention or removal of harm, or provision of benefit, is that this consideration frequently triggers paternalistic actions. In the order of experience, perception of risk to the patient, apart from intervention, usually precedes and provokes an assessment of the patient's competence to decide. Indeed, as I have already noted, Carlton's studies indicate that a patient's competence to consent to treatment is rarely examined unless there is a conflict between the physician's recommendation and the patient's wishes.[3] Thus, an apparent conflict of values provides the occasion for an examination of the patient's competence. In view of customary medical practice, there are two good reasons for beginning with the patient's incompetence as a necessary condition for justified paternalism. First, to begin with the prevention or removal of harm may appear to give this condition priority and may play into the hands of strong paternalists. Second, even though in practice there may be little interest in the patient's competence unless there are risks, from a moral point of view the assessment of the patient's competence should be somewhat independent of the risks. Otherwise, strong paternalism could masquerade as weak paternalism, since—the argument might go —no competent person would knowingly and voluntarily accept some risks.

For the first condition, as well as for others, I will only sketch prominent lines in this chapter, reserving more detailed explication for the applications in chapters VI–VIII. The first necessary condition for justified paternalism is that the patient have some defect, encumbrance, or limitation in deciding, willing, or acting. In explicating this first condition, we are interested in the criteria or tests by which a person may be found to be nonautonomous. The principle of respect for persons does not mandate identical treatment for autonomous and nonautonomous persons. It does not require acquiescence in a nonautonomous person's wishes.

Respect for a person's wishes, choices, and actions presupposes that the person is autonomous, that is, deliberating rationally and acting freely. A shorthand expression for several (but not all) capacities for autonomy is competence. In particular, I will focus on a person's competence in the range of wishes, choices, and actions that paternalism in health care sometimes refuses to accept. For purposes of this argument, I will emphasize people's competence, or incompetence, *to decide* what they are to do and what is to be done to them in matters of health care.[4] "Decision" is more appropriate than "consent," because what is at stake is not merely consent to or refusal of treatment—though this is important—but a person's role as a decision-maker in health care (broadly conceived) whether he or she is a patient in a narrow sense.

As I indicated in chapter III, a person's competence may vary from situation to situation and over time. Since a person may be competent to decide or to do X but not Y, it is appropriate to recognize limited or specific competence. A person who may not be competent to make some decisions may, nevertheless, be competent to accept or to refuse medical treatment. In addition, competence may be intermittent; a person may be competent one day but incompetent the next. His incompetence may stem from a temporary condition such as drug overdose. In some cases, permanent conditions, such as severe mental retardation, may render a person generally incompetent.

There should be a moral presumption—parallel to the accepted legal presumption—of an adult's competence to make decisions in health care. Then the burden of proof should fall on those who believe that a particular individual is incompetent. As Alan Meisel argues,

> Because of the legal presumption of competency . . . a patient must be *found* incompetent before he may be disqualified from participation in decisionmaking, that is, before the physician need not (and may not) rely on the patient's decision as either a valid authorization or refusal of treatment. Therefore, what we need is some sort of test to ascertain which persons, of all the persons who are presumed competent, are, in fact, incompetent.[5]

Thus, as Meisel continues, the tests that we seek should be tests of incompetence rather than of competence. We should presume competence and test for incompetence.

Several tests have been proposed for incompetence, but not all of them are defensible.[6] First, if a person is in a position where a decision (such as to accept or to refuse treatment) is clearly indicated, and he cannot or does not respond, he may be treated as incompetent. A clear case is a comatose patient. If there is "paternalism" in such a case, it is analogous to the parent-infant relationship rather than to the parent-adolescent relationship. This test of incompetence would exclude very few adults.

If a person makes a decision and expresses his or her preferences, health care professionals, as I have emphasized, usually do not raise questions about incompetence unless the decision itself appears to be mistaken. But the *content* of the decision is neither necessary nor sufficient to indicate incompetence, even if it rightly triggers an inquiry into incompetence. If this test were sufficient, it would support strong paternalism under the guise of weak paternalism. (Nevertheless, the content of the decision, such as refusal of treatment under certain conditions, may justify action against the patient's wishes where there is serious *doubt* about the patient's competence; I will return to this point below).

Other possible tests of a person's incompetence focus on his or her understanding or process of deliberating and reasoning. If a person does not understand a situation and does not deliberate rationally about it, he or she may be incompetent to make a decision. Often, of course, it may be possible to inform the patient in order to overcome deficiencies of understanding. Thus, lack of understanding cannot be used as an excuse for paternalistic intervention, unless efforts have been made—time

permitting—to increase the patient's understanding by disclosure of information. If, however, a person lacks the *ability* to understand because
of severe mental retardation or mental illness, the principle of respect
for persons does not mandate acquiescence in his or her wishes; that
person is not competent to decide. The inability to understand may be
limited and specific, rather than general. A person may have false beliefs
about a situation that are incorrigible; in case #15, a woman falsely
believed that her feet were not gangrenous, and in case #16, a woman
falsely believed that she did not have cancer. Such false beliefs may lead
a patient to pursue ineffective means to desired goals, such as survival.
While a person's false beliefs about some circumstances and means may
support a finding of incompetence, such beliefs should be distinguished
from beliefs about religious or metaphysical matters, which are not
empirically verifiable. An example is the Jehovah's Witness refusal of a
blood transfusion because Jehovah has prohibited the injection of blood
and will punish violators of the prohibition (see case #10). However
much such beliefs may be disputed, they do not provide grounds for a
finding of incompetence. Even when false beliefs are not used as premises, the process of deliberating and reasoning may be defective in other
ways. It may, for example, be internally inconsistent and even contradictory.

I have concentrated on incompetence in decisions, but wishes,
choices, and actions may be encumbered in other ways, for example, by
emotional stress, by compulsion, or by drug addiction. Such encumbrances may prevent a person from deciding or acting freely. A care
provider does not act with disrespect when she refrains from acquiescing
in a person's express wishes or actions under such circumstances. There
are, of course, numerous conceptual, moral, and practical difficulties in
determining that a person is encumbered or incompetent in a particular
decision or action.

Conceptions of incompetence and encumbrance are frequently ambiguous. Focusing on mental capacity, Daniel Wikler has identified two
conceptions of competence. According to the *relativist* conception, the
judgment that some persons are mentally impaired is always relative to a
perspective on some other level. The attribute of mental capacity,
viewed as intelligence, is a matter of degree; people have more or less.
The line between the competent and the incompetent is arbitrary. Indeed, it might be possible to make a case for what Wikler calls a

"benevolent hierarchy" in which the gifted would make many decisions for normal adults just as normal adults currently make many decisions for mildly retarded adults. But, according to the *threshold* conception of competence, competence is a property that is possessed equally by all who have it. On this understanding, mental capacity might be viewed as "intellect's power in meeting a challenge." Many challenges may be met by a certain amount of intelligence, and a person's additional intelligence will simply be "unused surplus": "Those lacking enough intelligence for the task will be incompetent to perform it; while those having sufficient intelligence will be equally competent however great the difference in their intellectual levels." People will pass the threshold test of competence if they can comprehend and avoid "downward risks," even though some who cross the threshold will be more competent than others to realize "upward gains."[7]

It might be argued that the principle of beneficence ought to lead to a relativist conception of competence, because beneficence is concerned with the promotion of goods and not only with the prevention or removal of evils.[8] But such an argument for a "benevolent hierarchy" is plausible only if the principle of beneficence is removed from its context of limitation and constraint by the principle of respect for persons. Because of the latter principle, there are good reasons for using a threshold conception of competence. Individuals who are competent in this sense may, of course, solicit the advice and aid of others, such as physicians, whose greater expertise may enable them to realize "upward gains," as well as to prevent any "downward risks" not included in the determination of the threshold of competence.

The second condition for justified paternalism is the probability of harm unless there is intervention. As I indicated earlier, altruistic beneficence takes both positive and negative forms. Positive beneficence promotes another's good, while negative beneficence prevents or removes evil or harm. Although the distinction is not always easy to draw, and although some acts may fall under both positive and negative beneficence, the distinction is still useful. And, as I argued earlier, negative beneficence takes priority over positive beneficence, *ceteris paribus*. Perhaps one reason for this priority is greater agreement about what counts as evils or harms (such as pain, disability, and death) than about what counts as excellence in health. An example—to be discussed in chapter VIII—is the distinction between reducing risks of morbidity and premature mortality, on the one hand, and promoting excellent health, on the other. Gert and Culver defend negative paternalism: "Although we have talked of 'S's good' and of 'benefiting S,' what is intended is the prevention or relief of S's suffering some evil, that is, death; pain; disability; or loss of freedom, opportunity, or pleasure."[9]

Although Gert and Culver use the language of "evils," I will use the language of "harms." The object of harm is always an *interest*.[10] But there are both broad and narrow definitions of "harm" according to the range of interests involved. In a narrow definition, harm is viewed as damage to physical and perhaps mental interests, which are distinguished from other interests. In a broad definition, various interests are included, such as life, health, property, familial relations, privacy, and liberty. Harm is damage to any of those interests. Proponents of a broad definition can then distinguish trivial and serious harms by the order and magnitude of the interests involved. For purposes of this discussion, I will use a broad definition of harm, but I will concentrate on physical harms, including pain, disability, and death, while not excluding other harms.

In paternalism, it is necessary to examine both the magnitude and the probability of the harm. Both elements are captured in the probabilistic term "risk," which may refer to the *amount* of possible loss or to the *probability* of that loss. While harms are sometimes certain, most have degrees of probability. Determination of the probability of harm, apart from intervention, is more technical than determination of the magnitude or severity of the harm; nonetheless, such a determination is not value-free since the analyst's values influence the resolution of uncertainty about potential harms.

Harms may range from minor to major. But even if there is a general consensus about what counts as harm—such as discomfort, pain, disability, and death—there may be serious disputes about how much particular harms count. (As I will emphasize later, such disputes make "soft" paternalism more attractive than "hard" paternalism). For example, it is not clear that the harm of death is always more serious than other harms such as pain; thus, it is not clear that the prevention of death should always have priority or should be pursued at all costs. Nevertheless, in general, where a harm such as death is irreversible, the paternalist has stronger reasons for intervening to prevent it than where harms are reversible. Even when a harm is minor, its irreversibility may offer a strong reason for intervention (if other conditions are met).

These first two conditions are necessary for justified paternalism, but they are not sufficient. It is not enough to show that, apart from intervention, there is a high risk of serious harm to a person who is incompetent to make his or her own decisions. Some other necessary conditions are simply specifications or amplifications of the first two conditions and the moral principles that support and limit paternalism, especially beneficence and respect for persons.

A third condition is *proportionality*: the probable benefit of intervention should outweigh the probable harm of nonintervention. According to this condition, the magnitude and probability of benefit have to be balanced against the magnitude and probability of harm apart from intervention. The benefit that is sought for the patient should outweigh both the moral rules that make some actions prima facie wrong (such as lying and coercion) and any goods that the patient will lose through the intervention. Even the nonautonomous patient has wishes that paternalism frequently thwarts, and paternalistic interventions themselves may cause pain, suffering, and disability. Thus, a patient's experience of pain and suffering as a result of involuntary hospitalization may outweigh the benefits of treatment. Not only should the paternalistic action be aimed at a net benefit for the patient; it should also have a reasonable chance of realizing this net benefit. Finally, the probable net benefit of the *proposed* intervention should also outweigh the probable net benefit of *alternative* interventions as well as nonintervention.[11]

Even if these standards are acceptable, they do not always provide clear answers. This point can be illustrated by the continuing controversy over the treatment of severely burned patients. Case #13 was drawn from an article "Autonomy for Burned Patients When Survival is Unprecedented" in *The New England Journal of Medicine*.[12] The authors, members of the burn team for the Los Angeles County-University of Southern California Medical Center, hold that "during the first few hours of hospitalization . . . even the most severely burned patient is usually alert and mentally competent." Thus, the burn team takes what the authors describe as "an aggressive approach to decision making to preserve patient autonomy." The severely burned patient is given sufficient information about his condition and prospects and is asked if he wishes to choose between full therapy and ordinary care. The authors contend that such patients exercise more "self-determination" and receive more "empathy" and that the mortality rates of burn patients have not increased.

Needless to say, this aggressive approach toward autonomy is controversial. It does not merely respect autonomy; it actively (aggressively) promotes autonomy under very difficult circumstances. Critics of this approach (including a National Institutes of Health consensus panel) contend that the conditions for justified weak paternalism are met in such burn cases. First, critics argue that the burn victim is under "physical and emotional shock" even in the early period and thus cannot really participate in the decision-making. According to them, the first condition for justified weak paternalism is met. Second, critics also hold that "there have been instances in which patients with as much as 90–95 percent third degree burns have been salvaged."[13] But withholding therapy at the patient's request guarantees death. In short, controversy rages about several conditions for justified paternalism, particularly the limitations on the patient's capacity to make decisions and the risks of nonintervention to the patient.

A major practical problem in paternalism concerns what should be done in doubtful or borderline cases. As the debate about severely burned patients indicates, several aspects of a case may be in doubt. Professionals and others may be uncertain about one or more of the conditions for justified paternalism: the patient's incompetence, the probability and seriousness of harm, and the probability that an intervention will produce a net benefit. They may also be uncertain about the patient's actual wishes and values.

How doubt is resolved will depend in part on the presumptions in the case. It is important to distinguish presumptions of morality from presumptions of fact. As I have argued, there is an irrebuttable presumption that the principle of respect for persons constrains and limits the principle of beneficence, at least in paternalism; beneficence toward one person cannot override respect for that person. But respect for persons does not require treating autonomous and nonautonomous persons in the same way. In particular, some rights of persons may not be exercised by nonautonomous persons when they are at risk of serious harm.

Then there are questions of fact: is this patient incompetent and is she at risk of serious harm? In our society, there is a rebuttable presumption that adults are competent to make their own decisions. This presumption also extends to adults as patients. Although some hold that "sickness" makes persons less "sovereign" and less "autonomous," such a claim is not defensible as a general proposition about patient decision-making. Nevertheless, the presumption of patient competence can be rebutted in cases where there is sufficient evidence of incompetence. Furthermore, certainty about the patient's high risk of serious and irreversible harm, such as death, may justify intervention against the patient's express wishes even when there are some doubts that the patient is incompetent. An example is suicide intervention, which will be discussed at length in chapter VII. Such an intervention can, however, only be temporary. It may be necessary to intervene in order to gain time so that a more adequate assessment can be made of the patient's competence and wishes, as well as his risks. Where, however, there is a probability of minor, reversible harm (such as the foolish expenditure of several hundred dollars), paternalistic intervention should not proceed if there is significant doubt that the person is incompetent. As in case #18, where there is a very narrow margin of probable net benefit from a risky intervention and the patient may be incompetent (because of denial), paternalistic actions are not warranted.[14] In short, how we resolve doubtful or borderline cases will depend on the circumstances but also on the weights assigned to the principles of beneficence and respect for persons.[15]

Whose values are relevant and decisive as we try to identify and balance harms and benefits? This question is not identical with the question, "who should make the decision?" Some paternalistic interventions impose *alien* values not accepted by the patient. But others only attempt to help the patient realize *his or her own values* whatever they are. The former are "hard," the latter are "soft." "Soft" paternalism warrants actions only when the patient's own values are threatened, whereas "hard" paternalism overrides the patient's values in the name of other values. Rosemary Carter, who draws this distinction, identifies "hard" paternalists as "those who believe that the subject's conception of the good is irrelevant to determining whether or not to interfere."[16] But "hard" paternalists need not hold that the patient's values are irrelevant, only that they are not decisive. They may accept his or her values as relevant but then override them in the name of other values.

"Soft" paternalism, which is easier to justify, *ceteris paribus*, than "hard" paternalism, takes different forms. Sometimes both the paternalist and the patient affirm a dominant value in the circumstances, but the patient for some reason cannot or will not follow the path that leads to it. In case #4 a man voluntarily entered a psychiatric clinic which teaches self-control of pain, but he falsely believed that he could not control his pain without his six daily doses of Talwin and thus refused to allow any modification in his medication. The therapists substituted a placebo which was successful. They and the patient concurred in the primary value (pain control), but they disagreed about whether his instrumental value (medication) was necessary. This was basically a disagreement about factual matters, not primary values; the therapists' deception was "soft" paternalism.

In other circumstances, "soft" paternalists may intervene to overcome a person's weakness of will; for example, he may not be able to stop smoking cigarettes or to stay on a diet to control obesity. In such cases the patient rationally affirms certain values as dominant but other values actually dominate his life. The paternalist helps him realize his values, as rationally affirmed, against his weakness of will.

Probably few primary values are alien to any patients. However much a patient may denigrate health and life, he has probably affirmed these values in various ways over the years. Thus, to keep a person alive against his wishes could have some warrant in his past values. Earlier I examined the relations between past consents and present refusals and, thus, between values previously affirmed and values currently rejected. But it is also necessary to distinguish values such as life and health from their rank in a personal hierarchy of values. This hierarchy is itself a value, not reducible to its parts. A person's life plan includes not only discrete values; it also ranks them. It is true that Jehovah's Witnesses value earthy life and do not want to die, but they value everlasting life more than earthly life. Much paternalism is "hard" because it imposes a hierarchy of values alien to the patient at that time. It overrides the patient's value-structure.

"Hard" paternalism is not categorically excluded unless it is (wrongly) identified with extended or strong (active) paternalism. Such an identification would mean that alien values are imposed not only against a patient's express will but also regardless of his or her competence. I distinguish "soft" and "hard" paternalism in terms of the *source* of the values that are used to justify intervention: the patient's own values or someone else's. Neither "soft" nor "hard" paternalism can be justified unless the patient suffers from defects, encumbrances, or limitations in decision-making or acting. When that condition is met, however, both "soft" and "hard" paternalism can sometimes be justified, even though it is easier to justify "soft" paternalism. Of course, as I indicated in chapter IV, one difficulty for the "soft" paternalist is the discernment of a person's values, especially when they conflict with his or her express wishes and actions.

Modes of Paternalistic Action

Even though the three conditions identified above—encumbrance, risk, and proportionality—are necessary to justify paternalistic interventions, they are not sufficient because the modes of paternalistic action vary greatly. While deception and coercion are perhaps the most common, there are several different modes of paternalistic nonacquiescence, and it is a mistake to identify paternalism with any single mode. For example, paternalism may involve nondisclosure of information (see case #6), violation of confidentiality (see case #7), forcible invasion of a person's body (see case #15), refusal to carry out a patient's request (see case #19), and provision of unwanted services, among other possibilities.

Various modes of paternalism require special and independent attention; their effectiveness alone will not justify them. Even if several modes of nonacquiescence are equally effective, they may not be equally justified. In some cases, an independent moral assessment of the means might even lead to the conclusion that while X would probably be more effective than Y, it should not be used, perhaps because it violates more stringent moral rules. For example, there may be considerable debate about whether to use deception or coercion in a particular case, and different judgments may depend on the weight attached to the rules against lying or the use of force. (This example will be discussed at greater length in chapter VI.)

One general principle applies to all modes or means of paternalism: the least restrictive, humiliating, and insulting alternative should be employed. The requirement that the least restrictive alternative be used is common in civil commitment. While effectiveness is important, it should justify only those means absolutely necessary to prevent the harms or realize the benefits in question for the nonautonomous patient. The moral principle of respect for persons and its associated requirements such as truthfulness and noncoercion continue to mandate the degree of respect that is compatible with the patient's condition (both his incompetence and his risk of harm). It would be a form of disrespect and insult to use more force or deception than is necessary to realize the ends in question. This principle is a limit on beneficence even in relation to nonautonomous persons.

Other guidelines are plausible for means and modes of action. In his discussion of a man attempting to cross an unsafe bridge, John Stuart Mill argued that it would be morally acceptable to "seize him and turn him back" if "there were no time to warn him of his danger."[17] Such an intervention would be temporary and reversible. After informing the man of the bridge's condition, the weak paternalist would have to let him cross the bridge, unless he were incompetent to make his own decisions. Temporary interventions, designed to determine the patient's capacity to make decisions and to ascertain the probability and magnitude of harm, are often justified when long-term interventions would not be (for example, suicide intervention). Similarly, if the interventions and their effects are irreversible (such as amputation of a leg or psychosurgery), they must meet a heavier burden of justification. Finally, invasion of a person's body through surgery or other means also has a heavy burden of justification.[18]

It is sometimes appropriate and even mandatory for a paternalist to accept means that are less effective than others in order to respect moral principles and rules. Effectiveness alone does not determine the morality of paternalistic modes of action. Sometimes particular paternalistic actions could be avoided altogether if the society accepted a different pattern of allocation of resources and distribution of burdens. Daniel Wikler contends that paternalism involves questions of justice and not merely beneficence and respect for persons. Indeed, he even argues that "the morality of paternalism *reduces to* a question about distributive justice."[19] While such a claim is too strong even for Wikler's own context—civil liberties such as mildly retarded persons' decisions to marry and have children—it nevertheless identifies an important (and frequently neglected) presupposition of most arguments about paternalism. In many cases the society could lower the "threshold of competence" required for certain tasks and/or protect persons from harm from their actions. An example would be allowing mildly retarded persons to marry and to reproduce while assigning the costs of child care to the society (see the debates reflected in case #22 on involuntary sterilization). Such a policy might be criticized on utilitarian grounds. But if so, what is at stake is not only paternalism, but the general social welfare. At the very least, arguments for restricting the rights of mildly retarded people to marry and to reproduce are mixed. Thus, it is appropriate to examine very carefully any claim that a paternalistic policy, such as restriction of reproduction, is a last resort to protect incompetent persons from harm or burdens. Such a policy may be necessary only because the society is unwilling to allocate more resources or to redistribute the "burdens of incompetence."

Earlier I distinguished active from passive paternalism, according to different modes of nonacquiescence. In active paternalism an agent refuses to accept a person's wish or request that he not intervene, whereas, in passive paternalism, an agent refuses to carry out a person's wishes or choices. While I have concentrated on active paternalism in this chapter, passive paternalism is also important, though easier to justify. In medical contexts, the problem of passive paternalism often appears under the rubric of "the demanding patient," that is, the patient who insists on a particular course of treatment that the physician believes to be inappropriate treatment and perhaps even malpractice. Considering three ways to treat a thyroid tumor—radiation therapy, surgery, and chemotherapy—a physician might be convinced that radiation therapy is inappropriate for a young woman who might want to have children later, and he might refuse to acquiesce in her wishes for that therapy. His refusal would be paternalistic (cf. cases #19 and 20). But unless a patient has a moral right to a specific mode of treatment from a particular physician, the physician's paternalistic action would not be morally unjustified. Where there are no positive rights, such as the right to assistance in a specific way, passive paternalism is easier to justify than active paternalism. Nevertheless, at the very least, the physician would have a duty to recommend another physician who might be more sympathetic with the patient's request.

Passive paternalism, in contrast to active paternalism, may be justified (or at least excused) even when the health care professional believes that the patient is competent to make a decision. Thus, some forms of justified passive paternalism may be strong rather than weak, or extended rather than limited. This conclusion is warranted, but its implications need to be drawn very carefully. In passive paternalism, the agent does not attempt to block the patient's wishes, choices, and actions; rather he or she refuses to be their instrument. Recognition of the moral legitimacy of passive paternalism stems from the principle of respect for persons and their autonomy—the same principle that accords patients their strong negative rights. If a physician conscientiously believes that providing a treatment requested by a patient (such as an antibiotic for a cold) is not in the patient's best interests, he is not compelled to violate his professional or personal conscience.

In short, the only active paternalism that can be justified is the limited or weak kind, but passive paternalism can be justified or excused in a broader range of cases, even when the patient is competent. Throughout this discussion, when I use the term "paternalism" without the modifier "passive," I refer to "active" paternalism, which is more prominent and more difficult to justify.

Limited Paternalism: Justified, Obligatory, or Praiseworthy?

In this chapter I have concentrated on *justified* paternalism by examining the conditions under which agents may rebut the presumption in favor of acquiescence in the patient's express wishes, choices, and actions. It is necessary to justify active paternalism because of this presumption; in addition, it is necessary to justify particular paternalistic acts such as deception and coercion because of other moral rules, several of which derive from the duty to respect persons. But to show that paternalism can be justified in some circumstances is only to show that it is not always wrong. While in some cases paternalism may be justified, a question remains as to whether it is ever obligatory.

One possible response is that paternalistic acts are never morally obligatory, but that they are sometimes praiseworthy.[20] For instance, we might praise professionals for acting paternalistically in some circumstances, but we might not blame them if they refused or failed to do so. Paternalistic acts may be plausibly construed as praiseworthy because of their foundation in beneficence, a principle whose status is frequently obscure. As I noted in chapter II, beneficence is sometimes an imperfect duty, which allows the agent great latitude and discretion in discharging it, and sometimes an ideal, especially when it involves burdens and risks for the agent. But I also argued that beneficence is often a duty because of an agent's role(s) and sometimes a duty for an agent because no one else can perform the action. Where a duty of beneficence rests on role relations, for example, weak paternalism may not only be justified; it may also be morally obligatory. Where the conditions for justified weak paternalism are met, the professional does not violate the principle of respect for persons, and his/her role-related duty of beneficence may require protective intervention against the patient's wishes.

Exactly when the duty of beneficence requires paternalistic intervention depends on several factors including the calculations that have been treated under the conditions for justified paternalism. But such a duty to intervene may also depend on the relationship between the parties. The duties that a health care professional has to a patient because of a prior and present relationship need to be distinguished from the duties that she has to a nonpatient. Disputes about what ought to be done for a person may emerge *within* or *outside* an established and continuing therapeutic relationship. It may be instructive to compare the cases of Otis Simmons and Mary Northern (cases #14 and 15). Otis Simmons, a 58-year-old derelict, suffered from gangrenous feet as a result of frostbite, and he voluntarily entered Roosevelt Hospital to obtain treatment. Nevertheless, he refused to allow doctors to amputate portions of his feet, saying "My two legs got to stay on." Mary Northern also had gangrenous feet because of frostbite and burns. In her case as in Simmons' case the physicians insisted that amputation was necessary in order to prevent death, but she too refused surgery. However, she had not sought help; acting upon the report of neighbors and friends, police forcibly entered her house and half-carried her to a vehicle which took her to the hospital. According to one report, "she kicked and elbowed them all the way." Whereas Simmons had voluntarily established a therapeutic relationship, Northern forcibly resisted it.

Voluntary entry appears to imply some agreement with the general goals of therapy without necessarily implying acceptance of specific courses of action. Certainly it creates some specific duties of beneficence. At the very least, such prior consent identifies agents who have special rights and duties to take care of a person. They have rights and duties to assess the person's competence and risks. But duties of beneficence, especially on the part of the society and public officials (as well as friends and neighbors), also extend to people who do not voluntarily seek medical treatment perhaps because they are not even able to make or to implement such a decision. And these duties may even mandate forcing an incompetent person into health care.

An act may possibly be justified on limited or weak paternalistic grounds but unjustified on other nonpaternalistic grounds, such as utility or justice. For example, in an institution where patients are involuntarily hospitalized, it may be morally appropriate to disallow some limited paternalistic acts, simply because allowing them would create greater dangers for the whole group of patients over time. What may be acceptable as an act may be unacceptable as a rule of practice. While this point may not hold for all paternalistic acts, it may hold for such acts in some settings.

While some philosophers would accept the moral legitimacy of many acts that I have counted as limited or weak paternalism, they would deny that they are instances of "paternalism." If such acts are justified, these philosophers would contend, they are justified on nonpaternalistic grounds. They object, in part, to justifying any paternalism, even limited or weak paternalism, because of what it might imply.

According to Tom Beauchamp, a rule-utilitarian, extended or strong paternalism is unacceptable mainly because "paternalistic principles are too broad and hence justify too much."[21] Even when thoughtfully restricted, such principles still allow "unacceptable latitude" that is "dangerous and acutely uncontrollable." In effect, Beauchamp offers a version of the wedge or slippery slope argument, holding that the principles that justify paternalistic interventions in cases we find defensible also justify such interventions in indefensible cases.

Two versions of the wedge argument merit attention. The first, prominent in Beauchamp's argument, focuses on the logic of moral reasoning. Because we are required by the principle of universalizability to treat similar cases similarly, we have to be sure that there are relevant dissimilarities between cases of "justified" and "unjustified" paternalism. Otherwise we will open the door to widespread paternalism even though we consider it unacceptable. Justification of an act that seems right may imply justification of an act that seems wrong. The second version of the wedge argument considers psychological, social, and cultural forces in order to determine the likely impact of a principle. Such forces may make it very difficult (if not impossible) to fetter and control even limited paternalism. While the first version of the wedge argument depends on logical analysis, the second depends on empirical analysis.

Both versions are legitimate in some cases. But neither one is decisive against the principle of limited paternalism. My specification of the principle of limited paternalism adequately restricts its scope in theory. But what is right in theory may not be right in practice. Even the principle of limited paternalism requires some interpretation (e.g., determination of incompetency). Jeffrie Murphy admits that rational persons, or parties in the Rawlsian original position, would accept a principle of limited or qualified paternalism, not very different from what I have defended in this chapter. While he stresses, just as Beauchamp does, that it may not be possible to specify the qualifications clearly enough, for him the more important problem is whether "any actual practice or human institution (necessarily staffed by fallible and often stupid and venal human beings) could be designed so as to guarantee the literal application of the principle." Rational persons might mistrust all suggested procedures and mechanisms for implementing the principle and decide that they had rather "take their chances of becoming incompetent and being left helpless than run the risk of suffering from an abuse of a paternalistic institution."[22] Procedures and mechanisms are indispensable. Whether any are acceptable for application of the principle of paternalism depends on several practical and empirical matters as well as on moral principles, some of which I will now explore.

Procedures

When there are disputes about values, procedures for resolving disputes and making decisions become increasingly important. Indeed, pluralism goes hand-in-hand with procedural morality. When the gods are silent, or their voices ambiguous, procedures are necessary. In this chapter, I have emphasized procedures of moral justification, that is, procedures to determine when paternalism is justified. In addition, it is essential to have procedures of responsibility and accountability. They specify the agents and mechanisms to determine when the conditions are present for justifiably overriding patients' express wishes, choices, and actions. The application of the principle of beneficence and the principle of respect for persons (including its derivative rules such as informed consent) hinges on *who* is authorized to invoke the exceptions. Of particular importance is who can declare a person incompetent and who can then make the proxy decision. First I want to indicate the importance of *some* procedures before offering brief and inconclusive suggestions about *which* procedures might be adopted.

Researchers, physicians, and other health care professionals frequently contend that even if informed consent is necessary, a "more reliable safeguard is provided by the presence of an intelligent, informed, conscientious, compassionate, responsible researcher," physician, or other health care professional.[23] But procedures are required in part because the compassionate or benevolent professional represents an ideal that is only approximated and in part because the ideal itself is too limited and too subject to distortion. The ideal is too limited because it emphasizes benefits rather than rights, and it is susceptible to distortion for the same reason. A spirit of "moral realism" is thus required not only because humans are imperfect but also because "moral passions," as Lionel Trilling notes, "are even more willful and imperious and impatient than the self-seeking passions." They tend to restrict as well as to liberate. We must be aware, Trilling insists, of "the dangers which lie in our most generous wishes. Some paradox of our nature leads us, when once we have made our fellow men the objects of our enlightened interest, to go on to make them the objects of our pity, then of our wisdom, ultimately of our coercion."[24] This sense of realism also appears in Justice Louis Brandeis' defense of the right to be let alone in his dissent in *Olmstead* v. *U.S.*:

> Experience should teach us to be most on our guard to protect liberty when the government's purposes are beneficent. Men born to freedom are naturally alert to repel invasions of their liberty by evil-minded rulers. The greatest dangers to liberty lurk in insidious encroachment by men of zeal, well-meaning but without understanding.[25]

Procedures to provide realistic protection against beneficence are especially important where the decisions are of "low visibility," as they frequently are in medicine and health care. Because the principle of patient-benefit is embedded in medical practice, some "external force" may be necessary to represent the principle of respect for persons.[26]

Procedures may be viewed in terms of their outcomes or in terms of principles they express and embody. First, let us consider the relationships between procedures and outcomes. As John Rawls suggests, there are at least three possible relationships between procedures and outcomes which depend on (1) whether there is an independent standard for evaluating outcomes and (2) whether the procedures can guarantee the right outcome. In "perfect procedural justice," there is an independent standard for assessing outcomes, and it is possible to devise a procedure to bring about the right outcome. Perfect procedural justice is, of course, rare. Indeed, Rawls uses a trivial example: if a fair division of cake is an equal division, the procedure to produce this outcome is to have one person cut all the pieces but with the warning that he or she will have the last piece after all others have chosen theirs. In "imperfect procedural justice," there is also an independent standard for assessing outcomes, but procedures are imperfect because they cannot guarantee the right outcome. An example is the criminal trial. The independent standard is that the guilty and only the guilty should be convicted, but no procedure can guarantee this result. Finally, in "pure procedural justice," there is no independent standard for assessing outcomes; whatever results from the procedure is right if the procedure is followed. An example is gambling. There is no right or wrong outcome; any outcome is acceptable as long as the procedure is fair and no one cheats.[27]

Of course, paternalists and patients disagree about the best outcome and thus about the best course of action. Even if the outcome is defined in such broad and vague terms as "the patient's best interests," there is dispute about whether those interests should include rights as well as needs and the patient's or the professional's hierarchy of values. Because of these disagreements, the debate about paternalism is a debate about procedure: who should decide? But now we are interested in procedures that should be followed before limited paternalism is implemented. And because the outcomes are in dispute, the procedures themselves become even more important. They should minimize the chances that a patient will be treated as a "child" under "parental" tutelage when in fact he or she is competent to exercise self-determination and self-direction. Fair and impartial procedures should decrease the possibility that individuals' rights will be overridden even to meet their needs. Basically they should express the moral principle of respect for persons. To prevent a person from making his or her own choices, or acting on them, without regard for such procedures is to deepen the personal insult and the affront to dignity. By assuming without actually meeting the relevant burden of proof in a public and accountable way, it assigns to a person the status of a child. Thus, procedures should be assessed both according to their outcomes and according to their symbolic significance—that is, what they produce and what they express.

A set of procedures that will cover all areas of paternalism is, of course, impossible to design. Some procedures may be desirable in some areas but not in others. Legal or legal-like adversarial procedures may be especially appropriate in cases of civil commitment, involuntary medical treatment, and involuntary sterilization. In such cases, there is a need for strict formality and structure, including the involvement of those who are not health care professionals. Less formal and less structured procedures may be sufficient in such cases as the violation of confidentiality by disclosing a patient's diagnosis to his or her family in order to ensure care, or withholding the diagnosis of terminal cancer in order to prevent anxiety. Such a division, which I will not defend at this point, may reflect judgments about the importance of the rights involved (such as the loss of freedom in civil commitment and the invasion of a person's body in involuntary treatment and involuntary sterilization). Not all paternalistic interventions violate rights equally or violate rights of equal importance. For the most part, philosophers have emphasized coercive interferences with liberty of action and have drawn analogies with criminal procedures. But whether it is better that ten incompetent persons be allowed to ruin themselves than that one competent person be helped unjustifiably will depend in part on the rights at stake.

Adversarial proceedings are unnecessary, according to many health care professionals, because everyone involved has the patient's best interests at heart while adversarial proceedings persuppose conflicts of interest. In the People's Republic of China, for example, adversarial relations are minimal in both health care and criminal law. When health care professionals and patients disagree about the best course of action, the professionals "persuade" patients to change their minds. For example, if a patient refuses treatment against his physician's and his family's wishes—reportedly a rare occurrence—he is "persuaded" to change his mind. Likewise if a woman is pregnant with her third child, she is "persuaded" to have an abortion. Sometimes "persuasion" appears to involve what Westerners might call undue influence, manipulation, and even coercion. Chinese physicians report that it is not easy to convince families to donate a deceased relative's kidneys or other organs for transplantation because they want to bury or to burn the body as a whole. As part of the process of "persuasion," a family may be taken to see the patient who would receive the organ. Such a request would probably be viewed as coercive in the United States.[28]

"Due process" is also different in Chinese criminal law, which presupposes that accurate identification and punishment of offenders can best be achieved by less adversarial and less public processes with fewer procedural safeguards for the suspect than in the West. A suspect in China, according to the government, should cooperate fully with the state; he can be confident "that the state will do the right thing, for it has his interests at heart." An appropriate analogy, Jerome Cohen suggests, is a parent's investigation of a child's destruction of some furniture while the parent was away from home. The parent proceeds by private interrogations with little attention to procedures such as a right to counsel. "Because parents have the best interests of the child at heart and the child is supposed to know this," Cohen continues, "our society generally accepts the practice as a reasonable way to proceed. This is the attitude that the People's Republic adopts toward apparently wayward citizens."[29] There is no need to presume that suspects are innocent until proven guilty and to protect their interests in other ways, for their interests and the state's are identical.

While Westerners are apt to find the paternalistic analogy quite strained for criminal law, where they find sharp differences of interest between the state and the suspect, they may not find it so strained in health care. Nevertheless, even if all parties seek "the patient's best interests," adversarial procedures may have a place as long as there is dispute about those interests and the patient has rights as well as needs. Such procedures do not presuppose conflicts of interest between parties; they may only presuppose conflicting interpretations of a single party's interests.

Procedures to implement limited paternalism can be costly, sometimes prohibitively so. They restrict professional autonomy, and consume time, energy, and money. Some adversarial proceedings may even damage the relationship between health care provider and patient, even if they also, in part, reflect a prior transformation. It is not necessary to deny or even to overlook these points in order to emphasize the importance of procedures. Whether adequate ones can be devised will depend on numerous factors, many beyond our purview. But where adequate procedures are unavailable, and significant rights are at stake, even limited paternalism may have to be rejected.

I will make further suggestions about procedures in the next three chapters when I apply the principle of limited paternalism to deception and nondisclosure of information, suicide and refusal of lifesaving medical treatment, and risky actions.

Notes

1. Although paternalism is frequently "impure," because paternalistic reasons are mixed with others in particular acts and policies, I will concentrate on "pure" paternalism in this chapter.
2. Some defenders of limited or weak paternalism include Joel Feinberg, *Social Philosophy* (Englewood Cliffs, N.J.: Prentice-Hall, 1973), Jeffrie Murphy, "Incompetence and Paternalism," *Archiv für Rechts- und*

Sozialphilosophie 60 (1974): 465–86, and John D. Hodson, "The Principle of Paternalism," *American Philosophical Quarterly* 14 (January 1977): 61–69. Feinberg concentrates on "nonvoluntariness," Murphy on "incompetence," and Hodson on "encumbrances." Contrast the justification procedures proposed by Bernard Gert and Charles M. Culver, "The Justification of Paternalism," *Ethics* 89 (January 1979): 199–210.

3. Wendy Carlton, *"In Our Professional Opinion. . . ." The Primacy of Clinical Judgment over Moral Choice* (Notre Dame, Ind.: University of Notre Dame Press, 1978), pp. 5–6.

4. This concentration on "decision-making" may be criticized as too narrow, because paternalism may appear in cases where the patient's decision-making is not involved. An example might be nondisclosure of a relative's illness or death to a dying person. It may be alleged that the dying person has not made a decision and could not make a decision regarding the use of the information. I do not claim that decision-making is always overridden in paternalistic acts. Nevertheless, decision-making identifies such a common and central feature in expressing wishes, making choices, and acting that it can serve as a shorthand expression for them for purposes of most of this discussion. See Bernard Gert and Charles Culver, *Philosophy in Medicine: Conceptual and Ethical Problems in Medicine and Psychiatry* (New York: Oxford University Press, 1982), pp. 135–36, which criticizes one of my earlier formulations.

5. Alan Meisel, "The 'Exceptions' to the Informed Consent Doctrine: Striking a Balance between Competing Values in Medical Decision-making," *Wisconsin Law Review* (1979): 442, fn. 104. As Meisel notes, "There is one class of individuals the members of which are *de jure* incompetent even though they have not been *adjudicated* incompetent, and may actually be *de facto* competent—namely, minors. It is well established at common law that minors are legally incapacitated from consenting to medical treatment" (p. 442, fn. 104).

6. My discussion of these tests is indebted to Meisel, "The 'Exceptions' to the Informed Consent Doctrine," and to Loren H. Roth, Alan Meisel, and Charles W. Lidz, "Tests of Competency to Consent to Treatment," *American Journal of Psychiatry* 134 (March 1977): 279–84. My discussion of these tests is not comprehensive or sufficiently detailed, but it indicates the direction in which determination of incompetency should be made if weak paternalism is to be justified.

7. Daniel Wikler, "Paternalism and the Mildly Retarded," *Philosophy and Public Affairs* 8 (Summer 1979): 377–92, especially 380–85.

8. Dan W. Brock makes a similar argument with great power. He contends that several conditions ("incompetence," "encumbrance," and "non-voluntariness") offered as necessary for justified weak paternalism are ambiguous, and that their most plausible interpretation "is consistent

with a consequentialist treatment of paternalism to the effect that it is justified just in case it maximally promotes its subject's good." See Brock, "Paternalism and Promoting the Good," an unpublished paper.

9. Gert and Culver, "The Justification of Paternalism," p. 200.

10. See Feinberg, *Social Philosophy*, pp. 25f., and chapter III above.

11. In arguing for these second and third conditions of justified paternalism, I am not withdrawing the reservations about beneficence that I identified in chapter II. At that juncture, I indicated deficiencies that weaken the appeal to the principle of beneficence in paternalism on its own terms. All those deficiencies remain, but within the limits set by the principle of respect for persons, it is, nevertheless, morally right and frequently obligatory to seek the patient's benefit, particularly when the patient's own values serve to identify and weight the relevant harms and benefits.

12. Sharon H. Imbus and Bruce E. Zawacki, "Autonomy for Burned Patients When Survival is Unprecedented," *New England Journal of Medicine* 297 (August 11, 1977): 308–11.

13. See *Medical World News* (January 22, 1979): 37f. and Seymour I. Schwartz, "Consensus Summary on Fluid Resuscitation," *Journal of Trauma* 19 (November 1979), Supplement, 876–77. Schwartz writes: "Ethically and morally, it is the physician's obligation to initiate fluid resuscitative therapy in all patients with major burn injuries. The limits of the potential of therapy have not been defined, and one factor, the frequent overestimation of the per cent burn, is a pertinent consideration in this regard. Physical and/or emotional shock in the burned patient makes it virtually impossible for this patient to contribute in the early decision-making process, as far early resuscitative therapy is concerned." But then he goes on to invoke a nonpaternalistic reason: "aggressive treatment" of the group of patients who have a high mortality can benefit future patients.

14. I should also add that where there is a high degree of certainty about a patient's incompetence to decide, intervention may be justified even though there is a low probability of harm apart from the intervention. There should, of course, be a high probability that the intervention will be successful without producing adverse consequences.

15. Jeffrie Murphy writes: "The real problem that will face us, then, is what to do in the borderline cases. When in doubt, which way should we err—on the side of safety or on the side of liberty? It is vital that we do not adopt analyses of 'incompetence' or patterns of argument that obscure the obviously moral nature of this question." "Incompetence and Paternalism," p. 479.

16. Rosemary Carter, "Justifying Paternalism," *Canadian Journal of Philosophy* 7 (March 1977): 138.

17. John Stuart Mill, *On Liberty*, ed. Gertrude Himmelfarb (Harmondsworth, Eng.: Penguin Books, 1976).

18. I have not discussed indirect modes of paternalism in this chapter. In

general, indirect paternalism is preferable to direct paternalism because the indirect mode is less restrictive and involves less overall coercion. See chapter VIII.

19. Wikler, "Paternalism and the Mildly Retarded," p. 392 (my italics).

20. Clifton Perry, concentrating on nondisclosure of information to patients, contends that such a paternalistic act is not obligatory (since the Hippocratic Oath does not require concern for the emotional state of the patient). Furthermore, he contends that it may be supererogatory because of the risk of "moral censure" the physician takes, regardless of his benevolent motives, because the information rightfully belongs to the patient. But such a position would, in effect, make various morally suspect actions potentially supererogatory because of the risk of "moral censure." See Perry, "Paternalism as a Supererogatory Act," *Ethics in Science and Medicine* 6 (1979): 155–61.

21. Tom L. Beauchamp, "Paternalism and Biobehavioral Control," *The Monist* 60, (January 1977): 77–78. Although unacceptable as a general moral theory, rule-utilitarianism cannot be avoided in some moral contexts. It cannot generate all moral principles and rules, but it can help to determine whether some are problematic.

22. Murphy, "Incompetence and Paternalism," pp. 484–85.

23. Henry K. Beecher, "Ethics and Clinical Research," *New England Journal of Medicine* 274 (1966): 1354–60.

24. Lionel Trilling, "Manners, Morals, and the Novel," in *The Liberal Imagination: Essays on Literature and Society* (New York: The Viking Press, 1950), p. 221. At the same time, Reinhold Niebuhr emphasized realism in morals and politics. See, for example, his *Christian Realism and Political Problems* (New York: Charles Scribner's Sons, 1953). Some of the difference in tone and substance in the biomedical ethics of Paul Ramsey and Joseph Fletcher can be traced to their different anthropologies, Ramsey emphasizing a more realistic and Fletcher a more idealistic interpretation of human beings.

25. *Olmstead* v. *United States*, 277 U.S. 438 (1928) (Dissenting opinion).

26. Meisel, "The 'Exceptions' to the Informed Consent Doctrine."

27. John Rawls, *A Theory of Justice* (Cambridge: Harvard University Press, 1971).

28. These comments are based on conversations with health care professionals in Peking, Shanghai, Canton, and Tsinan in August, 1979. For a report of observations of an interprofessional delegation under the auspices of the Kennedy Institute of Ethics, see *The Kennedy Institute Quarterly Report* 5, no. 2 (Fall 1979), including my essay "Reflections on Socialist Ethics" (pp. 11–14). For a discussion of *shuo-fu*, "to persuade by talking," see Victor Li, "Human Rights in a Chinese Context," in *The China Difference*, ed. Ross Terrill (New York: Harper and Row, 1979), p. 229.

29. Jerome Cohen, "Due Process," in *The China Difference*, esp. pp. 255–56.

VI

Paternalistic Deception, Lies, and Nondisclosure of Information

The Duty of Veracity

While paternalistic action takes many different forms, two of the most common are force and deception. Both can be used to get people to act against their will. As Sissela Bok notes, there is an analogy between the justification of force and the justification of deception. In cases of defense of oneself or others against an assailant, both force and deception would be justified, but deception would have moral priority over lethal or nonlethal force when they would be equally effective. But then Bok wonders whether force might not be preferable to deception in continuing relationships that involve intimacy and trust.

> The very fact that paternalism so often thrives in families and in other relationships of closeness and dependence has a special effect on the choice between manipulation by force and by deception. These relationships require more trust than most others, and over a long period of time. As a result, whereas in many crises such as that of the murderer seeking his victim, it may be as good or better to lie than to attempt force, the opposite may well be the case in family crises and wherever trust obtains.
>
> Consider, for example, two parents trying to keep a small child from

falling into a pond. They may try distraction or persuasion and resort to force if these do not succeed. But what if they choose instead to tell the child there are monsters in the pond? While such a tale might effectively avoid the danger of drowning and save the parents a certain amount of physical exertion, the strategy does not bode well for the family in the long run.[1]

Her point is that trust is more easily destroyed by deception than by force, particularly when the latter is openly acknowledged.

In an episode in "The Use of Force" by William Carlos Williams (himself a physician), a physician was called by a family he had not met to see their very sick daughter, who had had a fever for three days. Because there had been several cases of diptheria at the child's school, he asked the parents if she had a sore throat. She insisted that it didn't hurt, and the parents had been unable to see any problem. Because the physician needed to check, he and the parents tried to coax the child into opening her mouth. Persuasion failing, "the battle began. I had to do it. I had to have a throat culture for her own protection." The battle continued, amidst screams, splintered tongue depressors, and blood from her mouth. "The damned little brat must be protected against her own idiocy, one says to one's self at such times. Others must be protected against her. It is a social necessity. And all these things are true." When he finally succeeded, he saw both tonsils covered with membrane: she had diptheria.[2]

It is not clear that force was better than a lie in that setting, if a lie would have been effective. Mitigation of the negative effects of either force or deception on a continuing relationship among members of a family, or between a patient and a health care professional, will depend on several factors, including the explanation to the object of the force or deception after the crisis has passed. But whether Bok is right about the priority of (some degrees of) force over deception in familial and perhaps even therapeutic relations, she rightly emphasizes the moral *presumption* against deception, lies, and nondisclosure of information in all intimate relations including medical ones.

Actual and fictional patients have long complained about deception and incomplete disclosure of information in medicine. In Leo Tolstoy's classic story, *The Death of Ivan Ilych*,

What troubled Ivan Ilych most was the deception, the lie, which for some reason they all accepted, that he was not dying but was simply ill, and that he only need keep quiet and undergo a treatment and then something very good would result. He however knew that do what they would nothing would come of it, only still more agonizing suffering and death. This deception tortured him—their not wishing to admit what they all knew and what he knew, but wanting to lie to him concerning his terrible condition, and wishing and forcing him to participate in that lie. Those lies . . . were a terrible agony for Ivan Ilych.[3]

Martha Lear's recent *Heartsounds* tells the story of her husband's heart attacks, surgery, and postsurgical complications over a period of four years. One of its persistent themes is the incomplete medical disclosure to Harold Lear, the patient, himself a surgeon. Even Martha Lear participated in withholding information from her husband about the heart attack he had suffered while in the recovery room after heart surgery. When her husband discovered the truth, she defended the non-disclosure: "We thought it best. . . . What possible good could it have done to tell you?" Harold Lear responded, "Moe [his physician] may not have told me in order to protect me, or himself, and I think that was wrong, but I know he meant well. He didn't understand, though. *None* of you understood: *the truth would have been easier.*"[4]

In Tolstoy's and Lear's accounts, both health care professionals and members of the family collaborated in the deception, or incomplete disclosure of information, in the patient's interests, as they conceived them. They were paternalistic. In traditional conceptions of the physician-patient relationship, the duty of truthfulness has not been prominent. At times, it was even a compliment to say that a person "lies like a physician."[5] The duty of truthfulness, or veracity, does not even appear in the Hippocratic Oath or in the Declaration of Geneva by the World Medical Association in 1948.[6] For many years, according to the Principles of Medical Ethics of the American Medical Association, the physician had *discretion* about what to disclose to patients. Substitution of physician discretion for a duty of veracity is not surprising in view of the medical orientation toward patient benefit, a teleological or conse-quentialist perspective. Truthful information was simply viewed as another weapon in the physician's arsenal for use in the battle against disease and illness. Its use depended on its utility in the patient's care. Disclosure, or nondisclosure, of information was part of the "art of medicine." One moral question concerned the physician's motivation: "When you are thinking of telling a lie . . . ask yourself whether it is simply and solely for the patient's benefit that you are going to tell it. If you are sure that you are acting for his good and not for your own profit, you can go ahead with a clear conscience."[7] Or, "deception is completely moral when it is used for the welfare of the patient."[8] Thus, it became possible to justify "benevolent deception" or "benign trickery" or a "therapeutic privilege," which allows the physician to control the patient's access to information according to his or her perception of the patient's needs, regardless of the patient's wishes.[9]

Arguments for physician discretion in disclosure of information often confuse epistemological and moral claims. For example, according to one argument, physicians are not obligated to be truthful because they cannot know the truth. This claim might appear to be plausible because "ought" implies "can." But the inability of physicians to know the truth, or their fallibility in medical judgments, does not entail or even support the conclusion that they have no obligation to be truthful or that they have discretion about disclosure. Truthfulness means trying to convey what one believes to be true, and the duty of truthfulness can be discharged by an honest effort to state what one believes to be true.[10]

While many claim that the physician is not obligated to be truthful because he or she cannot know the truth, they sometimes also claim that physicians know enough about the psyches of their patients to be able to determine when truthfulness would be harmful (e.g., by causing them to become depressed, to refuse treatment, or to commit suicide). For example, just two paragraphs after Donald Kornfeld has rejected a duty of truthfulness because it appears to imply the ability to know the truth, he argues for physician discretion in disclosing information because of "the art of medicine": "The art of medicine is the ability of a physician to know what psychological approach would be best for each of his patients."[11]

Several mistakes are apparent. First, it is difficult to make both claims about prognostic powers at the same time: that prognostic powers are so limited as to undermine the duty of truthfulness and yet that they are so great as to warrant physician discretion in disclosure of information. Second, these claims are incongruous: a weak claim is made about prognostic power regarding physical matters, while a strong claim is made regarding psychological matters. The strong claim is difficult to maintain because prediction is even more problematic in psychological matters (studies show that there is a tendency to overpredict dangerousness), because physicians, for the most part, are not well-trained in psychological analysis and prediction, and because, in an age of specialized and bureaucratic medicine, physicians are not likely to know their patients well or to know their patients as a "whole" (in contrast to the "parts" they know in their specialties). While I have concentrated on claims about predictive ability in psychological matters, arguments for withholding information from patients for their own benefit also depend on an evaluation of different predicted outcomes for patients.[12] If this evaluation is "soft paternalism," i.e., based on the patient's own values, it presupposes intimacy with the patient. If it is "hard paternalism," i.e., the imposition of alien values, it is harder to justify.

Sometimes it is claimed that physicians and other health care professionals cannot *communicate* the "whole truth." The implication of this claim is that physicians should have *discretion* about disclosure of information, the amount and kind of information. Often this argument is only an extension of the epistemological argument: the "whole truth" cannot be known. But the epistemological argument usually focuses on the physician's limitations, while the communication argument usually focuses on the patient's limitations such as an inability to understand. But if the duty to be truthful does not presuppose that the physician knows the "whole truth," it likewise does not presuppose that the physician can communicate the "whole truth." Once we get beyond claims about the "whole truth," difficulties in communication are morally significant. But they cannot excuse the physician from the duty of *truthfulness*, even though they may make it difficult to discharge that duty. More time, effort, and imagination may be required. It may even be appropriate to involve other persons such as nurses and chaplains.

Several normative issues merit attention, even though they can only be briefly identified here. First, interpretations of the *grounds* or *foundations* of the duty of veracity vary greatly. Some philosophers hold that it is an independent duty, justified as other independent duties are justified, for example, by intuition, by divine commands, or by an analysis of the nature of human community.[13] The duty of veracity may, however, be derived from other duties, such as utility (e.g., the relationships of trust that we cherish depend on truthfulness), or fidelity (e.g., when we speak we make an implicit promise to be truthful), or respect for persons (e.g., to respect a person as an independent, choosing agent requires truthfulness). Although several grounds are plausible, it is sufficient for my purposes to indicate that the principle of respect for persons requires that we not lie to or deceive them. In special relationships, it may also require disclosure of information. Since the duty derives from respect for persons, patients may request nondisclosure. What is important is not their need for the information, but their wishes.

Second, the *strength* or weight of the duty of veracity is best characterized as prima facie. It is not absolute or merely relative; it is binding, *ceteris paribus*, and its violation requires justification.

Third, the strength of the duty will depend in part on the *meaning* of key moral terms such as "lying." Instead of relying on an elastic definition of "lie" (withholding information from or deceiving someone who has a right to the truth), or on a doctrine of "mental reservation," I shall define "lying" as intentionally telling a person what one believes to be untrue in order to deceive him.[14]

Fourth, the duty of truthfulness encompasses many different sorts of *positive* and *negative acts*. For example, it may require disclosure of information and prohibit deception and lying. The duty not to lie or to deceive depends less on roles and relationships than the duty to disclose information. Thus, the duty not to lie or to deceive is more general and more stringent than the duty to disclose information, which may depend on the particularities of relationships. There is no general duty to disclose information, for example, to let strangers know what we think about their dress or demeanor, but there is a general duty not to lie to them. In most cases, the physician has an affirmative duty to disclose information, not merely because he possesses specialized knowledge, but because he has a fiduciary relationship with the patient, who thus has a right to that information even where others do not.

> The relationship between patient and physician is one known to the law as a "fiduciary relationship." Any person such as a physician, attorney, priest or other who enters into a relationship of trust and confidence with another has a positive obligation to disclose all relevant facts. If an individual wishes to buy a pig from a farmer, the farmer is not obliged to point out defects of the pig. If specifically questioned, the farmer commits fraud if he answers dishonestly, but he is not obliged to volunteer information which may be detrimental to the sale. However, since the essence of a professional relationship is that the professional knows more about his subject than the person who seeks his help . . . an affirmative duty of disclosure has always existed.[15]

Some sociologists contend that control of information is a matter of power. They argue that physicians do not like to reduce patients' uncertainty especially in prognosis because of the effort to maintain power.

This explanation does not imply that physicians want power for their own ends rather than for the patients' needs. Their motivation may be genuinely benevolent and altruistic; they may believe that their actions are necessary to serve the patients' best interests, and to realize the "common" goal of therapy: "the physician's ability to make necessary therapeutic decisions may depend on his power position vis-a-vis that of the patient."[16]

In his classic discussion of truth and falsehood in medicine, Richard C. Cabot, a renowned physician and social ethicist early in this century, distinguished the applications of the principle of veracity in diagnosis, prognosis, and treatment.[17] It is more useful for our purposes to distinguish (1) dissemination of information regarding diagnosis and prognosis where consent is not required, and (2) dissemination of information regarding diagnostic and therapeutic procedures to which consent is required. Obviously these areas overlap; for example, disclosure of a diagnosis of cancer and a prognosis of death within three months may be conjoined with information about experimental therapeutic procedures which may benefit the patient in some way if he or she consents to undergo them. Nevertheless, the distinction usefully indicates two important areas of paternalistic deception and incomplete disclosure of information.

Informed Consent to Diagnostic and Therapeutic Procedures

In case law the rule of consent to diagnostic and therapeutic procedures evolved out of the torts of negligence and battery, especially the latter which involves touching a person who has not consented to the contact. Regardless of the health care professional's benevolence and qualifications, he or she has no right to touch a patient who is capable of consent without that person's consent. He or she has a moral (and a legal) duty to seek a patient's consent to diagnostic and therapeutic procedures. While many different reasons can be given for this rule (such as protection of patients' interests and social utility), the basic reason is respect for persons and their autonomous wishes, choices, and actions. As Justice Cardozo wrote, "Every human being of adult years and sound mind has a right to determine what shall be done with his own body."[18] Surgery without the patient's consent, Cardozo continued, is an assault, except in emergencies when surgery is necessary and the patient is unconscious or otherwise unable to make a decision.

In order for her consent to diagnostic or therapeutic procedures to be valid (i.e., to create a right on the part of the physician or other health care professionals), the patient must be *competent* to consent, must *understand* what she is about to undergo, and must *voluntarily* consent. Since I have already examined consent in chapter IV, as well as conditions of autonomy in chapter III, I want to concentrate on the physician's or other health care professional's duty to *disclose information* regarding the nature of the proposed procedures, their benefits, their risks, and alternative procedures in obtaining the patient's consent. In recent years this duty has been expressed in the rule or doctrine of "informed consent," which, as Alan Meisel notes, "allocates decisional authority within the doctor-patient relationship."[19] It is an affirmative duty because of the fiduciary relationship between physician and patient. It is more than a duty not to lie to or deceive patients. But what are the standards, scope, and limits of this affirmative duty of disclosure?

There are two distinct standards of disclosure of information in the process of obtaining voluntary, informed consent. The first standard is professional and ultimately paternalistic: it asks what a reasonable medical practitioner would disclose in the circumstances. It thus depends on a determination of customary medical practice which is presumed to be oriented toward the patient's needs but not necessarily toward his/her wishes.[20] What the physician ought to disclose is derived from the medical community's judgment about what would be in the patient's best interest. As a result, expert medical testimony is required in trials alleging breach of the duty to disclose information. This professional and paternalistic standard was invoked by the radiologist in case #6 when he withheld information about the risk of a fatal reaction from urography because it would have upset the patient without benefitting her in any way. He proposed that the American College of Radiology explicitly affirm that "our responsibility is to our patients and to do what is best for our patients medically. Informing patients of risks and possible death from urography may not be in the best interest of the patient and . . . it may be dangerous." Opponents of this professional standard of disclosure deny that disclosure is a *medical* judgment, contending that patients' rights rather than paternalistic definitions of patients' interests should determine what should be disclosed.

The second standard focuses on what patients want to know, and it may take two different forms: objective and subjective. In its objective form, this standard considers what the reasonable patient would want to know. Thus, the physician should disclose the amount and kind of information that a reasonable person would find materially relevant to his or her decision about diagnostic or therapeutic procedures. For example, in disclosure of risk, a "risk is material when a reasonable person, in what the physician knows or should know to be the patient's position, would be likely to attach a significance to the risk or cluster of risks in deciding whether or not to forego the proposed therapy."[21] At most, the reasonable person standard is only a minimum standard of disclosure, for particular patients, with their own life plans and risk budgets, may well desire more or different information. Thus, the objective test should be supplemented (but not replaced) by a subjective test: what this particular patient wants to know. In application, then, the physician should disclose what the reasonable person would want to know, adding the kind and amount of information that this particular patient wants. But the reasonable person standard cannot be invoked as an excuse for not providing the information requested by a particular person. Following is an example of a morally acceptable policy regarding the disclosure of risks of anesthesia, such as a 1-in-10,000 chance of death:

> At the present time, we feel the most reasonable approach is to tell all patients that there are serious, although remote, risks of anesthesia, but to allow the individual patient to decide how much additional information he or she wishes to obtain about these risks.[22]

There are signs that the rule of informed consent has become too formalistic and that following it has become mechanical sometimes to the extent of violating its spirit. First, there are ways to circumvent this duty of disclosure even when it is mandated by law and when a consent form is required. The operation of such procedures depends, in part, on virtuous health care professionals who are motivated by both benevolence and respect for persons.[23]

Second, the affirmative role-based duty of disclosure of information is not discharged by providing information that is not understood. This duty also requires that the physician or other health care professional endeavor to secure understanding; otherwise, the consent is not genuinely but only technically "informed." Here again the skeptical response that patients cannot understand the whole truth is irrelevant, for what is required is that they comprehend or understand the relevant information. If this is impossible, then proxy permission should be secured because the patient may not be competent in these circumstances to give valid consent—consent that authorizes the health care professional to proceed.

There is a line, perhaps a fine one, between ensuring understanding and forcing the patient to use information in deciding and acting. The former is part of the duty of disclosure of information; the latter is not. Patients may choose and act irrationally. Thus, for example, when working with potential organ donors the physician has a duty to disclose the risks of the donation and to make sure that they are understood, but he does not have a duty to make them actually use this information in their decision-making.[24] Indeed, patients may even waive their right to information in most circumstances. When they do, the physician has no duty to disclose, or to seek comprehension of, information. (I will return to waivers in the last section of this chapter.)

The use of a placebo merits special attention because it is perhaps the most common case of deception or incomplete disclosure of information in treatment. A placebo (from the Latin, "I shall please") is a substance or procedure that is thought by the provider to be pharmacologically or biomedically inert for the condition for which it is provided. It is important to distinguish two contexts for the use of placebos: research and therapy. On the one hand, placebos are used in clinical trials of drugs and therapies in order to reduce the chances that bias might distort the results of the research. For example, a patient may be asked to participate in a randomized clinical trial in which both a placebo and a new drug will be used. If the trial is double-blind, neither the patient-subject nor the physician-investigator can know who receives the placebo and who receives the drug. But as long as the patient-subject receives information about the placebo and drug and about the method of allocation, his consent can be valid, even though he does not know what he will receive. But not to disclose the fact that placebos will be used is morally wrong.[25]

On the other hand, placebos are sometimes used in therapy, where no research is underway. In this context, they are allegedly used for the patient's benefit rather than for the purity of research design. Studies indicate that placebos relieve some symptoms of approximately 35 percent of the patients who suffer from such conditions as angina pectoris, cough, anxiety, depression, hypertension, headache, and the common cold.[26] Placebos are perhaps most often used for pain and this use may actually have a biochemical basis in the release of endorphins.[27] The moral problem in the therapeutic use of placebos is deception or, at least, incomplete disclosure of information. In defense of placebos, Alan Leslie contends that "deception is completely moral when it is used for the welfare of the patient."[28] Can this paternalistic use of placebos be justified?

In trying to answer this question, we should first recall the distinction between lying to, deceiving, and withholding some information from the patient. It may be possible, for example, to give a placebo and say to a patient: 'Take these pills; there is a good chance that they will ease your pain." If there is good reason, perhaps based on previous studies, to think that this placebo may have this effect on this patient, the physician has not lied. And it is not even clear that he has deceived the patient, unless we assume that the patient supposes that all pills "work" through pharmacological mechanisms. But if the patient specifically asks about the substance, the physician should not lie.[29]

Second, there are often, perhaps usually, alternatives to deception and incomplete disclosure. There is some evidence, by no means conclusive, that some placebos may engender the "placebo effect" even if patients are informed that the substance is pharmacologically inert. It may thus be possible to use placebos and to gain positive placebo effects with the patient's consent.[30]

Third, as Howard Brody argues, "since the placebo effect can be elicited by other, nondeceptive means, placebos need not be resorted to." He considers several categories of cases in which medical commentators tend to find placebos justified, and he contends that the "healing context," involving physician (and other health care professional) and patient interaction and communication, can engender the placebo effect without the use of deceptive placebos. In response to the possible charge that his alternative techniques would have a high failure rate under the daily pressures of medicine, Brody notes that placebos generally have only a 30–40 percent success rate and are not likely to work if "the physician who administers [them] does not display compassion and concern."[31] Of course, Brody's proposal would require that health care providers spend more time in communication with and education of patients. From the standpoint of the allocation of resources, such an approach may not be as cost-effective as writing prescriptions, but if a broader cost-benefit analysis (including the effects of deception on trust) is used, it may be justified. Brody's own position depends on an *ideal* of the actualization of human capacities for responsible behavior.[32] But I have tried to avoid defending such an ideal, relying instead on the notion of respect for persons whatever their choices.

In case #4, Mr. X refused to accept further alteration in his pain medication although he had voluntarily entered a pain control clinic where adjustment in medication was a clear expectation. He had sought treatment for debilitating pain and drug dependency. When he refused further modification in his Talwin dosage level, the staff substituted a placebo over several days. In chapter IV, I analyzed this case in terms of implicit prior consent and probable future consent, indicating that they do not appear to nullify or to justify the paternalistic withdrawal of Talwin without the patient's present consent. If the staff had obtained the patient's general consent at the outset or during therapy to the administration of several drugs, including placebos, they could have avoided some of their moral difficulty. This general consent would have obviated the need for specific consent to the substitution of a placebo (saline) for the Talwin, unless, of course, the patient continued to insist that he could tolerate no further modification of his Talwin dosage level. In the face of such an insistence, the staff would have had to determine whether he had revoked the earlier general consent. Even this general consent is not free of difficulties; it may tend to reduce the amount and quality of communication between professional and patient because the former may no longer feel the need to discuss various procedures with the patient in the course of treatment.

Can the paternalistic use of a placebo be justified in this case? The patient apparently suffered from no defects, encumbrances, and limitations in his decision-making other than his false belief that he could not tolerate further modification in his medication. His fear was irrational, but irrationality of fears is not a sufficient reason for bypassing informed consent. It is dangerous to allow false beliefs to determine the presence or absence of defects in decision-making, but they cannot be avoided altogether, particularly when the false beliefs concern the patient's *condition* or *means* of treatment rather than the *ends* of treatment. In this case, the patient accepted the goals of treatment, but insisted that he could not tolerate further modification in his medication.

Because of his pain, Mr. X was somewhat depressed; he had poor personal hygiene and was unkempt; he had lost weight; and he had withdrawn socially because he had to assume awkward or embarrassing postures in order to control his pain. The injection of Talwin six times a day for more than two years had resulted in so much tissue and muscle damage that he had trouble finding injection sites. Furthermore, Talwin may be addictive. The patient wanted "to get more out of life in spite of [his] pain," and he admitted the need to control his Talwin, which in the clinic he reduced to four times a day. Because of his acceptance of these goals, the paternalism was "soft" rather than "hard." And the therapists had good reason to think that the placebo would probably produce the desired results. Apparently, a risk-benefit analysis, using the patient's own values, and considering both the amount and the probability of benefit from the intervention, would support the deception, particularly in an established context of care. It did not require intervention from the outside. It is not clear, however, that the therapists considered the possible decline in the patient's self-esteem as a result of the intervention. Furthermore, the risk-benefit analysis might have been different if the patient had not relied on Talwin but on an oral pain medication with only minor negative side effects.[33]

Throughout this discussion I have focused on the deceptive placebo as the mode of nonacquiescence in the patient's wishes, but some features of the situation merit more attention. The staff gradually diluted Talwin with normal saline at the rate of .25 cc over the four injections which the patient still received each day. After five days, he was receiving only saline, along with Elavil, which had been introduced to ease the withdrawal symptoms. While the staff did not use Elavil to deceive the patient, he attributed his nausea, diarrhea, and cramps to the Elavil when they were in fact the result of the withdrawal of Talwin. Elavil was discontinued, but saline was used for three more weeks while self-control training increased the interval between injections to twelve hours. Then the staff told him. At first he was incredulous and angry, but then he asked that the saline be discontinued and the self-control techniques continued. It is not clear that the staff actually lied to the patient at any point; because the record is not clear on this point, it would be interesting to know what they told him about the reason for prescribing Elavil. But within their relationship, the nondisclosure of information was morally suspect because disclosure for informed consent was expected.

In the justification of deception, whether paternalistic or otherwise, the deception must be *necessary* to obtain the goal. If the goal can be obtained by some other morally appropriate means, deception is unjustified. Believing that they had a duty to "use a treatment that had a high probability of success" rather than to protect "some standard of openness," the therapists "saw no option without ethical problems." For them, there was a moral dilemma: They had to choose between "openness" and "effectiveness" in seeking a goal which the patient also desired. It is not clear, however, that all moral options had been exhausted. I have already mentioned the possibility of getting the patient to consent to several drugs, including placebos. While the report does not indicate whether the staff considered this possibility, it does indicate that they did not favor aversive conditioning and that Mr. X would probably not have consented to it. In this case, as in so many others, how the "problem" is defined may be the most important matter. From the standpoint of the therapists, it was defined in terms of specific behaviors. But they may have underestimated Mr. X's ability to cope with his situation because they failed to pay "sufficient attention to the person responsible for those behaviors." If the therapists had conceived the problem in a different way, they might have considered alternative procedures with high probabilities of success and without ethical problems. As Herbert Kelman suggests,

> the course of treatment might have been different if the therapists had been prepared to work with the broader motives that the patient brought to the treatment and to draw on the increasing coping capacities that the patient developed as the treatment proceeded—in other words, to deal with him as a whole person. They might have found that deception was not necessary to initiate the withdrawal procedure. They might even have concluded that deception was more likely to retard than to advance the treatment process.[34]

In chapter V, I also emphasized the importance of various procedures to protect the rights of individuals who might be targets of paternalism. In part, these procedures would require consultation, preferably with lay persons as well as with professionals. In this case, the therapists "wrestled with the task of reducing Talwin dosage in a patient who had great apprehension about accomplishing such a goal" and finally reached their decision "after much discussion with colleagues." Perhaps it would have been useful to solicit the advice of the patient's wife, other members of his family, and friends. They could not offer "surrogate consent," but they could offer some corroboration or criticism of the therapists' judgment. It is possible that, despite their acceptance of treatment based on behavioral technology, the therapists

> adopted the traditional position—"the doctor knows best!" Indeed, the more certain one becomes that a particular treatment intervention will accomplish a preestablished goal, the more likely one is to accept such a traditional medical stance with all of its paternalistical and noncollaborative trappings.[35]

It may be instructive to compare this case, #4, with case #5. In the latter, for three months after thymectomy a 60-year-old patient was ventilator dependent. Gradually neuromuscular function returned, and the patient appeared to be ready for weaning from the respirator. He was depressed and totally dependent on the intensive care unit (ICU) staff whom he believed to be totally in command of his bodily functions. Even when he could breathe on his own for several hours (up to 24 hours), he was afraid he would die if he fell asleep with the respirator disconnected. In part because of his insomnia agitation and sleep deprivation, two attempts to wean him were unsuccessful. Finally, his physicians decided to reduce mechanically delivered breaths without informing him. Because of the noise from the machines he thought he was still connected, and he was not told that he was weaned until the ventilator had been totally off for three days and nights, during which the patient breathed spontaneously and slept soundly. When the physicians and nurses told him what had been done he expressed surprise and then broke into tears. He thanked the ICU staff for their patient and understanding care.

In both cases the argument for justified weak paternalism hinges on (a) the patients' defects, encumbrances, and limitations in decision-making, particularly their false beliefs about their conditions and about effective means to ends that they accepted, (b) a risk-benefit analysis, and (c) availability of alternatives short of manipulating the patient or his environment without the patient's consent. Both cases produced good outcomes, but the outcome in case #4 probably could have been obtained in other ways, and it is not clear in case #5 that the staff did everything possible to convince the patient that he would be able to breathe without the ventilator. In both cases, the paternalism was soft in that it pursued the agent's own goals rather than goals merely endorsed by outsiders.

Sometimes physicians prescribe placebos when a patient demands or requires "something tangible that can be interpreted as 'treatment.' "

> Such situations are common and present to the conscientious physician a real dilemma: On the one hand, he is faced with something very like an outright lie; on the other, by refusing to prescribe a "wonder drug," he may lose his patient to a colleague who will prescribe unnecessary and potentially toxic medication. The dilemma can be resolved if the placebo appears likely to provide some real benefit to the patient and to preserve a useful relationship between the patient and his physician.[36]

This rationale for placebo use fits with a functional and symbolic analysis of placebo use. Practitioners are expected to "do something," which for many patients means "prescribe something." But also physicians in general practice, according to one sociological study, use the act of prescribing as "a means of dealing with uncertainty and with patient management." It is efficient because it conserves the physician's time and energy. Placebos can be viewed "primarily as a function of the way in which doctors have come to use the prescription, and its attendant ritual, to solve fundamental problems inherent in their social situation and in their relations with their patients."[37]

But suppose a person suffering from a common cold comes to his or her physician and asks for antibiotics, which are, of course, ineffective for such viral conditions. While I have concentrated on pharmacologically inactive or inert drugs, active drugs can be placebos when they will not be effective for a given condition or at the level of dosage prescribed.[38] It is customary to distinguish *pure* from *impure* placebos; pure placebos are known or thought to be pharmacologically or biomedically inactive, while impure placebos are known or thought to have active ingredients, even if the dosage is too low or not indicated for the specific condition. Although some commentators insist that this distinction "is of no consequence,"[39] impure placebos may be harder to justify on a risk-benefit analysis. For example, antibiotics are not only ineffective for the common cold, but they may be harmful to the patient, are costly, and may contribute to the deleterious effects of the excessive use of antibiotics (such as the development of bacteria that are resistant to certain antibiotics). In addition, the physician's refusal to provide antibiotics under these circumstances would be a form of passive nonacquiescence in the patient's wishes. And in purely paternalistic terms, it is easier to justify than active nonacquiescence.

Disclosure of Diagnostic and Prognostic Information

Where informed consent is not required, deception or incomplete disclosure of diagnostic or prognostic information is sometimes viewed as a "therapeutic privilege." Some physicians even contend that "every physician should cultivate lying as a fine art" because of its benefits to the patient. Indeed, they claim, some lies "contribute enormously to the success of the physician's mission of mercy and salvation."[40]

Obviously such claims presuppose the physician's duty of beneficence —to remove or to prevent harm or to provide positive benefit. But there is an even stronger claim about the "therapeutic privilege": because the physician's primary duty is to do no harm (*primum non nocere*), he or she sometimes should withhold information when that information would probably *harm* the patient. Some commentators even accept a presumption against disclosure of a fatal illness "if there is the slightest chance that such knowledge may further impair the physical or mental well-being of the patient. . . . Only in exceptional circumstances should the true facts be divulged to the patient."[41] Because the most widely debated examples of the nondisclosure of information (where consent is not required) are the diagnosis of cancer and the prognosis of death, I will concentrate on them.[42] (See case #3.)

Before undergoing exploratory intestinal surgery, Charles Wertenbaker asked his wife Lael Tucker Wertenbaker to promise to tell him the truth. She agreed because deception or incomplete disclosure "would be to try to reduce you." But in a long conversation with Jim, their physician and friend, after the tests indicated that her husband had fatal cancer, she had to face the charge that disclosure might be "cruel."

> "Now," said Jim gently, "what shall we tell Wert?"
> "Tell him the truth," I said.
> "You can't," said Jim. "You can't take hope away from a human being."
> "*Is* there any hope?" I asked him.
> "No," said Jim. . . .
> "Then," I said, "that's that."
> ". . . Lael, I tell you, it is better if they hope. It is one thing to take a brave chance on dying and another to know that you are going to die—soon. You cannot take hope away from Wert."
> "I cannot lie to this man," I said. "That would take his dignity away from him. He would rather have dignity than hope."
> "You cannot know *any* man that well," said Jim.[43]

As this dialogue suggests, the major tension is between dignity and hope, or between the principle of respect for persons, on the one hand, and the principles of beneficence and nonmaleficence, on the other. According to the principle of respect for persons, it is "*insulting* to patients for us [physicians] to make the decision that they [patients] should not be told what their problem is on the grounds that they will 'go to pieces.' "[44] According to the principle of beneficence, it is important to *reassure* patients so that they will continue to fight for survival; according to the principle of nonmaleficence, it is important not to deprive patients of hope. Physicians worry about the consequences of the loss of hope. First, they fear that the patient might stop the battle against the disease, even if victory is impossible. Norman Cousins contends that the truth "should not be allowed to become a battering ram against the patient's morale, impairing his ability to cope with the greatest challenge of his life."[45] Second, the patient might choose to commit suicide or to refuse further treatment. Third, the patient might turn to "quacks" to find hope.[46] While these fears have generally been exaggerated, they are very real in particular cases. But it is not clear that such actions are always irrational; it is not always irrational to withdraw from the medical system or from life itself. But even if the feared actions are irrational, the physician has no right to withhold information from a competent patient who wants the information. To do so would be insulting and disrespectful.

For many years, according to opinion surveys, most physicians had a policy of not disclosing a diagnosis of cancer to patients, while laypeople generally indicated that they wanted disclosure if they had cancer. But in recent years, there has been a dramatic increase in the number of physicians who affirm a policy of generally or always telling patients that they have cancer. In a 1961 study, 88 percent of the physicians surveyed had a policy of not telling, while in a 1979 study, 98 percent had a policy of telling.[47] As in all opinion surveys, it is difficult to determine whether the responses accurately reflect contemporary practices. At any rate, it is clear that statements about policy have changed. Numerous factors account for this change: changes in public perception of "the big C" in part because of improvements in therapy and prospects for some types of cancer; the need to get informed consent to enroll patients in experimental and research protocols; fear of malpractice suits; focus on chronic care, which requires more active patient participation than acute care; involvement of several parties in bureaucratic medicine, some of whom (perhaps especially nurses) may believe that information should be disclosed; and recognition of patients' rights to information.[48]

At least two different moral perspectives appear in these reasons for the new policy of generally telling patients: (1) a consequentialist perspective, oriented toward the patient's interests and dependent on a risk-benefit calculus, and (2) a deontological perspective, oriented toward patient's rights and dependent on an analysis of the patient's wishes and preferences. From the first perspective, physicians can defend a policy of generally telling patients because there is little evidence that disclosure harms patients and because patients can participate more effectively in their care if they are informed. Thus, in general, the benefits of disclosure outweigh the risks. Even though its adherents currently accept disclosure, this perspective remains *paternalistic*. It grants patients information because of an analysis of patients' interests and needs, not because of what patients want or have a right to. Disclosure is contingent at best. From the second perspective, physicians pay attention to what patients want and respond accordingly because they recognize that patients have a right to diagnostic and prognostic information. Disclosure does not hinge mainly on a risk-benefit calculation.

Dennis Novack and his colleagues worry that the second perspective may have dictated the new policy of disclosure:

> Our respondents' written comments seem to indicate that the current policy of telling the patient is accompanied by increased sensitivity to patients' emotional needs. There is some evidence that telling is the best policy. Yet how rational is the process of deciding what to tell the patient with cancer? Even though the policies have reversed, many physicians are still basing their communication with cancer patients on emotion-laden personal convictions. They are relying on honesty, sensitivity, and patients' rights rather than focusing on the following relevant scientific psychological question: Does telling the diagnosis of cancer help or harm (which) patients and how?[49]

His formulation of the question, his setting of the problem, presupposes the first moral perspective which expresses beneficence, or nonmaleficence, rather than the second moral perspective, which expresses respect for persons and their wishes, choices, and actions.

In Novack's study 100 percent of the respondents stated that patients have a *right to know*. Fearing that this implies abdication of medical judgment in particular cases, Novack wonders whether "patients also have a right not to know." But this question misses the logic of a right to know. If a patient has a right to know, it does not follow that he has a duty to know. He may or may not have such a duty, but if he does, it does not follow simply from his right to know. And a patient may waive his right to know. Thus, as I will argue in the last section of this chapter, exactly what should be told and when it should be told can only be determined by sensitive communication with the patient. Within the second moral perspective, the patient's desire to know would take priority over a risk-benefit calculus because of the principle of respect for persons. Instead of determining first of all whether the disclosure would "help or harm," the physician should try to determine what the patient wants to know.

Patients sometimes do not want to know and information should not be forced upon them. This too is a form of respect for persons. In view of various opinion polls, there should be a presumption that disclosure is what patients want, but this can only be a presumption. For example, a Gallup opinion poll in 1978 indicated that 82–92 percent of the population wanted to be told if they had a fatal illness.[50]

It is possible, of course, that a policy or even a presumption should not be based on what *well* people say. In a recent study, 74 hospital patients with diagnosed but undisclosed malignancy were interviewed and observed to determine their awareness of their condition and their desire for information about it.

> While 88% either knew or suspected that they had a malignant tumour at admission to the ward, the great majority of them had no wish to augment that knowledge. The fact that their diagnosis or prognosis was not revealed to them allowed many patients to maintain the hope either that they might not have cancer or that the outlook might be favorable.[51]

They did not, however, indicate that they did not want the information they already had. Perhaps the best policy is to assume that patients want some information even about cancer and impending death and to be guided by their verbal and nonverbal signs and signals as to how much, what, when, and how to tell. Nondisclosure or deception when the patient wants to be told can be justified only if the conditions for weak paternalism are satisfied.

A Patient's Request for Nondisclosure of Information

It is presumptively wrong to deceive patients or to withhold information from them even for their own benefit. However, such actions may not be wrong or even paternalistic in some cases. Earlier I criticized definitions of paternalism that omit nonacquiescence in a patient's wishes, choices, and actions. It is not sufficient to define paternalism as coercing people or deceiving them for their own benefit because patients may, for example, ask physicians to withhold information from them. If a patient declines information, withholding it is not paternalistic but in accord with her wishes. Indeed, *disclosure* of information against a patient's wishes for her own good is paternalistic and prima facie wrong.[52]

Are there any solid reasons for overriding a patient's express wish for nondisclosure of information about his illness? One clear reason is not paternalistic: to protect the welfare of others. This protection might be secured in some cases by a nonpaternalistic breach of confidentiality. For example, a physician might be able to protect members of a patient's family by discussing his illness with them. But when this protection cannot be ensured by informing others, the physician may have sufficient (nonpaternalistic) reasons to disclose the information to the unwilling patient.

A second reason sometimes given for overriding a patient's refusal of information focuses on his or her welfare, defined in terms of autonomy and dignity. Because this argument is clothed in the language of autonomy and dignity, its paternalistic nature is often overlooked. Sometimes the argument appeals to self-regarding duties. "Even in this extreme case, where the patient has freely chosen to avoid knowledge of his condition and no one else will suffer directly from his refusal," suggests Robert Veatch, "there may still be a moral duty to know one's self and one's fate."[53] While Veatch does not conclude that the physician should force the patient to discharge this moral duty, some ethicists have drawn this conclusion. For example, in *Morals and Medicine*, Joseph Fletcher held that physicians should confront resistant patients with truthful information and could withdraw from such cases if patients persisted in their resistance.[54]

In back of such a position is a conception of an ideal way of living and dying, which makes autonomy or dignity a goal or value to be promoted. From such a standpoint, individuals should seek as well as accept information about their condition and should live and die with lucidity. Despite its language, this position is paternalistic: it refuses to acquiesce in a patient's wish not to receive information for his or her own *benefit* (defined in terms of autonomy or dignity rather than physical goods). An alternative position, which I have defended in these chapters, is that respect for persons, including their autonomy and dignity, is a side constraint, a limit, and a boundary in our promotion of their welfare, however that welfare is defined. Thus, people may choose to live in ignorance of their condition and fate, as long as others are not adversely affected. They should not be forced to be free or to live up to an ideal of personal autonomy. Their freedom to choose their own styles of living and dying should be respected.

The conflict between these two conceptions of respect for personal autonomy, which I identified in chapter III, emerges most dramatically and poignantly in the care of the dying. There are various styles of dying, not all of which presuppose full information about one's condition and fate. A person might want to die while denying that he is dying. According to Elizabeth Kübler-Ross' interpretation of the dying process, denial is the first and the least adequate of the five stages of dying; the other stages are anger, bargaining, depression, and acceptance.[55] But denial is widespread, and the physician has no duty, and no right, to force patients and their families to face reality. It is one matter to develop a paternalistic policy of nondisclosure on the basis of a general claim that "human kind cannot bear very much reality," as T. S. Eliot puts it.[56] It is another matter altogether to respect a patient's wishes not to confront reality. As Eric Cassell, a physician, notes,

> The ways in which denial operates are many, and its power to protect is wondrous. Sometimes the person simply fails to hear what has been said. Unpleasant facts are told and minutes later the person speaks and acts as if nothing had occurred. I remember telling a patient with normal hearing some bad news. She kept saying, "I'm sorry, I can't hear you," after each louder repetition. I finally had to yell. Sometimes only selected parts of the conversation are remembered, and at other times the patient or family make up a whole new set of facts to fill the gaps. Denial being a process occurring through time, the person may gradually remember what was told him over a period of days as he becomes able to accept the news. On other occasions the patient clearly tells the doctor what he must not be told. It doesn't require much practical experience before physicians have encountered all the various forms in which denial pre-

> sents itself. Most doctors feel that the patient's right to deny is as basic as his right to be told the truth. The fundamental right of patients in such matters is to have their wishes respected whether their doctor agrees with them or not. The fact that denial has become unpopular or that it is a mode that I do not really like seems irrelevant in the presence of a dying person who has chosen to deny knowledge of that fate.

Cassell continues, "Where denial is very strong, I feel no obligation to breach it. . . ."[57]

A patient's denial and request for nondisclosure may present practical problems for the staff. For example, a patient on the cancer ward may deny that she has cancer, noting how fortunate she is and how unfortunate all the other patients are. For this denial to remain intact, onlookers such as physicians and nurses have to participate in a charade, which places a heavy responsibility and burden on the staff.[58] How far the staff should go in *supporting* and *maintaining* this patient's denial depends on their conception of its importance for her total welfare. The duty to respect the patient's denial by not forcing unwanted information on her does not engender a duty to help her maintain her denial by supporting it in various ways (e.g., by lying). The latter duty, if it exists, would derive from the principle of beneficence as well as from the principle of respect for persons. Here again the distinction between negative and positive duties is important: the requirement not to impose unwanted information is stronger than the requirement to buttress the denial.

In some cases when patients request nondisclosure of information, there may be a moral and even a legal duty to disclose the information, even though no one else will be directly harmed by the nondisclosure. Several of these cases involve persons who enter *nontherapeutic* spheres of medicine and research. For example, a person enrolling in phase I drug testing may insist that he does not want to be bothered with the details. Or a person wanting to donate a kidney to a dying relative may make up his or her mind before receiving the information about risks and may insist that this information is irrelevant to his decision. In such cases, a healthy person is being used to benefit others through the generation of scientific knowledge or through the donation of an organ. There may be good reasons for making sure that such people understand what they are doing, for insisting upon *informed* consent, in order to make sure that we are not using them merely as means. These reasons include our conception of our society, the significance of these acts of voluntary beneficence, and the risks of malpractice, as well as paternalistic considerations.

How does a health care professional know, or have reasonable certainty, that a patient does not want some information? When a patient expressly requests information, it should be provided. When a patient expressly declines information, usually it should not be provided (within the limits indicated above). But the process of communication between physician and patient is often more complicated and extends over time, as chapter IV indicated. Rarely is it a matter to be resolved in a moment. And rarely is it a matter merely of direct expressions of wishes. Eric Cassell notes some of the complexity in dealing with dying patients:

> My own preference is to try to find out what the patient wants to know and to supply that much information truthfully. I am uncomfortable with an open lie. Determining what the patient wants to know may mean asking directly, indirectly, or metaphorically, or by sensing feelings. Uncomfortable, awkward feelings in a patient's hospital room proclaim unmistakably—louder than words—that an unanswered question must be dealt with.[59]

When in doubt about a patient's wishes, a physician should disclose the information that a reasonable person would want. Of course, this disclosure may take place over time and, in the process, the patient's own wishes may be clarified. Furthermore, a patient's express wishes at one point may not be determinative for all points. Certainly, respect for persons requires recognition that they may change their minds. The process of communication should be sensitive to the patient's wishes as they emerge and evolve over time.

Suppose the patient wants to be informed about her condition, but the family insists that "she couldn't take it" (see case #3). Although this situation may be difficult to handle practically, it is not difficult morally. Respect for the patient as a person requires disclosure against the family's wishes. This position does not presuppose the existence of an autonomous person, disconnected from family and other communities, as some critics of respect for personal autonomy maintain. But it does assign priority to the patient's desire for truthful information over the family's desire to deny her access to that information. Nevertheless, the family's interpretation of the patient's general condition may be useful to the physician as he or she determines whether nondisclosure might be warranted because of defects and encumbrances in the patient's decision-making. What the family says may augment evidence about the patient's condition and effects of disclosure, but it should not override her wishes.

Notes

1. Sissela Bok, *Lying: Moral Choice in Public and Private Life* (New York: Pantheon Books, 1978), pp. 213–14.

2. William Carlos Williams, "The Use of Force," *The Farmers' Daughters* (New York: New Directions, 1938), pp. 131–35.

3. Leo Tolstoy, *The Death of Ivan Ilych* (New York: New American Library, 1960), p. 137.

4. Martha Weinman Lear, *Heartsounds* (New York: Simon and Schuster, 1980), pp. 137–40, 266–67, et passim.

5. See Joseph Fletcher, *Morals and Medicine* (Boston: Beacon Press, 1960), p. 42.

6. For the texts of these codes, see Tom L. Beauchamp and James F. Childress, *Principles of Biomedical Ethics* (New York: Oxford University Press, 1979), Appendix II.

7. Richard C. Cabot quotes one of his teachers to this effect, but he goes on to oppose this position on grounds of his own very different experience. Cabot, "The Use of Truth and Falsehood in Medicine: An Experimental Study," *American Medicine* 5 (1903): 344–49, reprinted in *Ethics in Medicine: Historical Perspectives and Contemporary Concerns*, ed. Stanley Joel Reiser, Arthur J. Dyck, and William J. Curran (Cambridge: The MIT Press, 1977), p. 213. Other selections in this volume helpfully delineate 19th and 20th century attitudes in the medical profession. In addition, see Sissela Bok, "Truth-telling: Ethical Aspects," in *The Encyclopedia of Bioethics*, ed. Warren T. Reich (New York: Free Press and Macmillan, 1978), as well as Steve Holve, "Truth-telling in Medicine: A Historical Perspective," *Health and Human Values: Winning Essays of the Essay Contest for Students in the Health Professions* (Philadelphia: Society for Health and Human Values, 1980), pp. 5–21.

8. Alan Leslie, "Ethics and Practice of Placebo Therapy," *American Journal of Medicine* 16 (1954): 854–62, reprinted in *Ethics in Medicine*, ed. Reiser, Dyck, and Curran, p. 242.

9. The phrase "benevolent deception" appears in Henry Sidgwick, *The Methods of Ethics*, 7th ed. (London: Macmillan, 1907), p. 315; the phrase "benign trickery" appears in Miriam Siegler and Humphry Osmond, *Patienthood: The Art of Being a Responsible Patient* (New York: Macmillan, 1979), p. 119: "The good doctor engages in benign trickery from time to time in order to meet the human but often irrational needs of his patients." The so-called "therapeutic privilege" is well-recognized in case law, even though it is rarely decisive in cases; it "allows the physician to withhold information that he would otherwise

be obliged to disclose if disclosure would be 'harmful.' " See Alan Meisel, "The 'Exceptions' to the Informed Consent Doctrine: Striking a Balance Between Competing Values in Medical Decisionmaking," *Wisconsin Law Review* (1979): 460. At least one court has held that this privilege "does not accept the paternalistic notion that the physician may remain silent simply because divulgence might prompt the patient to forego therapy that the physician feels the patient really needs." *Canterbury v. Spence*, 464 F. 2d 772, 789 (D.C. Cir.), cert. denied, 409 U.S. 1064 (1972).

10. The failure to distinguish the moral and the epistemological questions can be seen in Norman Cousins, "A Layman Looks at Truth Telling in Medicine," *Journal of the American Medical Association* 244 (October 24/31, 1980): 1929–30. The distinction is emphasized by Bok, *Lying* and by Fletcher, *Morals and Medicine*, p. 40.

11. Donald S. Kornfeld, "Doctor's Dilemma: What Truth for Which Patient at What Time?" *CA—A Cancer Journal for Clinicians* 28 (July–August 1978): 256, reprinted from *The New York Times*, Tuesday, May 16, 1978.

12. For a fuller discussion, see Allen Buchanan, "Medical Paternalism," *Philosophy and Public Affairs* 7 (Summer 1978): 157–72.

13. See, for example, the Decalogue; Bernard Gert, *The Moral Rules* (New York: Harper and Row, 1970); and G. J. Warnock, *The Object of Morality* (London: Methuen, 1971), pp. 85–86.

14. For further discussion of these second and third issues, see Tom L. Beauchamp and James F. Childress, *Principles of Biomedical Ethics*, pp. 41–47. For "mental reservations" in Catholic moral theology, see Charles J. McFadden, *Medical Ethics*, 4th ed. (Philadelphia: F. A. Davis Co., 1956), pp. 410–14.

15. Angela Roddey Holder, *Medical Malpractice Law* (New York: John Wiley & Sons, 1975), p. 225. Even if the patient has no moral (or legal) right to the information, there would still be an important moral question about responding to the patient's wishes. But where a moral (and legal) right is involved, a stronger moral presumption emerges. I have not dealt with the question as to *who* has the duty of disclosure. This question is very important in relationships among members of the health care team, particularly since some may believe that they ought to disclose information and others may not. See, for example, Case #1, which also raises the issue of the nurse's *right* to disclose information if the physician orders nondisclosure.

16. Howard Waitzkin and John D. Stoeckle, "The Communication of Information about Illness," *Advances in Psychosomatic Medicine* 8 (1972): 185–89; reprinted in part in *Ethics in Medicine*, ed. Reiser, Dyck, and Curran, pp. 232–35.

17. Richard C. Cabot, "The Use of Truth and Falsehood in Medicine: An Experimental Study," in *Ethics in Medicine*, ed. Reiser, Dyck, and Curran, pp. 213–30.

18. *Schloendorff v. New York Hospital*, 211 N.Y. 125, 127, 129; 105 N.E., 92, 93 (1914). See also *Natanson v. Kline*, 186 Kan. 393, P. 2d 1093 (1960), rehearing denied, 187 Kan. 186, 354 P. 2d 670 (1960).

19. Alan Meisel, "The 'Exceptions' to the Informed Consent Doctrine," p. 418. For the evolution of legal standards of informed consent, see Walter Wadlington, Jon R. Waltz, and Roger Dworkin, *Cases and Materials on Law and Medicine* (Mineola, N.Y.: The Foundation Press, 1980), to which the following paragraphs are indebted, and Charles Fried, *Medical Experimentation: Personal Integrity and Social Policy* (New York: American Elsevier Publishing Co., 1974). For a valuable discussion of theories of informed consent and a defense of self-determination as the basis of the rule of informed consent, see Robert M. Veatch, "Three Theories of Informed Consent: Philosophical Foundations and Policy Implications," the National Commission for the Protection of Human Subjects of Biomedical and Behavioral Research, *The Belmont Papers*, Appendix Vol. II, pp. 26–1 through 26–66, DHEW Publication No. (OS) 78–0014.

20. I have conflated two standards that the court in *Canterbury v. Spence* distinguished; they come out at the same point if we assume that customary medical practice would reflect the standards of the reasonable practitioner. See *Canterbury v. Spence* 150 U.S. App. D.C. 263, 464 F. 2d 772, cert. denied. 409 U.S. 1064 (1972).

21. Jon R. Waltz and Thomas W. Scheuneman, "Informed Consent to Therapy," *Northwestern University Law Review* 64 (1970): 640. The *Canterbury v. Spence* decision drew heavily on this article.

22. This proposal was actually based on a prospective, randomized study of emotional responses to risk disclosure, but I would defend it in terms of the principle of respect for persons. See James W. Lankton, Barron M. Batchelder, and Alan J. Ominsky, "Emotional Responses to Detailed Risk Disclosure for Anesthesia, a Prospective, Randomized Study," *Anesthesiology* 46 (April 1977): 294–96.

23. Gregory Pence rightly emphasizes that virtues are indispensable because "almost any experimenter can get around any informed consent document if he really so desires." But formal requirements and procedures are not dispensable even if they are not adequate. See Pence, *Ethical Options in Medicine* (Oradell, N.J.: Medical Economics Company, 1980), p. 177.

24. Studies of kidney donors indicate that they tend to make their decisions before receiving information about the procedure and its risks. See C. H. Fellner and J. R. Marshall, "Kidney Donors—The Myth of Informed Consent," *American Journal of Psychiatry* 126 (1970): 1245. See also the study of patients in family planning by Ruth R. Faden, "Disclosure and Informed Consent: Does It Matter How We Tell It?" *Health Education Monographs* 5 (1977): 198–215, and Ruth R. Faden and Tom L. Beauchamp, "Informed Consent and Decision Making: The Impact of

Disclosed Information," *Social Indicators Research* (1979). Only 12 percent of the patients actually used the information in their decisions, even though 93 percent felt they had benefitted from the information.

25. See James F. Childress, *Priorities in Biomedical Ethics* (Philadelphia: The Westminster Press, 1981), chap. 3, esp. pp. 65–69, and Charles Fried, *Medical Experimentation*. The latter is the best extended discussion of ethical problems in randomized clinical trials.

26. See the summary in Howard Brody, *Placebos and the Philosophy of Medicine: Clinical, Conceptual, and Ethical Issues* (Chicago: University of Chicago Press, 1980), pp. 10–11, and Herbert Benson and Mark Epstein, "The Placebo Effect: A Neglected Aspect in the Care of Patients," *Journal of the American Medical Association* 232 (1975): 1225.

27. See J. D. Levine, N. C. Gordon, and H. L. Fields, "The Mechanism of Placebo Analgesia," *Lancet* 2 (1978): 654–57.

28. Alan Leslie, "Ethics and Practice of Placebo Therapy," in *Ethics in Medicine,* ed. Reiser, Dyck, and Curran, p. 242.

29. Contrast Brody, *Placebos and the Philosophy of Medicine*, pp. 98–100, which calls into question the distinction between "outright lying and avoiding lying by judicious silence."

30. See L. C. Park, et al., "Effects of Informed Consent on Research Patients and Study Results," *Journal of Nervous and Mental Disease* 145 (1967): 349–57, and L. C. Park and L. Covi, "Non-blind Placebo Trial: An Exploration of Neurotic Outpatients' Responses to Placebo When Its Inert Content Is Disclosed," *Archives of General Psychiatry* 12 (1965): 336–45.

31. Brody, *Placebos and the Philosophy of Medicine*, pp. 110, 113. For a confirmation of this viewpoint in the reduction of postoperative pain, see Lawrence D. Egbert, et al., "Reduction of Postoperative Pain by Encouragement and Instruction of Patients: A Study of Doctor-Patient Rapport," *New England Journal of Medicine* 270 (April 16, 1964): 825–27.

32. Brody, *Placebos and the Philosophy of Medicine*, p. 114. For other helpful analyses of the ethics of giving placebos, see Sissela Bok, "The Ethics of Giving Placebos," *Scientific American* 231 (November 1974): 17–23, and Beth Simmons, "Problems in Deceptive Medical Procedures: An Ethical and Legal Analysis of the Administration of Placebos," *Journal of Medical Ethics* 4 (1978): 172–81.

33. See Stuart Cook, "Comments on Ethical Considerations in 'Self-Control Techniques as an Alternative to Pain Medication,'" *Journal of Abnormal Psychology* 84 (1975): 169.

34. Herbert C. Kelman, "Was Deception Justified—And Was It Necessary? Comments on 'Self-Control Techniques as an Alternative to Pain Medication'," *Journal of Abnormal Psychology* 84 (1975): 172–74.

35. Leonard D. Goodstein, "Self-Control and Therapist-Control: The Medical Model in Behavioral Clothing," *Journal of Abnormal Psychology* 84 (1975): 179.

36. Henry R. Bourne, "The Placebo—A Poorly Understood and Neglected Therapeutic Agent," *Rational Drug Therapy* 5 (November 1971): 3–4.

37. Jean Comaroff, "A Bitter Pill to Swallow: Placebo Therapy in General Practice," *Sociological Review* 24 (February 1976): 94. Comaroff also indicates that the data do not clearly support the view that the vast majority of patients want a prescription.

38. See Brody, *Placebos and the Philosophy of Medicine*, p. 102.

39. See Alan Leslie, "Ethics and Practice of Placebo Therapy," in *Ethics in Medicine*, ed. Reiser, Dyck, and Curran, p. 242.

40. Joseph Collins, "Should Doctors Tell the Truth?" in *Ethics in Medicine*, ed. Reiser, Dyck, and Curran, p. 221.

41. See Fred Rosner and Rabbi Moses D. Tendler, *Practical Medical Halacha*, 2nd. ed. (New York: Philipp Feldheim Inc., 1980), p. 55. When Rosner states his own position, he alters the presumption: "a patient with an incurable illness should be told about his illness, unless there is strong reason not to tell." See Rosner, "Emotional Care of Cancer Patients: To Tell or Not to Tell," *New York State Journal of Medicine* 74 (July 1974): 1469.

42. Genetic counselling is another area of important issues of disclosure of diagnostic and prognostic information. For a helpful discussion of truthtelling to both dying patients and genetic counselees, see Robert Weir, "Truthtelling in Medicine," *Perspectives in Biology and Medicine* 23 (Autumn 1980): 95–112. See also case #2.

43. Lael Tucker Wertenbaker, *Death of a Man* (New York: Bantam Books, 1957), pp. 44–45.

44. Charles Wright, "Personal View," *British Medical Journal* 4 (October 6, 1973): 43.

45. Cousins, "A Layman Looks at Truth Telling in Medicine," p. 1930. See also Neil Kessel, "Reassurance," *Lancet* (May 26, 1979): 1128–33.

46. Some of these reasons can be seen in the rest of the dialogue in Wertenbaker, *Death of a Man*, p. 45.

47. See Donald Oken, "What to Tell Cancer Patients: A Study of Medical Attitudes," *Journal of the American Medical Association* 175 (April 1, 1961): 1120–28; William D. Kelly and Stanley R. Friesen, "Do Cancer Patients Want to Be Told?" *Surgery* 27 (1950): 822–26; Dennis H. Novack, et al., "Changes in Physicians' Attitudes Toward Telling the Cancer Patient," *Journal of the American Medical Association* 241 (March 2, 1979): 897–900. I will not analyze the methodological shortcomings of these studies. For a valuable survey and analysis of the various studies, see Robert M. Veatch and Ernest Tai, "Talking about Death: Patterns of Lay and Professional Change," *Annals of the American Academy of Political and Social Science* 447 (January 1980): 29–45.

48. For several of these reasons, see especially Veatch and Tai, "Talking About Death," and Novack, et al., "Changes in Physicians' Attitudes Toward Telling the Cancer Patient."

49. Novack, et al., "Changes in Physicians' Attitudes Toward Telling the Cancer Patient," p. 900.

50. See M. Blumenfeld, N. B. Levy, and D. Kaufman, "The Wish to Be Informed of a Fatal Illness," *Omega* 9 (1978–79): 323–26, and their letter to the editor, *New England Journal of Medicine* 299 (November 16, 1978): 1138.

51. Jim McIntosh, "Patients' Awareness and Desire For Information About Diagnosed but Undisclosed Malignant Disease," *The Lancet* (August 7, 1976): 300. There may be important differences between Britain and the United States. For an indication of some differences between Britain and Canada, see Charles Wright, "Personal View," *British Medical Journal* 4 (October 6, 1973): 45. For one patient's argument for incomplete disclosure, see Natalie Davis Spingarn, "Doctors Who Tell All," *Washington Post*, Sunday, July 30, 1978, B8.

52. Allen Buchanan tries to show that the "Contract Version of the Prevention of Harm Argument" does not provide a general justification for paternalistic deception or nondisclosure; however, as Donald Vandeveer contends, the "Contract Version" does not even offer a justification of paternalism but, rather, a reason for viewing the deception or nondisclosure as non-paternalistic. As Vandeveer notes, "If a patient contracts to authorize his physician to withhold information under certain conditions, then the physician's doing so *under those conditions* is not a case of interference and, hence, not paternalistic interference." Buchanan's difficulty at this point stems, in part, from his failure to connect paternalism to nonacquiescence in a patient's wishes, choices, or actions. Allen Buchanan, "Medical Paternalism," pp. 370–90, and Donald Vandeveer, "The Contractual Argument for Withholding Medical Information," *Philosophy and Public Affairs* 9 (Winter 1980): 198–205.

53. Robert Veatch, *Death, Dying, and the Biological Revolution: Our Last Quest for Responsibility in a Technological Age* (New Haven: Yale University Press, 1976), p. 247.

54. Joseph Fletcher, *Morals and Medicine*, p. 62. Now, as a strict consequentialist, balancing various goods, Fletcher would not draw that conclusion unless he believed that more good than harm would result from the forced disclosure.

55. Elizabeth Kübler-Ross, *On Death and Dying* (New York: Macmillan, 1969). I will discuss these stages in Chapter VII.

56. T. S. Eliot, *The Four Quartets* (New York: Harcourt, Brace, Jovanovich, 1971), p. 14.

57. Eric Cassell, *The Healer's Art: A New Approach to the Doctor-Patient Relationship* (Philadelphia: J. B. Lippincott, 1976), p. 224.

58. *Ibid.*, p. 191.

59. *Ibid.*, p. 198.

VII

Suicide and Refusal of Lifesaving Medical Treatment

Suicide and Suicide Intervention

In the last chapter I discussed one of the most common reasons for deception or incomplete disclosure of information: to sustain hope in order to prevent suicide or refusal of lifesaving medical treatment. Now I want to explore whether paternalistic reasons are sufficient to intervene, particularly through coercion, to prevent suicide and refusal of lifesaving medical treatment.[1] In this chapter I will consider public policies and professional actions toward people who choose the certainty of immediate death; in the next chapter I will consider public policies toward the reduction of risk-taking, sometimes labelled "slow suicide."

In 1975 in the United States, there were 27,000 reported suicides (and probably many others not reported as suicides). At a rate of 12.6 per 100,000 in the United States, suicide is the tenth leading cause of death in the general population, but much higher for certain populations such as white males, ages 10 to 55.[2] If society wants to reduce premature death, reduction of the rates of suicide should have high priority. But because suicide appears to be voluntarily undertaken in many cases, beneficence may conflict with respect.

Most definitions of "suicide" include the agent's intention and action to bring about his own death. But then there are major disputes about the relevance of such factors as time, directness and indirectness of action, and motivation. For example, there is disagreement about whether Captain Oates, a sick member of Scott's Antarctic expedition, committed suicide when he walked into a blizzard so that his comrades would not be further delayed by their efforts to care for him. R. F. Holland appeals to several criteria to suggest that Oates did not commit suicide:

> Oates simply walks away from his companions—and in the act of doing so becomes exposed to the blizzard: he needs to put distance between himself and them and he cannot do so in any other way. He is concerned only with their relief. And he is well on the way toward death already. Such are the features of the case which in combination make it possible, though not obligatory, to say of him unsophistically what would naturally be said of a martyr, namely that he goes to his death.[3]

In addition to time and indirectness of action, Holland adduces Oates' motivation and his terminal condition. If, however, Oates had shot himself, Holland would have described his act as suicide, regardless of Oates' motivation (acting for others) and his terminal condition.

I will not try to resolve these disputes about the concept of suicide. Such a resolution is not necessary for our purposes as long as we recognize that what would be justified "exceptions" to a rule against suicide within one tradition may be built into the definition of the rule in another tradition. In this section I will concentrate on cases such as #8 and 9, which most people would recognize as suicide or attempted suicide. Then in the next section I will examine cases of refusing lifesaving medical treatment, which may in some instances, and for some traditions, also count as acts of suicide. At any rate, determining that an act is or is not suicide does not conclusively determine its morality. And certainly it does not determine the morality of societal and professional intervention in attempted suicide.

It is important to distinguish two kinds of acts of suicide or attempted suicide. Following Max Weber, we can call them "goal-rational" (*zweckrational*) and "value-rational" (*wertrational*), or "instrumental" and "expressive."[4] In goal-rational or instrumental conduct, an agent attempts to realize some goal or end and to bring about some effect in the world. For this conduct, the language of cause/effect, effectiveness, and efficiency is very important. For example, an agent may commit suicide because he believes that death is better than his current life of pain and suffering. In case #9, John K. tried to commit suicide because of his Huntington's chorea. He intended to bring about a result or state of affairs that he considered better than (or, at least, not as bad as) his life prospects. In "expressive" acts of suicide, an agent conveys a meaning or makes a statement. For example, a person attempting suicide may convey his contempt for the world or affirm some value. Frequently, suicides or attempted suicides are efforts to punish the survivors, or they are pleas for help. According to some interpreters, acts with such intentions are not appropriately called "suicide" or "attempted suicide."

Obviously, these two categories of instrumental and expressive suicide are not mutually exclusive; some acts fall under both. For example, in case #8, Jo Roman committed suicide because she had cancer and felt that death was better than suffering from her disease and from chemotherapy, and because she wanted to create "on my own terms the final stroke of my life's canvas." Sometimes the intended result is sought by symbolic actions including suicide (e.g., the self-immolation of protesters of the war in Vietnam). Because Jo Roman also wanted to publicize her belief in the right to die, she made her suicide a quasi-public event by having a cameraman videotape conversations with her family and friends on this subject (later used in a PBS documentary "Choosing Suicide") and by completing her book *Exit House*, which advocates a right to die.[5] Her act of suicide was one of a series of acts designed to achieve a result (awakened public consciousness) by their expression and communication of meaning. While she could have obtained her goal of avoiding suffering by a private act, she pursued her larger goal of changing public consciousness by her quasi-public act.

Judgments about the rationality of instrumental suicide will depend on an assessment of alternative states of affairs and their probability. For example, an autopsy indicated that Jo Roman's cancer had not spread beyond the lymph nodes to any vital organ. Furthermore, she had to determine whether her act of suicide would be likely, even in conjunction with her other activities, to contribute significantly to her public goal, and whether other acts would be as effective. But in addition to considerations of probability, there are valuational matters. How much weight should be given to avoiding suffering and prolonging life? How much weight should be given to the end of arousing public consciousness over against the end of staying alive? These depend, of course, on the agent's life plan, but the observer may have a different view and consider the act irrational.

Judgments about the rationality of expressive suicide hinge on different criteria, such as adequacy, appropriateness, and fittingness.[6] Somewhat similar to aesthetic criteria, these standards suggest the difficulty of determining the rationality of expressive suicide.

Although he concedes that suicide can be rational, Stanley Hauerwas contends that it is a mistake to hold that if a suicide is autonomous and if there are no strong utilitarian reasons or "reasons of human worth and dignity standing in the way, then we ought to allow the person to commit suicide, because we would otherwise be violating the person's autonomy."[7] According to Hauerwas, viewing the problem in this way "reveals the insufficiency of autonomy either as a basis or ideal for the moral life" and also "simply fails to provide an appropriate account of why any of us decide or should decide to stay alive." In contrast to Hauerwas, I would argue that to affirm that respect for another person sometimes requires nonintervention or limited interventions in suicide attempts does not imply that autonomy is "a basis or ideal for the moral life."

It is important to distinguish "A has a right to do X" from "it is right for A to do X" or "A is rightly doing X." All A's negative right to do X implies is that others have a duty not to interfere with A's exercise of that right. Of course, others may question the rightness and the rationality of what A is doing, but in so questioning they need not deny A's right to act in this way. This distinction between "rights" and "right conduct" is exceedingly important.[8] We may be interested in whether A should or may commit suicide in terms of his traditions and values, or we may be interested in whether B should intervene to stop A's attempted suicide. We might say with Hauerwas that there are strong (even decisive) reasons for the Jew or the Christian to repudiate suicide because of the belief that life is a *gift* from God. But unless it is right to compel others to live out that religious conception, it is not clear that the belief that life is a gift from God authorizes anyone to intervene in attempted suicide.

Furthermore, to recognize that we should sometimes respect a person's right of self-determination even when he or she attempts suicide is not to hold that autonomy is the basis for or an ideal of the moral life. It is simply to respect a person's wishes, choices, and actions as a constraint on what we may do even to promote his or her own welfare. Hauerwas rightly emphasizes that medicine should gesture care, but he does not emphasize that it should also gesture respect. He loses the tension between beneficence and respect for persons, and the latter appears to have no weight in his determination of societal and medical policies toward suicide and attempted suicide. But if respect for persons is taken seriously as a principle, it does not imply that interventions in attempted suicide are never morally justified. It simply sets a limit on those interventions. Suicide prevention and intervention are important not only because of the principle of beneficence but also because of the principle of respect for persons.

Suicide prevention may take many different forms. While in earlier times, suicide was criminal conduct, which subjected the perpetrator's body and estate to severe penalties, it has been decriminalized in most states. Paternalistic and other reasons are not strong enough to support legal prohibition of suicide and legal penalties for attempted suicide. The society may, however, allocate resources to reduce the incidence of suicide by providing tangible and symbolic care. For example, there is some evidence that voluntary Samaritan organizations, devoted to "befriending" people who are considering suicide, may reduce the rate of suicide.[9]

While a health care professional's intervention to prevent a particular suicide may take several forms, such as wrestling a gun from a patient, the most common is involuntary hospitalization for a limited period. Such hospitalization may be permitted or even mandated, in part, because of a person's dangerousness to himself or to others. Because of my focus on paternalistic justifications, I will not consider dangerousness to others. There may, however, be a tendency for psychiatrists to overpredict both sorts of dangerousness, in part, as Loren Roth suggests, because "dangerousness" is "a political and not a medical concept."[10] To determine dangerousness, it is necessary to determine both probability and magnitude of harm. I do not here consider whether other harms such as destruction of one's own property may satisfy this condition, but the irreversible harm of death may justify intervention (if other conditions are met). It is also necessary to determine that the person will probably attempt suicide. The mere possibility of such an attempt is not sufficient.[11]

Just as John Stuart Mill justified forcibly stopping someone from crossing a dangerous bridge, at least temporarily in order to inform the person of the danger, so it is possible to justify emergency detention of persons threatening suicide in some circumstances. Such involuntary hospitalization may be justified on the grounds that the person is at risk of a serious, irreversible harm and that he may suffer from some defect or encumbrance in his decision-making. For example, he may have psychotic depression. When it is probable that the person will attempt suicide, and there are doubts about the person's mental state, temporary intervention or postponement of suicide may be justified. It is often necessary to gain time in order to determine the person's mental condition and also what he or she really wants (e.g., to call attention to his or her plight or to die).[12] But in order to detain a person for longer than a brief period (such as 72 hours), there should be clear and compelling evidence that the person suffers from some defect or encumbrance in decision-making that renders him incompetent to make his own decisions in this area. Furthermore, the criterion of least restrictive alternative applies.[13]

When a person who has attempted suicide is brought to the emergency room, treatment should be immediate and vigorous, even if the person refuses treatment as John K. did by his note in case #9. In most situations, the physicians and others in the emergency room will have no way to determine whether John K. was competent and wanted to die. Both care and respect demand treatment in such cases.

Acts of "attempted suicide" are frequently symbolic, and agents may convey many different messages through these acts. Thus, as an implication of the principle of respect for persons, it is very important to determine what these agents are saying, even when their messages are garbled or ambivalent. They may not want to die, and they may actually be crying for help. To ignore this possibility in order to respect their "autonomy" is to turn the principle of respect for persons into an excuse for indifference.[14] Furthermore, treatment does not foreclose future options for the patient; each year 1–2 percent of the people who have unsuccessfully attempted suicide are successful in another attempt.[15]

Refusal of Lifesaving Medical Treatment

Nowhere is paternalism more rampant than in the care of patients who are terminally ill and dying. At least in the past, many health care professionals tended to withhold information from such patients. In recent years, some health care professionals have also tended to impose a model of dying on patients, forcing them through predetermined stages. For example, on the basis of her study of dying patients, Elizabeth Kübler-Ross used the metaphor of stages to illuminate processes of dying. Many patients, she discovered, go through five stages: denial, anger, bargaining, depression, and acceptance.[16] Her work legitimated discussion of an area that had been sadly neglected, and it afforded several insights. Unfortunately, for some of her followers the interpretive metaphor of stages became a prescription for proper dying. Patients were expected to go through the four negative steps followed by positive acceptance, the fifth and highest stage. Obviously such an approach converts a person's dying into a professionally directed process. It becomes a form of paternalism. In a cogent critique of this approach, Larry Churchill observes, "To put the dying into stages is to control them and to deny them the needed opportunity to tell us what dying means to them. . . . Persons should both die, and understand their dying, in the manner they deem most appropriate, so long as the rights and wellbeing of others are not significantly abridged."[17] His point is epistemological as well as ethical: only the dying can determine the meaning of their lives and their deaths. He proposes that professionals think about the care of dying patients not in terms of rigid stages but in terms of the metaphors of drama, narrative, and stories, within which people locate the meaning of their deaths. For example, locating her life within the Christian story and the death of Christ, Flannery O'Connor wrote in the last year of her life: "I haven't suffered to speak of in my life."[18] Often the style of death will be chosen, explicitly or implicitly, as part of one's style of life. As a character in T. S. Eliot's *The Cocktail Party* comments about a woman's death,

> Because it was for her to choose the way of life
> To lead to death, and, without knowing the end
> Yet choose the form of death. We know the death she chose.
> I did not know that she would die in this way.
> *She* did not know. So all that I could do
> Was to direct her in the way of preparation.
> That way, which she accepted, led to this death.
> And if that is not a happy death, what death is happy?[19]

Major conflicts often erupt when patients refuse lifesaving medical treatment against the advice of health care professionals and family members. As I indicated earlier, it is not necessary to draw a hard and fast line between suicide and refusal of lifesaving medical treatment. Wherever the line is drawn for conceptual and moral reasons, important issues will emerge from both actions. In case #9, John K. attempted suicide after having pinned a note to his shirt to refuse medical treatment if he should be taken to the emergency room. I argued that intervention was justified in this case, and that physicians and others in the emergency room had an obligation to treat him vigorously. But there are many cases in which people have a moral and a legal right to refuse lifesaving medical treatment. Rights are both active and passive: they involve determination of both what one shall do and what may be done to one. In the discussion of suicide, the emphasis is largely, but not exclusively, on the former; in the discussion of refusal of treatment, the emphasis is largely, but not exclusively, on the latter.

There are two contexts for discussion. First, some people outside medical relationships refuse treatment. Then the question is whether health care professionals and others have a right to compel them to enter a medical relationship, e.g., by hospitalizing them. Second, some patients within medical relationships refuse further lifesaving treatment. They may want further care (such as relief of pain), but not prolongation of their lives. For example, Christian Scientists often remain outside medical relationships, while Jehovah's Witnesses often accept medical treatment but refuse blood transfusion even when it is believed to be essential to survival. In case #15, Mrs. Northern refused to enter into medical relationships, while in cases #10, 14, and 17 patients within medical relationships refused further lifesaving treatment. In both contexts, it is important to determine when, if ever, it is justified to override a person's express refusal of lifesaving treatment for that person's own benefit. The relevant issues are similar, but not identical, in both contexts.

My claim is that competent persons in either context have the moral right and have, or should have, the legal right to refuse lifesaving medical treatment for whatever reasons they find appropriate. The right to consent to and the right to refuse medical treatment are two sides of the same coin. Both are derived from the principle of respect for persons. Nevertheless, the customary language of " 'consent,' as opposed to 'decision,' in the legal concept of informed consent introduces a bias, especially in therapeutic transactions, for perceiving refusals as uninformed."[20] Thus, the language of decision may be more desirable.

How strong is the right to refuse lifesaving medical treatment? Paul Ramsey has argued that the right of refusal is only a "relative right": "There are medically indicated treatments (these used to be called 'ordinary') that a competent conscious patient has no moral right to refuse, just as no one has a moral right deliberately to ruin his health."[21] Thus, Ramsey would justify strong paternalistic interventions at least under some conditions. For him, the right of refusal is relative to medical indications for treatment of a patient who is not dying. The important medical line is between dying and nondying. For patients who are irreversibly dying, the choice is between further palliative treatments and no treatments. For the nondying, there is an obligation to use medically indicated treatments to save life. This obligation falls on both the patient and the professional.

Ramsey focuses on physicians as agents who have to make decisions about patients in the context of their commitment to care for and preserve life rather than to serve patients' wishes. Their decisions, he claims, should be based on medical factors (e.g., whether a patient is dying) that are objective even though they cannot be infallibly determined. Instead of emphasizing a right of refusal, Ramsey acknowledges the right of conscious, competent patients to "participate" in decisions affecting them.[22]

In contrast to Ramsey's paternalism, it is important to distinguish medical facts and values, even though they cannot be separated, and to allow patients and their agents to make decisions about treatment, which cannot be reduced to medical indications. It is impossible to refer to "medically indicated treatments" without presupposing a set of values.[23] Indeed, in the guise of medical indications, Ramsey assumes a set of values—the importance of sustaining the life of a nondying person regardless of its anticipated quality. In effect, Ramsey would recognize refusal of treatment only when that treatment merely prolongs *dying*, in contrast to treatments that prolong life. His fears about societal trends toward active involuntary euthanasia of incompetent nondying patients have led him to subvert, or unduly restrict, the competent patient's right of refusal.[24]

Ramsey's appeal to "medical indications" recalls some of the inadequacies of the distinction between ordinary and extraordinary means of treatment. This distinction was developed in the Roman Catholic context to resolve moral conflicts about surgery prior to the discovery of antisepsis and anesthesia. But it is now used by others, for example, the American Medical Association and several courts. Although it was originally applied to decisions of patients as well as proxies, including physicians, it is now mainly applied to proxy decisions about incompetent patients. Nevertheless, within certain contexts, especially religious ones, it is still sometimes used to distinguish legitimate and illegitimate refusals of treatment by competent patients.

The language of ordinary and extraordinary means of treatment should be discarded because of its imprecision and its tendency to support strong paternalism. At most, it is a shorthand expression that presupposes moral grounds for determining which treatments are obligatory and which are optional. Indeed, the language of "obligatory" and "optional" is more appropriate than "ordinary" and "extraordinary," because it suggests that moral reasons undergird the distinction. According to Gerald Kelly, S.J., treatments are extraordinary, or optional, if they do not offer a reasonable prospect of benefit, or if they involve excessive expense, pain, or other inconvenience.[25] But physicians and other health care professionals often ground the distinction in medical practice. Thus, for them, "ordinary" is equated with "usual," and "extraordinary" with "unusual" or "heroic" medical practice. If it is customary to treat disease X with treatment Y, treatment Y is ordinary and thus required. Paternalism, aided by the imprecision of the language, appears in two ways. On the one hand, what is customary medical practice determines what ought to be done. On the other hand, the disease entity and the medical technology to treat it displace the patient as the center of concern. The patient as a person is subordinated to the patient as a bearer of a disease. Neither customary medical practice, nor medical technology, nor medical indications can provide adequate grounds for distinguishing obligatory and optional means of treatment. Thus, no treatment as such is obligatory or optional; everything depends on the patient's condition. The only adequate grounds or standards can be found in the ratio of benefits and burdens of the treatment to the patient. But the competent patient should make his or her own assessment, while a proxy must make it for an incompetent patient, using that patient's previously expressed wishes or values when they can be determined.

In affirming the competent adult patient's right to determine his or her own assessment of the benefits and burdens of treatment, I do not accept simplistic views of personal wishes, autonomy, and competence. What appear to be criticisms of the right of refusal often are only criticisms of inadequate interpretations of the meaning of the principle of respect for persons. For example, in an article entitled "Patient Autonomy and 'Death with Dignity,'" Jackson and Youngner contend that preoccupation with autonomy and dignity can lead to bad medical judgments.[26] While they sometimes appear to challenge appeals to patient autonomy as such, they usually challenge appeals that are "precipitous," "automatic," and "superficial." Their cases also indicate that the real issue is what to do when patients are ambivalent or lack some conditions for self-determination. Even if there is a presumption—as I contend there is—that the adult patient is competent to make his or her own decisions, that presumption can be rebutted under certain conditions, as chapter V argued. And even if the patient is competent, it may not be easy, as chapter IV suggested, to determine his or her will, for there may be conflicting signals.

While the principle of beneficence by itself might support medical interventions regardless of the patient's wishes, it is constrained by the principle of respect for persons. But the principle of respect for persons does not preclude medical judgment; it only establishes presumptions and limits for the exercise of medical judgment. Furthermore, this principle requires, rather than precludes, attention to the patient's competence and to what he or she is really saying, which may not be fully and clearly expressed in current statements such as "I do not want this treatment." Thus, while there will sometimes be tensions between medical judgments, grounded on the desire and intention to benefit the patient, and patient choices, these tensions should not be exaggerated. There are important bridges between these two principles of beneficence and respect for persons, when they are fully analyzed.[27] One bridge, as we have seen, is weak or limited paternalism. These bridges have also been recognized by the courts, which have affirmed a patient's right to refuse lifesaving treatment except where he or she is incompetent, or ambivalent, or would impose burdens on others.[28] Sometimes all three features are present, as in a famous case at the Georgetown Hospital: A Jehovah's Witness refused a blood transfusion, but the court authorized physicians to administer it to the woman because she was incompetent and ambivalent and because she had a young child.[29] In order to concentrate on paternalism, I will not consider the possible harms or burdens of a patient's death to others, which may sometimes justify medical intervention even when the patient is competent and clearly refuses medical treatment in order to die.

Suppose a patient refuses to give reasons for his or her refusal of treatment: "I just don't want any more treatment, and I don't want to talk about it." In principle, such a refusal should be accepted; but in practice such a refusal probably should be rejected or at least deferred until it is possible to determine the patient's reasons. In some cases, the physician may know the patient well enough to determine the authenticity of the refusal. But without an indication of reasons, it may be impossible to determine whether the patient is competent and what he is saying or wants.

The processes of trying to determine the patient's competence and his or her will are not totally separate even though they are distinguishable. While patients will frequently display signs of both incompetence and ambivalence, sometimes only one is present. For example, in case #15, Mrs. Northern was not ambivalent though she was perhaps incompetent. She decisively refused treatment for her gangrenous feet, not because she wanted to die, but because she did not believe that they were gangrenous. And a patient who is clearly competent to make a decision, who has the conditions for self-determination, may, nevertheless, be ambivalent. In chapter IV, I analyzed the different consents and refusals people may offer over time—past, present, and future. In such contexts it is often difficult to determine which "person" or which "will" to respect. But even when we concentrate on the present, it may be difficult to determine what the patient really wants amidst his or her conflicting signals, as was evident in my analysis of suicide and suicide intervention. It is important, as Jackson and Youngner emphasize, that physicians not precipitously act on the side of the ambivalence that makes the most sense in their view of the patient's condition. Respect for persons, as well as beneficence, requires communication and discussion. In order to gain this time for communication and discernment of the patient's will, it may be necessary to continue treatment in some cases even though the patient says stop. The irreversibility of death and, in some cases, of the decision to terminate treatment is, of course, relevant. When competent patients are involved, it may be desirable that the courts not prematurely freeze the positions of the patients and the physicians.[30] It may be important that the process of discussion and even negotiation continue, as the case of Mr. C. suggests (see case #12).

I have already discussed the complications of Jehovah's Witness cases (see chapter IV), particularly those in which the patient wants to live, cannot consent to a transfusion, and yet believes that a court-ordered transfusion would not adversely affect his or her religious life. Even though several legal decisions appeal to the patient's incompetence and harm to third parties, a central moral question is the patient's ambivalence, as an examination of the court records indicates.[31] Sometimes the patient appears to want the transfusion, and yet cannot consent to it. In a few cases it may be a matter of both beneficence and respect for persons to help such patients through the loophole in their beliefs: a court-ordered transfusion would not harm them morally or religiously.

Interpreting legal trends, Robert Veatch notes, "There is a clear right of the competent person to refuse treatment for any reason, but the right not to be declared incompetent while exercising that refusal is only beginning to emerge."[32] His observation rightly emphasizes that rights can be denied in ways other than by directly overriding them. And yet a putative right not to be declared incompetent while exercising the right to refuse medical treatment cannot be absolute. After all, the right to refuse medical treatment can only be exercised by competent persons. While there is a moral and legal presumption in favor of an adult's competence to make such decisions, this presumption is rebuttable. In addition to the obvious cases where patients cannot communicate their wishes at all, other patients may be incompetent to make decisions because of serious defects, encumbrances, and limitations in their decision-making.[33] Both beneficence and respect for persons may require overriding their express wishes in some cases.

As I noted earlier, competence may be intermittent and limited or specific. There are several implications of these claims. First, because competence may be intermittent, it is necessary to continue to assess the patient's competence; the determination of competence or incompetence can not always be final. Second, a person may be incompetent in several other areas and perhaps even institutionalized, but he may be competent to make decisions about his medical care. Third, a person may be competent in other areas of life, but not in decisions about medical care. While it is not possible to say that medical care is so technical that laypeople cannot make decisions about their care, because of specific encumbrances some patients may be incompetent to consent to or refuse therapy. Thus, it is necessary to determine the competence of this patient to make this decision about medical treatment at this time. For example, in case #15, Miss Northern denied that she had gangrene of both feet and was in danger of dying; she insisted that her feet were black because of soot or dirt. According to the court which authorized the Commissioner of the Department of Human Services to consent to amputation of her feet, Miss Northern is an intelligent, lucid, communicative and articulate individual who does not accept the fact of the serious condition of her feet and is unwilling to discuss the seriousness of such condition or its fatal potentiality . . . because of her inability or unwillingness to recognize the actual condition of her feet which is clearly observable by her, she is incompetent to make a rational decision as to the amputation of her feet.[34]

In such a case, a false belief may render a patient incompetent to decide. The patient may not want to die, but may deny that he or she has a terminal illness (e.g., case #16) or deny the importance of a particular treatment for survival (e.g., amputation of a leg in cases #14 and 15). It is important to distinguish a patient's allegedly false beliefs about her condition and about means to her ends from her allegedly false evaluations, such as a preference for death over life under these circumstances. It is not necessary or possible to draw a sharp dichotomy between facts and values, but in different situations disputes may center more on one than on the other. While false beliefs about a medical condition may be a reason for viewing a patient as incompetent, false beliefs about goods are not.

Intervention for the patient's benefit when he or she is not competent to make a decision is weak paternalism that can sometimes be justified, particularly when it is also a form of soft paternalism (expressive of values affirmed or goals sought by the patient). In these situations of false belief, such as the case of Miss Northern, the patient may affirm the goal of survival, while disputing the facts about his or her medical condition or the effectiveness of means to ends. Where there is also medical uncertainty or dispute about the patient's diagnosis and prognosis, or about the effectiveness of proposed means to the patient's own ends, the case for paternalistic intervention is weakened. Such a dispute weakens the claim that the treatment refused by the patient is necessary and also the claim that the patient is incompetent because of false beliefs in this area. Even if the patient's incompetence is more profound and more extensive, it may sometimes be appropriate to let the patient decide in view of conflicting evidence. Justified weak paternalism requires evidence of incompetence and of risk of harm from the patient's own decision.

Siegler and Goldblatt argue that paternalism is justified in some cases of "acute, critical, treatable illness," which they define as "an unanticipated, immediately life-threatening condition which begins acutely and is caused by factors beyond the patient's control."[35] In such cases there is a high probability of mortality or of severe long-term disability without treatment, and the treatment is relatively easy, standardized, and conventional. One example is case #17, in which a young man with high fever, headache, and stiff neck appeared at the emergency room and gave permission for a spinal fluid examination. The diagnosis was bacterial (pneumococcal) meningitis, which can be cured easily with antibiotics. Without treatment, it is fatal in three out of four cases, and those who survive without treatment usually have severe physical and mental impairment. But this patient refused antibiotics. Siegler and Goldblatt recognize that some patients in acute, critical cases are able to choose for themselves, while others are not. But they contend that "the acutely, critically ill patient who refuses immediately necessary, lifesaving treatment more closely resembles the trauma victim and the profoundly irrational patient than a patient asked to consent to elective medical procedures." Implicit in their contention is also a distinction between treatments that prolong or even save life and treatments that merely prolong dying. Siegler and Goldblatt are thus more likely to acquiesce when the patient refuses the latter. In short, they defend a form of weak paternalism that emphasizes the patient's defects and encumbrances in decision-making and the harm of nontreatment of the patient's condition. In case #17, the probability and immediacy of serious harm are clear enough, and it is probable that the patient's meningitis caused metabolic brain derangement. Hence, overriding this patient's refusal was justified on weak or limited paternalistic grounds. In such cases, when there is reason to believe that the patient is not competent to decide, it is justifiable to treat the condition against the patient's express wishes.

In most disputes, the physician wants to prolong life, and patients or their representatives want to terminate life. But paternalism appears in other guises too. Let us suppose a patient is dying and the physician believes that letting him die would be in his best interests, but the patient wants to have his life prolonged. (I will ignore questions of the allocation of resources in this context in order to focus on paternalism.) If the patient is competent, his wishes should be respected. To let him die against his wishes would be paternalistic, for it would be nonacquiescence in his wishes for his benefit, as defined by the physician. But even if the patient is probably *incompetent*, his current express wish to live should be respected. Such a judgment is not strictly required by the principle of respect for persons, and it does not depend on a right to health care. But it can be supported by utilitarian considerations: the dangers of letting patients die against their wishes. For example, in a case in Massachusetts, the family sought to terminate dialysis for Earle Spring, who suffered from "end-stage kidney disease" and "chronic organic brain syndrome," or senility. He was legally incompetent, and he was completely confused and disoriented. According to the Court, "there was no evidence that while competent he had expressed any wish or desire as to the continuation or withdrawal of treatment in such circumstances, but his wife and son were of the opinion that if competent he would request withdrawal of treatment."[36] Nevertheless, nurses involved in this case reported that Earle Spring continued to indicate by gestures that he did not want to die.[37]

Authorizing termination of treatment against an incompetent patient's current expressed wishes is dangerous because it may be the thin edge of the wedge for *involuntary* termination of treatment. In many cases there is *nonvoluntary* termination, i.e., termination not requested or not consented to by an incompetent patient. But nonvoluntary termination is different from involuntary termination, i.e., termination against the express will of the patient.

Decision-Making for Incompetent Patients

Incompetent patients include the severely defective newborn and the comatose adult as well as patients who express their wishes even though they are incompetent to make decisions. It is too simple to say that proxy decision-makers should act in the best interests of these patients, because the controversy hinges, in part, on whose values, or which values, should be used to determine those interests. Thus it is necessary to distinguish different categories of incompetent patients. For our purposes, there are two major categories: (1) the previously competent, and (2) the never competent.

When decisions have to be made about previously competent patients, it is important, where possible, to take account of their past, their history, and their biographies, which express their values. But, of course, there are different degrees of explicitness and formality. In some cases, previously competent patients may have signed a "Living Will," which indicates explicitly and formally what they would like to have done. In other cases, they may have indicated their wishes to family or friends or professionals. Brother Joseph Fox, an 83-year-old member of the Society of Mary, told his close friend, Father Philip Eichner, that he wanted no "extraordinary care" if he could not make his own decisions.[38] After Brother Joseph Fox suffered a heart attack and became comatose, the court appointed Father Eichner as the guardian to make the decision to terminate treatment. Judge Meade indicated that Father Eichner was not to substitute his own judgment but to pass on Brother Fox's request "as a conduit." This metaphor nicely expresses the significance of previous explicit statements: Since those statements remain an expression of the patient's will unless he revoked them, they are both relevant and decisive. Unless they were subsequently repudiated, or unless the person was not competent, they determine what ought to be done. Indeed, to act contrary to them on grounds of the patient's best interests is unjustified, strong paternalism. Apart from such explicit statements or a "living will," it may be possible to infer a patient's desires from her life plan and her former activities. Even though such inferences can only be drawn cautiously, they are relevant to judgments about what ought to be done. They provide the values for the benefit-burden calculation.

Matters are very different for the never competent, such as the severely defective newborn or the severely retarded adult. For example, Joseph Saikewicz was 67-years-old, with an I.Q. of 10 and a mental age of approximately two years and eight months. He had been in a state institution for over 40 years, and he could communicate only by gestures and grunts. He developed acute myeloblastic monocytic leukemia, which is inevitably fatal. Chemotherapy has a 30–50 percent chance of bringing about temporary remission of 2–13 months, but it often has serious side effects. A court-appointed guardian decided that "not treating Mr. Saikewicz would be in his best interests."[39]

Even when a patient is incompetent and a proxy decision-maker is required, medical paternalism may not be warranted. "Medical paternalism" may indicate the sphere of decision-making (i.e., medical treatment), or it may identify the decision-makers (i.e., physicians and other health care professionals). Unless technical considerations are dominant in such decisions, medical paternalism in the second sense may be inappropriate. For example, if the patient has been previously competent, his wishes or values may be more accessible to family members or to friends. And if the patient has never been competent, the appropriate standard is the patient's best interest, but its determination may be assigned to the family, to the physician and other health care professionals, to a hospital committee, or to the courts. Which proxy decision-maker is appropriate will depend on the importance of such considerations as technical expertise and impartiality. In general, a serial or lexical ordering of decision-makers makes sense where the patient's current or previous will cannot be known: family, physicians and other health care professionals, hospital committees, and the courts. This order is appropriate unless the patient has designated a specific decision-maker. The family can make the decision only in consultation with the physician and other health care professionals, but the physician remains a moral agent and should appeal to another decision-maker if he or she believes that the family's decision is not in the patient's best interest. The court's involvement may be indispensable when it is necessary to adjudicate a conflict between the family's interests and the patient's interests.

While physicians should sometimes preempt familial decision-making in order to protect the interests of incompetent patients, some of them preempt it for paternalistic reasons. For example, pediatricians do not always present treatment options to parents of defective newborns because they want to relieve the parents of the burden of decision-making in such difficult circumstances. They hold that it is "cruel to ask the parents whether they want their child to live or die. . . ."[40] They assume the burden themselves. Their actions are paternalistic vis-a-vis the parents, but they rarely satisfy the burden of proof for justified limited paternalism.

Similar problems appear elsewhere. A common way to let a patient die is to withhold cardiopulmonary resuscitation efforts when the patient suddenly needs them for survival. According to the policy in many hospitals, efforts will be made to resuscitate all patients unless the physician has written an order for "no code." But who should make, or participate in, the "no code" decision? Even though the physician has to sign the order, should a competent patient and the family of an incompetent patient be involved in the decision? Steven Spencer, a physician, argues that a competent patient's "no" to resuscitation should be final. But when the patient has not already clearly expressed his wishes, for example, through a "living will," he recommends that the physician assume the responsibility for the decision and then "explain to family members why resuscitation will not be attempted [rather] than to ask them whether or not they want it attempted." His recommendation is based on patient and family trust in the physician, the physician's superior knowledge, and the family's confusion, lack of objectivity, fear of responsibility, and possible guilt, as well as their concomitant tendency to overtreat. While Spencer's paternalism toward the family is evident, his paternalism toward the patient is even more striking, for explanations to the patient are "thoughtless to the point of being cruel, unless the patient inquires, which he is extremely unlikely to do."[41] In the last chapter I argued against strong paternalism in withholding information from the patient. It is even more suspect when the information in question is that the patient will not be resuscitated. But my objection is more fundamental: There is no warrant for this strong paternalistic preemption of the patient's or the family's decision-making regarding resuscitation.

Throughout this discussion, I have used the language of "letting die." Sometimes this phrase and the alternative phrase "allowing to die" are criticized because they seem to presuppose paternalistic control and permission.[42] But these phrases are very useful for several reasons. First, rather than suggesting paternalistic control and permission, they reflect the notion of a negative, passive right, a right to noninterference as one dies. Because of the patient's rights, the physician should stand by (under the conditions sketched in this chapter) and "let the patient die," while providing appropriate palliative care. These phrases suggest respect through noninterference rather than a privilege granted by a professional. Second, this language is useful because it focuses on ways of bringing about death. It emphasizes the distinction between killing the patient and letting the patient die. But suppose the patient requests that he or she be killed?

Active Euthanasia and Assisted Suicide

Most theologians, philosophers, and health care professionals concede that care, mercy, kindness, or benevolence can justify and even require the use of pain-killers and sleep-inducers for patients who need and want them even though their use may hasten death in some cases. Thus, when it is beneficent to relieve pain in accord with a patient's wishes, even though death will be hastened, the action is not considered to be morally problematic because the hastened death is an indirect effect of a legitimate medical procedure. However the goal of medicine is defined, it cannot reasonably be limited to life-prolongation at all costs, particularly at costs of pain and suffering. Of course, if a patient prefers to endure pain rather than to take medication that will shorten his life, the physician should respect his wishes.

A more controversial question is whether care, mercy, kindness, or benevolence can justify or even require killing in some cases and whether such exceptions should be incorporated into our practices. Marvin Kohl, a humanist philosopher, and Arthur Dyck, a Christian ethicist, have engaged in an extended debate about mercy and euthanasia. Kohl argues that beneficent euthanasia (painless inducement of quick death resulting in benefit for the recipient) is a prima facie obligation because individuals and society have a prima facie obligation to treat people kindly and because beneficent euthanasia is kind. Furthermore, allowing the notion of dignity to control his conception of kindness, i.e., to determine what would benefit others, Kohl does not limit beneficent euthanasia to cases that involve the patient's request for or consent to euthanasia, the imminence of death, and the presence of pain. Indeed, one of his paradigm cases of beneficent euthanasia involves a severely defective newborn who is not in pain and whose death is not imminent. Dyck agrees with Kohl that we have a prima facie duty of mercy or kindness, but he insists that it has two components: nonmaleficence and beneficence. The former takes precedence over and controls the latter. The prior, more stringent duty is to do no harm, which includes killing. Over against beneficent euthanasia, Dyck proposes an ethic of "benemortasia," which would extend the following kinds of care to patients whose death is imminent: relief of pain and suffering, respect for the right to refuse treatment, and provision of health care without regard for ability to pay. Furthermore, using a form of the wedge or slippery slope argument, Dyck contends that the notion of dignity, which determines the content of mercy for Kohl, is so broad and flexible that it would justify morally unacceptable acts. While Dyck holds that direct killing is absolutely wrong, at least when it is intended to benefit the one who is killed, Kohl would make beneficent euthanasia a rule of practice.[43]

There are good reasons to reject both positions. Against Dyck, it is possible to argue that while death may always be a harm, it is not always a net harm. Thus, killing does not always violate the duty of nonmaleficence, and it may be an expression of care, mercy, kindness, or benevolence. An example appears in Jack Cady's short story, "The Burning," in which a trucker was trapped in the cab of a burning tanker after an accident.[44] Unable to release the screaming victim as the flames roared about him, another trucker finally took a pistol and shot him. While not common, such acts have occurred after accidents and on the battlefield. Even if such direct killings are illegal, they are frequently excused. And they may sometimes be morally praiseworthy as well as morally right. In addition, they may manifest respect for personal wishes and choices when the "victims" request death.[45] They may represent both beneficence and respect.

But whatever we say about isolated *acts*, there are good reasons for rejecting Kohl's insistence on a *rule* or *practice* of euthanasia, even to benefit and to respect patients who request death. These reasons are not necessarily paternalistic. More persuasive are considerations of justice and social utility, which require that a rule of practice avoid exploitation and produce more benefit than harm.

While accepting cessation of medical treatment under some conditions, the House of Delegates of the American Medical Association ruled out "mercy killing" and the "intentional termination of the life of one human being by another." Its reasons had to do with the integrity of the medical profession. Likewise, in all jurisdictions in the United States, to my knowledge, active euthanasia, or mercy killing, is illegal. Thus, if a physician tells a patient that she cannot in good conscience actively terminate the patient's life, despite the patient's interests and wishes, her refusal may not be paternalistic. She may simply appeal to a professional and societal rule, whether she accepts the legitimacy of the rule or only worries about the sanctions attached to the rule. And the rule to which she appeals may itself have grounds other than paternalism. Furthermore, such grounds as social utility and justice are adequate to support the rule.

There are two distinct issues, which require separate analysis: First, should rules of practice be changed so that professionals have an obligation to kill patients at their request under certain conditions, and, second, should rules of practice be changed so that professionals and patients can execute their own contracts regarding active euthanasia?

Regarding the first issue, Raanan Gillon writes, "Occasionally the argument is heard that euthanasia should not be permitted because it is an unpleasant obligation for doctors to have to assume. This may well be true: nevertheless, it need hardly be said that a doctor's first duty is to his patient, who for his part may prefer euthanasia to prolonging his fatal disease."[46] Gillon apparently wants to establish a physician's obligation or duty to kill patients who request death at least under certain circumstances and, correlatively, a patient's right to be killed. A positive right to be killed is not entailed by the negative right to die (i.e., a right to noninterference in one's dying) that I argued for in the last section. If taken seriously, it would make the physician an "animated tool," a mere servant of the patient's wishes. It cannot be maintained without violating the physician's integrity and conscience and without subverting professional autonomy. Even though it is true that the physician's first duty is to the patient, it is important to distinguish a duty to P, from a duty to P to do X. From the physician's primary duty to the patient, we cannot infer a physician's duty actively to kill patients. Indeed, the phrase "mercy killing" captures not only the element of motivation ("mercy") but also suggests that the act is more than the other can claim as a matter of right.

Gillon apparently defines the physician's duty to the patient in terms of the patient's wishes rather than the patient's needs. I have contended that the physician's duty of beneficence requires that he or she seek to benefit the patient, to meet the patient's needs, as defined to a great extent by the patient's values. In addition, pursuit of the patient's needs, however defined, should be limited and constrained by the patient's wishes. But simply to make the physician a servant of the patient's wishes, including the wish to be killed, would establish positive rights and correlative obligations that are not defensible. At the very least, the physician should have a right of conscientious refusal.[47]

Even if there is no moral right to be killed and if professional codes and societal rules should not create a professional duty to kill mercifully, should the codes and rules *permit* "mercy killing" when a patient requests it and when physicians agree that death would be in the patient's best interests and are willing to carry out the patient's wishes? There are nonpaternalistic reasons of social policy for not permitting killing even when it results from a process of negotiation between physician and patient and is genuinely voluntary for both parties. According to Antony Flew, the burden of proof rests on supporters of the practice of prohibiting killing, because it violates the principle of liberty.[48] Determining which side has the burden of proof—supporters or critics of the prohibition of killing—may determine the outcome of the argument in view of the uncertainties about current realities and probable consequences. But even if the burden of proof rests on the supporters rather than on the critics of current practice, the supporters can show (1) that there is insufficient need for a change in professional and societal rules, and (2) that the probable effects are more negative than positive.

Since I have developed these arguments in detail elsewhere,[49] I will present only a few points here. If the negative right to die is recognized, and if sensitive care, including appropriate medication, is provided, as in hospices, it is not clear that a change in the rules is needed. In the medical context, in contrast to the scene of accidents or to the battle-field, it is usually possible to relieve patients' pain and to make them comfortable without killing them. If, however, the need is not relief of pain or provision of comfort, but the patient's wish for death now rather than later, it cannot always be met by letting the patient die. In some situations, of course, the patient can kill himself or herself, but in others the cost of the current policy is extension of the dying process.

If the need that is usually adduced—relief of pain and suffering—is exaggerated (because it can usually be met in other ways than by kill-ing), the probable and possible negative effects of a change in social practice would have to be taken very seriously. It is risky to remove a barrier that has been so widely accepted in medical practice and in the society and that has been built on significant moral considerations. Some of these risks include (1) a shift in the basis of trust between health care professionals and the society because of an explicit redefinition of the professional role to include causation of death, and (2) the possibility of abuse of an explicit exception. Even if the possibility of abuse were reduced by procedures to ensure voluntariness, the redefinition of the professional role, which would necessitate a new basis of trust, would be undertaken for a limited benefit.

Our professional and societal rules should retain the prohibition of killing, despite the arguments for the rightness of killing patients who request death in some circumstances. This prohibition serves a peda-gogical function in that it reminds friends, relatives, and professionals of the presumption against killing and directs them to seek alternative ways to meet the needs and wishes of patients. Its threat of sanction also creates hesitancy. Nevertheless, our rules of practice are not and should not be inflexible. In their application, it is important to distinguish *jus-tifying* killing from *excusing* it and to distinguish both from *mitigating* circumstances in determining penalties for violations of the rule. In addition to the discretion of prosecutors and judges, in several cases juries have found agents of active euthanasia not guilty, often by reason of temporary insanity. In June, 1973, George Zygmaniak was paralyzed from the neck down as a result of a motorcycle accident.[50] Because the paralysis was considered to be irreversible, George begged his brother, Lester, to kill him. Three days later, Lester entered the hospital with a sawed-off shotgun under his coat, and killed his brother. The jury's verdict was not guilty by reason of temporary insanity. Such a verdict reaffirms the rule because it does not justify killing as an exception; it rather excuses the agent. This mode of "accepting" killing in some cases leaves the agent considering killing in an uncertain position. Gaining certainty through an explicit exception in the law would create greater social risks by erasing a line that has offered some protection and a condition of trust.

In case #9, John K., who had learned that he had Huntington's chorea, requested help from his psychiatrist in committing suicide. Can a stronger case be made for accepting assisted suicide than for accepting active voluntary euthanasia within professional and societal rules? While acts of suicide and attempted suicide have been decriminalized, aiding and abetting suicide is still a crime in many jurisdictions. The main difference between assisted suicide and active voluntary euthanasia is the final agency: who performs the *final* act that brings about death? In assisted suicide, a person kills himself with the assistance of another; in active voluntary euthanasia, someone else kills the person at his request or with his consent. Of course, there are many kinds and degrees of assistance, such as providing information about means of suicide, offering encouragement, providing means, helping a patient use the means (e.g., holding a gun while a patient pulls the trigger), and offering several services as in the "Ethical Suicide Parlors" depicted by Kurt Vonnegut.[51]

Richard Brandt argues that the "moral obligation of other persons toward one who is contemplating suicide is an instance of the general obligation to render aid to those in serious distress, at least when this can be done at no great cost to one's self."[52] This statement is unobjectionable as it stands, and it can be strengthened by indicating the specific obligations that health care professionals, family members, friends and others may have toward the person considering suicide. What is objectionable is his inference from this obligation: "if he needs help in executing the decision, there is a moral obligation to give him help." It is not clear that we would or should blame people, even in close relationships, who refuse to help others commit suicide, even when that suicide is rational. Furthermore, if there were such a moral obligation, there might still be reasons for prohibiting some kinds or degrees of assistance in suicide. They are not, however, as decisive as the arguments against the institution of active voluntary euthanasia, for in assisted suicide the final agency remains with the suicide.

Notes

1. Important issues of beneficence and respect also emerge in situations that are not life-threatening, but I cannot analyze them in detail in this book.
2. These figures are given in David H. Smith and Seymour Perlin, "Suicide," *The Encyclopedia of Bioethics*, ed. Warren T. Reich (New York: Free Press and Macmillan, 1978), Vol. IV, p. 1618. There is considerable debate about statistics in this area, in part because many suicides are not reported as such and many occur in ways that are not easily detected (e.g., automobile accidents). For some of this debate, especially in Britain, see H. G. Morgan, *Death Wishes? The Understanding and Management of Deliberate Self-Harm* (Chichester: John Wiley and Sons, 1979).
3. R. F. Holland, "Suicide," in *Moral Problems*, ed. James Rachels (New York: Harper and Row, 1971), p. 353. For some of the debate about the definition of suicide, see Joseph Margolis, *Negativities: The Limits of Life* (Columbus, Ohio: Charles E. Merrill Publishing Co., 1975); Tom L. Beauchamp, "What is Suicide?" in *Ethical Issues in Death and Dying*, ed. Tom L. Beauchamp and Seymour Perlin (Englewood Cliffs, N.J.: Prentice-Hall, 1978), pp. 97–102; Tom L. Beauchamp, "Suicide," in *Matters of Life and Death*, ed. Tom Regan (New York: Random House, 1980), pp. 67–108; and Glenn C. Graber, "The Rationality of Suicide," in *Suicide and Euthanasia: The Rights of Personhood*, ed. Samuel E. Wallace and Albin Eser (Knoxville: University of Tennessee Press, 1981), pp. 51–65.
4. See Max Weber, *Max Weber on Law in Economy and Society*, ed. Max Rheinstein and trans. Edward Shils and Max Rheinstein (New York: Simon and Schuster, 1967), p. 1. See also the excellent analysis, to which my discussion is indebted, by David Wood, "Suicide as Instrument and Expression," in *Suicide: The Philosophical Issues*, ed. M. Pabst Battin and David J. Mayo (New York: St. Martin's Press, 1980), pp. 151–60.
5. See Jo Roman, *Exit House: Choosing Suicide as an Alternative* (New York: Seaview Books, 1980).
6. For these criteria, see Wood, "Suicide as Instrument and Expression," p. 157. Joyce Carol Oates contends that the artistic suicide often uses "false metaphors" that allow him or her to construe the act of destruction as an act of creation. "The Art of Suicide," in *Suicide: The Philosophical Issues*, pp. 161–68.

7. Stanley Hauerwas, "Rational Suicide and Reasons for Living," in *Rights and Responsibilities in Modern Medicine: The Second Volume in a Series on Ethics, Humanism, and Medicine*, ed. Marc Basson (New York: Alan R. Liss, 1981), p. 187; the position quoted in the text and criticized by Hauerwas appears in Tom L. Beauchamp and James F. Childress, *Principles of Biomedical Ethics* (New York: Oxford University Press, 1979), p. 93. In part, Hauerwas argues against viewing the problem in terms of principles and rules, rights and obligations, contending that virtue and character are more important. See Stanley Hauerwas, *Truthfulness and Tragedy* (Notre Dame, Ind.: University of Notre Dame Press, 1977); see also James Bogen, "Suicide and Virtue," in *Suicide: The Philosophical Issues*, pp. 286–92.

8. A. I. Melden, *Rights and Right Conduct* (Oxford: Basil Blackwell, 1959).

9. See Christopher Bagley, "The Evaluation of a Suicide Prevention Scheme by an Ecological Method," *Social Science and Medicine* 2 (1968): 1–14. But critics have charged that this study is not methodologically sound, because of its selection of controls, and, using other controls, have found no reason for attributing a decline in the suicide rate to the work of the Samaritans. See B. M. Barraclough, C. Jennings, and J. R. Moss, "Suicide Prevention by the Samaritans: A Controlled Study of Effectiveness," *The Lancet* (July 30, 1977): 237–38.

10. Loren H. Roth, "A Commitment Law for Patients, Doctors, and Lawyers," *American Journal of Psychiatry* 136 (September 1979): 1126.

11. The standard of proof of dangerousness should not be as high as the standard of proof in criminal law: proof beyond a reasonable doubt. Even though liberty may be lost through both civil and criminal proceedings, there are good reasons for not requiring the same standard of proof in both. There are important differences between trying to help a person and trying to punish him for his acts. While it would be inadequate to rely on a "preponderance of evidence" for involuntary hospitalization, it should be sufficient to find "clear and convincing evidence." See *Addington v. Texas* 441 U.S. 418 (1979). This standard can, of course, be required for both proof of the person's dangerousness and proof of his or her defects or encumbrances in decision-making.

12. See David Heyd and Sidney Bloch, "The Ethics of Suicide," in *Psychiatric Ethics*, ed. Sidney Bloch and Paul Chodoff (Oxford: Oxford University Press, 1981), pp. 185–202. Jerome A. Motto, a psychiatrist, contends that if a patient has more than "minimal ambivalence" (which he does not specify), the psychiatrist is justified in limiting the person's exercise of his or her right to suicide: "I make the assumption that if a person has no ambivalence about suicide he will not be in my office, nor write to me about it, nor call me on the telephone. I interpret, rightly or wrongly, a person's calling my attention to his suicidal im-

pulses as a request to intercede that I cannot ignore." "The Right to Suicide," in *Suicide: The Philosophical Issues*, p. 217.

13. A thorough moral assessment is needed of operational criteria and legal procedures for involuntary hospitalization, but I cannot provide such an assessment here.

14. Alfred Alvarez notes that the "Church's condemnation of self-murder, however brutal, was based at least on a concern for the suicide's soul. In contrast, a great deal of modern scientific tolerance appears to be founded on human indifference." *The Savage God: A Study of Suicide* (New York: Random House, 1973).

15. See Smith and Perlin, "Suicide," p. 1618.

16. Elizabeth Kübler-Ross, *On Death and Dying* (New York: Macmillan, 1969).

17. Larry R. Churchill, "The Human Experience of Dying: The Moral Primacy of Stories Over Stages," *Soundings* 62 (1979): 27 and 32. See also Churchill, "Interpretations of Dying: Ethical Implications for Patient Care," *Ethics in Science and Medicine* 6 (1979): 211–22.

18. Flannery O'Connor, *The Habit of Being*, ed. Sally Fitzgerald (New York: Farrar, Straus, Giroux, 1979), p. 536.

19. T. S. Eliot, *The Cocktail Party* (New York: Harcourt, Brace & World, 1950), pp. 183–84. On styles of dying, see H. Tristram Engelhardt, Jr., "Tractatus Artis Bene Moriendi Vivendique: Choosing Styles of Dying and Living," in *Frontiers in Medical Ethics: Applications in a Medical Setting*, ed. Virginia Abernethy (Cambridge, Mass.: Ballinger Publishing Co., 1980), pp. 9–26.

20. Joseph Goldstein, "For Harold Lasswell: Some Reflections on Human Dignity, Entrapment, Informed Consent, and the Plea Bargain," *Yale Law Journal* 84 (1975): 691.

21. Paul Ramsey, *Ethics at the Edges of Life: Medical and Legal Intersections* (New Haven: Yale University Press, 1978), p. 156.

22. *Ibid.*, pp. 157, 187.

23. See Richard A. McCormick, S. J., "The Quality of Life, the Sanctity of Life," *Hastings Center Report* 8 (February 1978): 30–36.

24. For a fuller discussion of Ramsey's position, see James F. Childress, "Ethical Issues in Death and Dying," *Religious Studies Review* 4 (July 1978): 180–88. Also, Ramsey's policy of "medical indications" is not as flexible or as patient-centered as his position in *The Patient as Person: Explorations in Medical Ethics* (New Haven: Yale University Press, 1970).

25. Gerald Kelly, S. J., "The Duty to Preserve Life," *Theological Studies* 12 (December 1951): 550.

26. David L. Jackson and Stuart Youngner, "Patient Autonomy and 'Death with Dignity,'" *New England Journal of Medicine* 301 (August 23, 1979): 404–08.

27. The metaphor of "bridges" appears in Bruce L. Miller, "Autonomy and

the Refusal of Lifesaving Treatment," *Hastings Center Report* 11 (August 1981): 22–28.

28. For an analysis of relevant court cases, see Virginia Abernethy and Keith Lundin, "Competency and the Right to Refuse Medical Treatment," in *Frontiers in Medical Ethics*, ed. Virginia Abernethy, pp. 79–98, and Robert M. Veatch, *Death, Dying and the Biological Revolution* (New Haven: Yale University Press, 1976), chap. 4.

29. See *Application of President and Directors of Georgetown College*, 331 F. 2d 1000, (D.C. Cir. 1964), cert. denied, 377 U.S. 978 (1964). Excerpts from this case appear in Beauchamp and Childress, *Principles of Biomedical Ethics*, pp. 261–62.

30. See Robert A. Burt, *Taking Care of Strangers: The Rule of Law in Doctor-Patient Relations* (New York: Free Press, 1979), chap. 1.

31. See James F. Childress, "Moral Responsibility and Blood Transfusion: Ethical Issues in the Treatment of Jehovah's Witnesses," *The Journal of Religion*, forthcoming.

32. Veatch, *Death, Dying, and the Biological Revolution*, p. 146.

33. For some tests of incompetence, see chapter V.

34. Quoted in Abernethy and Lundin, "Competency and the Right to Refuse Medical Treatment," p. 87.

35. Mark Siegler and Ann Dudley Goldblatt, "Clinical Intuition: A Procedure for Balancing the Rights of Patients and the Responsibilities of Physicians," in *The Law-Medicine Relation: A Philosophical Exploration*, ed. S. F. Spicker, J. M. Healey, Jr., and H. T. Engelhardt, Jr. (Boston: D. Reidel Publishing Co., 1981), pp. 5–31. Contrast Siegler's earlier article, "Critical Illness: The Limits of Autonomy," *Hastings Center Report* 7 (1977): 12–15, and also Eric Cassell, "The Function of Medicine," *Hastings Center Report* 6 (1976): 16.

36. *In the Matter of Earle N. Spring*, Mass., 405 N. E. 2d 115, at 118 (1980).

37. See Fred Barbash, "Resumed Life Aid Sought for 'Right-to-Die' Patient," *Washington Post*, January 23, 1980, and "Treatment Resumption Denied in 'Death-With-Dignity' Case," *Washington Post*, January 24, 1980.

38. *In the Matter of Eichner*, 73 N. Y. App. Div., 2d Dept., 431 (March 27, 1980).

39. *Superintendent of Belchertown State School* v. *Saikewicz*, Mass., 370 N. E. 2d 417 (1977).

40. Quoted by Anthony Shaw, "Dilemmas of 'Informed Consent' in Children," *New England Journal of Medicine* 289 (October 25, 1973): 886.

41. Steven Spencer, " 'Code' or 'No Code': A Nonlegal Opinion," *New England Journal of Medicine* 300 (January 18, 1979): 138–40. For hospital policies that have different roles for patients, see "Optimum Care for Hopelessly Ill Patients: A Report of the Clinical Care Committee of the Massachusetts General Hospital," and Mitchell T. Rabkin, Gerald Gillerman, and Nancy R. Rice, "Orders Not to Resuscitate," *New*

England Journal of Medicine 295 (August 12, 1976): 362–64, 364–66. The patient's role is clearer and stronger in the latter than in the former, but the latter is limited to resuscitation.

42. See Churchill, "Interpretations of Dying," p. 221. Also of interest is Eric Cassell," Permission to Die," *Bioscience* 23 (August 1973): 475–78.

43. See Marvin Kohl, *The Morality of Killing* (New York: Humanities Press, 1974), and Arthur J. Dyck, *On Human Care: An Introduction to Ethics* (New York: Abingdon, 1977), as well as their essays in *Beneficent Euthanasia*, ed. Marvin Kohl (Buffalo, N.Y.: Prometheus Books, 1975) and elsewhere.

44. Jack Cady, "The Burning," *Atlantic Monthly* 216 (August 1965): 53–7.

45. Of course, involuntary, active euthanasia could be an expression of paternalism, but my arguments against involuntary termination of lifesaving medical treatment also apply to involuntary, active euthanasia. To kill a patient against the patient's wishes is unjustified paternalism, not respect for persons.

46. Raanan Gillon, "Suicide and Voluntary Euthanasia: Historical Perspective," in *Euthanasia and the Right to Die: The Case for Voluntary Euthanasia*, ed. A. B. Downing (London: Peter Owen, 1969).

47. See James F. Childress, "Appeals to Conscience," *Ethics* 89 (July 1979): 315–35.

48. Antony Flew, "The Principle of Euthanasia," in *Euthanasia and the Right to Die*, pp. 30–48.

49. See Beauchamp and Childress, *Principles of Biomedical Ethics*, chap. 4 and *Priorities in Biomedical Ethics* (Philadelphia: The Westminster Press, 1981), chap. 2.

50. See Paige Mitchell, *Act of Love: The Killing of George Zygmaniak* (New York: Alfred Knopf, 1976).

51. Kurt Vonnegut, Jr., *God Bless You, Mr. Rosewater* (New York: Dell Publishing Co., 1965), pp. 20–21. Some proponents of the legalization of assisted suicide distinguish "solicitation" (such as commanding, requesting, or encouraging) from "aid." See Leslie Pickering Francis, "Assisting Suicide: A Problem for the Criminal Law," in *Suicide: The Philosophical Issues*, p. 262.

52. Richard Brandt, "The Morality and Rationality of Suicide," in *A Handbook for the Study of Suicide*, ed. Seymour Perlin (New York: Oxford University Press, 1975), p. 73.

VIII

Prevention of Ill Health
and Early Death:
Intervention in Personal Lifestyles

Prevention

Benjamin Rush, an 18th-century physician, praised prevention of disease and ill health: "There is a grade of benevolence in our profession much higher than that which arises from the cure of diseases. It exists in exterminating their causes."[1] In the last two centuries prevention's successes have altered the causes of morbidity and mortality, and prevention now faces different obstacles.

In the United States during the past century, a major shift in the nature of health problems has occurred—from a burden imposed primarily by infectious diseases (the leading killers in 1900 being pneumonia, influenza, tuberculosis, and combined diarrhea and enteritis) to a burden imposed by chronic diseases, accidents and violence. Many of the chronic diseases arise out of changes in the environment and personal life-styles—exposure to new environmental pollutants, increased stress, decreased physical activity, and increased consumption of certain foods, cigarettes, alcohol, and other substances. . . . Considering the population as a whole, today's major medical problems are the chronic diseases of middle and later life: heart disease, cancer, and stroke. For the population under 44, the leading causes of death, in order, are: accidents, heart disease, cancer, homicide, and suicide. For persons under 25, accidents are by far the most common cause of death, with homicide and suicide the next leading causes.[2]

Many commentators insist that the best, perhaps the only, way to improve the nation's health is through *prevention*. DHEW's *Forward Plan for Health*, Fiscal Years 1977–81, contends: "Only by preventing disease from occurring, rather than treating it later, can we hope to achieve any major improvement in the Nation's health."[3]

This interest in prevention has several roots. One is the recognition that many diseases result from an interaction between a person's genetic endowment and his or her environment, broadly conceived to include behavioral patterns as well as physical, socioeconomic, and familial settings. Another is the concern for the most effective and efficient use of society's health care resources. A third root is a sense of the limits of medicine, exaggerated by the "therapeutic nihilists" such as Ivan Illich. Finally, even many who affirm medicine's goals and praise its achievements also try to contain its costs, another problem that makes prevention attractive.[4]

"Prevention," of course, is ambiguous. It is possible to distinguish primary, secondary, and tertiary prevention. Primary prevention consists of actions to avoid disease or ill health prior to its manifestation or occurrence in a particular individual. Secondary prevention involves detection of a disease before its symptoms have become evident and intervention to stop it or slow it down. An example is screening for asymptomatic hypertension and trying to control it; another example is screening for phenylketonuria in newborns and then instituting a dietary regimen. Tertiary prevention, which converges with conventional therapy, occurs after the disease or ill health has become clinically manifest and attempts to stop or slow its progression. An example is treating a person who has pernicious anemia with Vitamin B-12 in order to prevent its recurrence.[5]

Secondary and tertiary prevention obviously involves health care professionals who can detect a disease prior to or after its clinical manifestations. Primary prevention, our major interest in this chapter, includes strengthening individuals to make them less susceptible to disease and ill health (e.g., through vaccinations), altering the physical or socioeconomic environment (e.g., reduction of pollution), and changing individual lifestyles and behavioral patterns (e.g., diet and exercise).

Because governmental interventions in individual lifestyles and behavioral patterns raise important issues of paternalism (such as which policies are paternalistic and which are justified?), I will concentrate on them.

But why concentrate on prevention of ill health instead of promotion of health? Within the categories of beneficence discussed in Chapter II, promotion of good is a less stringent requirement than prevention of evil or harm. And there is often greater disagreement about what is good than about what is bad or harmful. I do not, however, wish to take one side or the other in the debate about conceptual and normative questions in health and disease.[6] However these questions are answered (e.g., whether health should be defined as the absence of disease), governmental policy should be analyzed first of all in relation to prevention. If the arguments do not support a policy of prevention, they will not support a policy of promotion, because of the priority of the prevention of harm and greater agreement about what counts as harm.

Some hard questions face any preventive program, not merely one that concentrates on changes in lifestyles and behavioral patterns. First, we may not know enough about causal links between environment or conduct and ill health to implement a preventive program. Any call for prevention must be able to point to an adequate knowledge base, and our ignorance in certain areas may indicate that society ought to allocate more funds for research than for application. The polio vaccine is an example of what can be accomplished in some areas, but end-stage renal failure, to take another example, results from numerous diseases and conditions and is not as amenable to prevention as polio.

Second, in some cases prevention may be less cost-effective and efficient than treatment.[7]

Third, medical care often has priority over prevention in public policy because it deals with "identified lives" rather than "statistical lives" and thus, according to some analysts, can better express social compassion and the value of life.[8] In effective prevention, "statistical lives" are saved, whereas in medical care "identified lives" are saved. The phrase "statistical lives" refers to unknown persons in possible future peril. Although they may be alive now, we do not know which of them will be saved by a successful preventive strategy. Whether and to what extent this apparent societal preference for "identified lives" over "statistical lives" and, thus, for personal medical care over prevention should be defended is a difficult question. At the very least, it sets a social and political constraint on public policy. It would sacrifice (some) effectiveness and efficiency in order to express society's compassion and in order to symbolize the value of life. Effectiveness and efficiency may conflict with symbolic value.

In short, preventive strategies are subject to careful scrutiny because they may not be effective or efficient or because they save statistical lives rather than identified lives. Primary prevention that focuses on lifestyles and behavioral patterns faces another constraint: the principle of respect for persons.

Lifestyles and Behavioral Patterns

In *The Republic*, Socrates argues for prevention rather than critical or chronic care. Drawing on Homer and others, Socrates recommends a simple lifestyle—no sauces and sweets, no Attic pastry, and no Corinthian girls. His argument is, in part, aesthetic: "And to need doctoring, isn't that ugly—except for wounds, or the attacks of some seasonal illnesses?" To need medical care "because of sloth or the manner of life" is ugly.[9]

According to several studies, an individual's lifestyle is a key determinant of his or her health. For example, the epidemiological data gathered by Lester Breslow and his colleagues at the University of California at Los Angeles support seven familiar rules for good health: don't smoke, get seven hours sleep each night, eat breakfast, keep your weight down, drink moderately, exercise daily, and don't eat between meals. At age 45, a person who has followed six of these rules has a life expectancy 11 years longer than a person who has followed fewer than four rules. In addition, at age 55 his health indices are comparable to those of a 35-year-old person who has followed fewer than four rules.[10]

In his book, *Who Shall Live?*, Victor Fuchs contrasts the states of Utah and Nevada, which have roughly the same levels of income and medical care, but are at the opposite ends of the spectrum of health. For example, mortality for persons ages 20–59 is approximately 39 percent higher in Nevada than in Utah. Fuchs asks:

> What, then, explains these huge differences in death rates? The answer almost surely lies in the different lifestyles of the residents of the two states. Utah is inhabited primarily by Mormons, whose influence is strong throughout the state. Devout Mormons do not use tobacco or alcohol and in general lead stable, quiet lives. Nevada, on the other hand,

is a state with high rates of cigarette and alcohol consumption and very high indexes of marital and geographical instability. The contrast with Utah in these respects is extraordinary.[11]

Another example is the increase and the decline in coronary heart disease mortality. From the 1930s through the 1950s coronary mortality increased before it reached a plateau in the 1960s. From the late 1960s to the present it has declined by approximately 2.5 percent annually. A major cause of the decline appears to be dietary change (especially less consumption per capita of animal fats and oils, butter, cream, and eggs) and decreased cigarette smoking (especially among male adults).[12]

Numerous other examples could be mentioned from such areas as physical activity, diet, psychosocial stress, accidents, violence, and the use of drugs, alcohol, and tobacco.[13] Our lifestyles and behavioral patterns increase the risk of morbidity and early mortality.

Life is inherently risk-filled, if we understand "risk" as a chance of injury or loss.[14] In ordinary discourse "risk" refers to the *amount* of possible loss and to the *probability* of that loss. We both run risks and impose them on others. It is important to distinguish between *risk-taking* and *risk-imposition*. The former refers to conduct that creates risks for the actor, while the latter refers to conduct that imposes risks on others. One important issue, to be considered later, is whether much or most individual risk-taking also imposes risks or, more generally, costs on others. "Risk-taking" implies that the actor is aware of the risks and voluntarily assumes them. He or she may, or course, engage in "risky" action without "taking risks" in this sense.

A second and related distinction is between *voluntary* and *involuntary* risks. Often we voluntarily assume risks because we desire certain benefits, either for ourselves or for others (e.g., eating rich foods). But risks are also imposed on us against our wills (e.g., by reckless drivers). Apparently we are willing to tolerate more risks in voluntary activities, over which we have some control, than in involuntary activities.[15]

To use Charles Fried's language again, each person has a *life plan* consisting of ends and values.[16] It also includes a *risk budget*, for we are willing to run certain risks to our health and survival in order to realize some ends and express some values. As Fried suggests, "a person's life plan establishes the magnitudes of risk which he will accept for his various ends at various times in his life." While Fried concentrates on budgeting risks of death for our ends and values, as well as for the life plan as a whole, at different periods of life, a person's life plan also implies budgets of other sorts of risks as well as of time, energy, and money. Some people may live unreflectively or have incoherent projects, but even they appear to have some ends and values that they are not willing to sacrifice in order to reduce risks to health or to survival. Indeed, a person's "lifestyle" is determined to a great extent by the ends and values for which he or she will voluntarily take risks. Our willingness to take the risk of ill health or death for success, or friendship, or religious beliefs discloses their importance for us and gives our lives their style. In one survey of several different communities, health was assigned the highest value by no more than 31 percent of the respondents across field tests. It was in the first two or three ranks for approximately 50 percent of the respondents but in the fifth rank or lower for as many as one-third.[17] At the very least, governmental intervention in lifestyles and behavioral patterns must meet a very heavy burden of proof because it appears to violate the principle of respect for persons and their self-determination through their life plans and risk budgets.

Ends of Governmental Intervention

In order to justify governmental intervention into personal lifestyles and behavioral patterns, several conditions should be met. First, justification requires that the intervention have an important end or purpose. This first condition is necessary but not sufficient, for other conditions also have to be met. And several ends and purposes are relevant but not necessarily decisive. They are invoked, for example, in arguments for statutes to require motorcyclists to wear helmets.

Most states have revoked their mandatory helmet statutes in the last few years. But arguments for such statutes have emerged again because of studies that indicate that riders without helmets are at greater risk of fatal head injury than riders with helmets.[18] Proponents of mandatory helmet legislation appeal to the different sorts of reasons introduced in chapter I: (1) prevention of harm to others or to the society (e.g., motorcycle accidents deprive society of able-bodied people), (2) prevention of unfair burdens for others or the society (e.g., the excessive use of society's resources), (3) moralism—control of the immoral lifestyles of motorcyclists, and (4) paternalism—protection of motorcyclists themselves. While the third reason is rarely explicit, it frequently emerges in subtle ways, for example, in the terms employed and in the behavior singled out for attention. Because both the first and second reasons focus on harms or costs to other individuals or to the society, they can be combined. But, for the present, I will distinguish them on the grounds that it is possible to emphasize either the harms and costs themselves or their unfairness.

These various reasons are frequently intermixed. It is important to determine whether any reason by itself can satisfy this first condition, whether a policy of intervention has stronger support if several reasons are combined, and whether the presence of one reason in an argument can vitiate the others. Our major interest is paternalism, but it is also important to see how it is combined with other reasons. In order to do this, it may be useful to examine one of the strongest defenses of self-determination in lifestyles and behavioral patterns, John Stuart Mill's classic essay "On Liberty."[19]

That essay asserts what Mill calls "one very simple principle," which is more complex than he realized:

> That principle is that the sole end for which mankind are warranted, individually or collectively, in interfering with the liberty of action of any of their number is self-protection. That the only purpose for which power can be rightfully exercised over any member of a civilized community, against his will, is to prevent harm to others. His own good, either physical or moral, is not a sufficient warrant (pp. 68f.).

Mill's principle depends on a distinction between *self-regarding* and *other-regarding* conduct. This apparently neutral language of "regard," "concern," and "affect" might appear to yield too much to society, for practically all actions regard, affect, and concern others. But it was meant negatively. Mill was interested in conduct that has adverse effects on others. Conduct that concerns, regards, or affects others or the public adversely may be regulated and even prohibited under certain conditions. But conduct that affects only the agent adversely should fall under his/her own self-determination. "In the part which merely concerns himself, his independence is, of right, absolute. Over himself, over his own body and mind, the individual is sovereign" (p. 69). On health, Mill held that "each is the proper guardian of his own health, whether bodily *or* mental or spiritual" (p. 72). Each person is "sovereign" and "final judge" in matters that affect only him or her adversely and is free to conduct "experiments of living" and to make various plans of life (p. 120).

The following chart may illuminate Mill's position.

Adverse Effects

	Self-Regarding	Other-Regarding
Voluntary	1	2
Nonvoluntary	3	4

Voluntariness of action

First, let us examine other-regarding conduct (#2 and #4). By other-regarding conduct, Mill meant not only conduct that affects others adversely. Such conduct must also affect others directly and without "their free, voluntary, and undeceived consent and participation" (p. 71). If others in the maturity of their faculties consent to the agent's risk-imposition, his action is not other-regarding in Mill's sense. An agent's other-regarding conduct may be either voluntary or nonvoluntary. If it is voluntary (#2), if the agent understands the risks and voluntarily imposes them on others without their consent, society may prohibit and punish the conduct through the criminal law. When the agent nonvoluntarily harms others, or imposes risks on them, society may also intervene. Contemporary examples include vaccinations or genetic screening.

When we distinguish voluntary and nonvoluntary conduct, we see that Mill's simple principle that self-regarding conduct may not be legitimately restricted or prohibited is complex. He contends that society should not interfere in *voluntary self-regarding conduct*. Such interference would be extreme or strong paternalism. It would override a person's wishes, choices, and actions for his/her own benefit, regardless of his/her condition (e.g., competence). It would be unjustified because it would fail to treat people in the maturity of their faculties as equals; it would be a sign of disrespect.

But interventions in self-regarding conduct that is substantially non-voluntary because of defects in deciding, willing, and acting may be justified. They are instances of limited or weak paternalism, which does not treat a person with indignity or disrespect. Mill used the example of a person about to cross a dangerous bridge. If we see such a person, and there is "no time to warn him of his danger," we might "seize him and turn him back, without any real infringement of his liberty; for liberty consists in doing what one desires, and he does not desire to fall into the river" (p. 166). But in such a case if the person is not a child, or delirious, etc., only temporary intervention is justified. Once the restrainers determine that the person is acting voluntarily, they must cease and desist. Likewise, Mill argued only for labelling dangerous drugs rather than prohibiting them.

Critics of Mill's principle have tried to take the sting out of it largely by contending that category #1 (voluntary self-regarding conduct) is practically a null class because our risky actions are other-regarding and/or nonvoluntary. Thus, they insist, the issue is not whether strong paternalism can be justified but whether most interventions in personal life plans and risk budgets are paternalistic at all, at least in the strong sense. To a great extent, the question is where the boundaries of the self and its actions are to be drawn, that is, whether various influences on the agent determine his actions and thus make them nonvoluntary, and whether the adverse effects of his actions extend beyond himself.

Traditional categories such as private and public are somewhat misleading, because they suggest that self-regarding conduct is interested only in the private sphere. In chapter III, I indicated that autonomy and self-determination should not be construed to eliminate concern for the expressive and communicative aspects of the self, and I used Jo Roman's suicide as an example (see case #8). Likewise, risky behavior often is expressive and communicative in that risk-takers choose to project a certain identity in the world. The choice of a vocation, of associations, and of activities—to name only a few—is usually expressive. Furthermore, one of the main (implicit) reasons for requiring motorcyclists to wear helmets presupposes this interest in communication: Helmetless riders suggest or symbolize a way of life that calls into question dominant social values.[20]

Adverse Effects on Others

Many critics of Mill contend that few lifestyles and behavioral patterns affect only the agent adversely. Rhetoric abounds: "No man is an island. . . ." "Our society is interdependent." "The distinction between private and public breaks down." Mill did not deny this interdependence (p. 146). He too recognized that most actions affect others, frequently in adverse ways. But harm to others or to the society is only a necessary condition for justified intervention; it may not be sufficient, at least for coercive intervention. Whether the harm is primary or secondary, whether it has the consent of the victim, whether the agent has a definite obligation, and whether the harm outweighs the loss of liberty are all relevant considerations. Mill insisted that an agent's liberty should be overridden only when there is a definite harm, particularly one that violates "a distinct and assignable obligation to any other person or persons . . ." (p. 148). A major question is whether society has a right to claim certain conduct from individuals. Mill was also suspicious of attempts to expand the category of harms and obligations to others, particularly in the care of one's own health. He noted, "If grown persons are to be punished for not taking proper care of themselves, I would rather it were for their own sake than under pretence of preventing them from impairing their capacity or rendering to society benefits which society does not pretend it has a right to exact" (p. 149). The implications of this preference are not fully clear, for Mill admitted that each person should bear his/her share of the social burdens, based on some equitable principle, and that society could enforce this obligation through the law (p. 141).

In the case of ill health and early death because of lifestyles, it is often difficult to find direct adverse effects on others. In general, the earlier model of infectious diseases, which justified coercive governmental interventions on grounds of beneficence and justice to others, is inapplicable. But some actions such as smoking cigarettes in the workplace and drunken driving do have direct and significant adverse effects on others, and the society may prohibit them if it can also meet other conditions (which will be sketched later). But such prohibitions would need to be carefully circumscribed. Neither smoking nor drunkenness as such should be prohibited. Only smoking or drunkenness in settings that result in direct and significant adverse effects on others should be the target of coercive governmental intervention.

Some critics of Mill appear to suppose that it is sufficient to identify some adverse effects on others, however trivial, indirect, or remote. For example, one recent study focuses on "the energy cost of overweight in the United States."[21] The authors admit that "overweight (excess body fat) has heretofore been considered mainly a personal problem with important implications for personal health and well-being." But, they contend, "with the rising specters of energy shortage and world hunger, overweight must become a social problem." For them, overweight is a social problem because of the use of fossil fuel energy to supply the extra food calories to maintain excess body fat.

> We have calculated the total fossil energy equivalent of the food calories saved by reducing the present degree of overweight (2.3 billion pounds for the adult United States population) to optimum body weight and the annual fossil energy reduction once all Americans reached their optimum weight. The energy saved by dieting to reach optimal weight is equivalent to 1.3 billion gallons of gasoline and the annual energy savings would more than supply the annual residential electrical demands of Boston, Chicago, San Francisco, and Washington, D.C.

While the authors have established that being overweight involves some moral issues beyond lifestyle, they have not established an adequate end for coercive governmental intervention in obesity. The government may, of course, disseminate information and provide services to overweight persons who accept them. This example also indicates the dangers of vague and expansive definitions of costs.

In a complex society, with welfare commitments, it may be possible to emphasize the financial burdens of ill health that certain lifestyles impose on the society and thus on individual taxpayers. These burdens might be construed as harmful (e.g., violation of pecuniary interests) or as unjust (e.g., violation of the principle of fairness in the imposition of burdens). People who engage in risky behavior may increase the health care costs of others in private insurance schemes and in Medicare and Medicaid programs. In a national health insurance program, we can expect widespread opposition to paying for the avoidable afflictions of others.

But more evidence may be needed to establish the cost (especially the net cost) of certain lifestyles and behavioral patterns. "Slow suicide" cannot be condemned and prohibited on these grounds without hard evidence that it does in fact impose major costs and unfair burdens on others. Indeed, on a straight cost-benefit analysis, it may be difficult, if not impossible, to criticize those who, in the words of the country-western song, want "to live fast, love hard, die young, and leave beautiful memories" or who, in the words of the rock song, seek "life in the fast lane." Their deaths might actually cost society less than many others. They may die early, without requiring costly care. Thus, a case-by-case analysis is required. For example, even if it is true that motorcycle helmets reduce the number of deaths, we have to consider whether they also lead to survival at a marginal and costly level (e.g., with extensive injuries which require massive medical and social care).

While such considerations may appear to be callous, they are required by an argument for interventions based on the putative costs of certain lifestyles to the society. More than any other factor, concern about the mounting costs of medical care directed attention to lifestyles.[22] But, as we have seen, some risky lifestyles may require less medical care and some rescue medicine may be more cost effective than prevention. Furthermore, when a broad cost-benefit analysis (including social security and retirement programs) is used, there may be even less reason for governmental intervention. Howard Leichter argues this case: "Over the long run, under public or private health and retirement systems, one can expect an increase rather than decrease in social expenditures as a result of avoiding health risks."[23] Finally, he contends, society can only appeal to "humanitarian impulses" to support intervention: the suffering endured by the individuals and their families. But this humanitarian impulse ultimately becomes paternalistic.

In short, it may be possible in some cases to show that individual risk-taking is actually risk-imposition on others. In such cases, it may be possible to restrict the area of risk-taking without prohibiting it altogether. And while there may be increased costs for other individuals and the society in individual risk-taking, they tend to be indirect, secondary, and difficult to substantiate. At the very least, they have been greatly exaggerated, and there is reason to be cautious about the expansion of the category of costs to others as a justification for interventions in lifestyles. Furthermore, where there are costs, they are often outweighed by other savings. In most cases, if there is to be governmental intervention, it cannot rest solely on adverse effects on others. It will have to be paternalistic, whether strong or weak.[24]

Nonvoluntary Actions

Other critics of the Millian position hold that even if some risky conduct is *self-regarding*, it is often *nonvoluntary*. Thus, they justify weak or limited paternalistic interventions—to protect people from themselves because their choices and actions are substantially nonvoluntary. They sometimes defend forms of social determinism ("societal constraints on individual will") that deny almost any individual responsibility for conduct that leads to morbidity and early death.[25] For example, Victor Sidel contends:

> most health and illness are socially determined rather than individually determined. I refer not only to the obvious instance of environmental pollutants and other unhealthy conditions but also to the fact that most personal health practices are culturally and societally determined.[26]

While cultural and societal forces surely influence our personal choices such as exercising, eating, smoking, and drinking, Sidel's denial of personal responsibility is too sweeping. Actions can be influenced without being determined and without becoming nonvoluntary or involuntary. And a person may exercise second-order autonomy by affirming those influences or by trying to break them (e.g., by seeking or not seeking help for drug addiction). If social and cultural determinism could be established—which I doubt—it might justify some interventions under the principles of justice and prevention of harm to others: the government could intervene to prevent exploitation of the victim by forces beyond his or her control. If we suppose that a company is producing, advertising, and selling a harmful product which the consumer finds irresistible, society might prevent this exploitation. If, however, we assume that the consumer's choice is largely voluntary, even if irrational, intervention would be paternalistic. Whether the intervention is direct (stopping the consumer) or indirect (stopping the producer), it would be a form of strong paternalism.

One argument that reduction of self-regarding risks is not paternalistic appeals to the consent of the actors. Its most strained version contends that interventions are not paternalistic because they are in accord with the person's "real will." As I noted in earlier chapters, there are both theoretical and practical difficulties in defending and identifying the "real will." A major problem is its denial that liberty is restricted, or that individuals are coerced, when they are forced to act in accord with their real wills. It is more plausible to admit that they are coerced in the name of a good which they do not recognize, even if they should. Such a view actually rests on either hard paternalism or moralism, in the absence of any evidence that this particular person affirms the ends or weights them in a way that is supposedly consistent with the real will.[27]

Some individuals may, of course, suffer from weakness of will. They may lack the will power to stop X, which they want to stop. Intervention in such cases could manifest both benevolence and respect for persons. But it is difficult to make a case for a "social insurance" policy which would prohibit risky self-regarding conduct that some individuals might find tempting and even irresistible.[28] One problem is distinguishing those who are acting voluntarily from those who are not. It might be appropriate to provide assistance for those who exercise their second-order autonomy to seek to overcome their weakness of will, rather than to prohibit the conduct in question.

In other cases, individuals may not act in accord with their own values because of ignorance of risks. For example, they might choose to avoid some risks if they were aware of them. Mill's own example is forcibly (but temporarily) stopping a person about to cross a dangerous bridge to make sure that he is aware of the risks. Provision of information, including warnings, can be justified and even required by the principle of respect for persons.

Many proponents of prevention are also concerned about evaluative mistakes in the face of accurate information. For example, risk-takers may discount probable harms that will not appear for thirty years. Some defenders of intervention use the analogy of "slow suicide." If suicide intervention can be justified, they contend, so can intervention in risky conduct. But there are important differences between "suicide" and "slow suicide," such as the degree of certainty of death and the irreversibility of the action as well as the length of time available for intervention and change.[29] As Mill emphasized (p. 166), "when there is not a certainty, but only a danger of mischief, no one but the person himself can judge of the sufficiency of the motive which may prompt him to incur the risk. . . ."

The choice of unhealthy practices or risky conduct is not itself a sign of nonvoluntariness. It cannot rebut the presumption against interfering in personal wishes, choices, and actions. Furthermore, nonvoluntariness of conduct can be established only by examining each case. Thus, governmental policies to reduce self-regarding risks will have to be very flexible, and it may be difficult to secure or maintain that flexibility. Nevertheless, provision of information to ensure voluntariness is appropriate under any circumstances. Whether other modes of intervention can be justified will depend on several conditions, which I will now examine.

Other Conditions for Justified Intervention

So far I have concentrated on the *ends* that are relevant to the justification of governmental interventions in lifestyles and behavior patterns. For paternalistic ends, it is also necessary to show that those who engage in risky conduct are not really "taking risks" because their conduct is essentially nonvoluntary. Thus, only weak or limited paternalism would be justified. Furthermore, soft paternalism, which might help individuals realize their own ends, is more easily justified than hard paternalism, which imposes alien ends. But in order to protect other individuals or the society from harm or injustice, the government may restrict conduct that is either voluntary or nonvoluntary. There are, however, other necessary conditions for the justification of governmental intervention for any of these goals. These ends (and in the case of paternalism, the nonvoluntariness of the risky conduct) are not sufficient to rebut the presumption against interference in lifestyles and conduct.

Not only do we need strong evidence that the ill health or disease constitutes a net harm to the society or a net harm to the individual (who is not acting voluntarily); we also need strong evidence that the lifestyle or behavior in question really contributes to ill health or disease. Consider, for example, the controversy about whether a high fat, high cholesterol diet contributes to heart diseases.[30] Of course, the government should present even controversial evidence so that people can make their own informed choices. But when the evidence is inconclusive, the government should do little more than conduct research and provide information. The history of proposed legislation in health is sobering. For example, in the 1920s Joseph Collins argued that people 45-years-old and older should have bi-yearly thorough physical examinations: "Should we ever feel the need of a new law in this country, the one I suggest would exact such examination."[31] Of course, current evidence indicates that such a practice would have only limited health benefits at great cost.

It is necessary to insist on solid evidence of causal links because terms like "health" and "disease" appear to be more objective than they really are. And they can be used to impose value-judgments that are not clearly articulated or defended. For example, when John Knowles, late head of the Rockefeller Foundation, criticized individual lifestyles and behavioral patterns, he naturally used the language of traditional vices: "The cost of sloth, gluttony, alcoholic intemperance, reckless driving, sexual frenzy, and smoking is now a national, and not an individual responsibility."[32] Such language may reflect a new moralism. The "moral police" may operate in the guise of the "health police" in order to enforce a certain style of life which has little to do with health and more to do with "morality" and "salvation." Indeed, "moral" and "religious" beliefs may account for the focus on some actions rather than others. If legislatures concentrate on requiring motorcyclists to wear helmets rather than motorists to use seat belts, their discrimination may reflect a desire to control "the life style bareheaded cyclists *suggest* rather than the life style they *pursue*."[33] For them helmetless motorcyclists suggest, express, or symbolize a way of life of bravado and defiance that merits condemnation. Obviously what is at stake is a moral assessment of a way of life rather than reduction of risk-taking because of other harms to the individuals involved or to the society.

Another condition is that the intervention in the lifestyle really be necessary to obtain the end in question. In some cases, ill health results from several different causal factors, such as the interaction of lifestyle and working environments. In such cases, because of the importance of lifestyle choices for individuals and the principle of respect for persons, the intervention should first of all alter the environment if that is feasible. Thus, in behavior-related disease, policy-makers should give priority to altering situational or environmental factors rather than directly intervening in lifestyles.[34] For example, stress is correlated with high risk for several diseases. Policy-makers should concentrate on situational factors (e.g., societal conditions) rather than on individual change (e.g., teaching individuals to cope with stressful situations). In general, in governmental policies to reduce risky behavior, indirect intervention is preferable to direct intervention. In paternalism, for example, the "indirect method of paternal interference" can reduce the total amount of attempted coercion by punishing the trader rather than the consumer.[35]

Neither direct nor indirect interventions are justified unless there is a reasonable assurance that they will realize the ends that are sought and that the good effects will outweigh the bad effects. Judgments about proportionality—balance of good over bad effects—are more difficult than judgments about effectiveness, as I indicated in my analysis of adverse effects of lifestyles. But both are required because ineffective interventions or counterproductive interventions are morally unjustified. If we consider a range of policy options, we face the paradox that "the very conditions under which paternalistic interventions seem most justified are those in which many of the methods available are least likely to succeed."[36] For example, if a person's actions are essentially nonvoluntary because of social constraints, it is not clear that provision of information or even incentives will be effective.

Any assessment of the mode of governmental intervention should be partially independent of the question of effectiveness. Indeed, some effective means should be excluded because of their long-term effects or because of their lack of respect for persons. I have concentrated on coercion and deception as modes of paternalistic intervention. There are very strong reasons for ruling out governmental deception in efforts to reduce risk-taking and risk-imposition. Many of them are utilitarian in character: the loss of trust between government and citizen and the danger of abuse. Even if an act of governmental deception of its citizens were justified, it would set a dangerous precedent. Thus, most discussions of prevention focus on coercion rather than deception because coercion can be open and public and controlled.

But whether coercion or some other means is used, there is a general rule that the least intrusive, least restrictive, and least humiliating means be employed. Of course, this rule may be in tension with effectiveness, and the adjudication of this conflict may be difficult. But in civil commitment to protect the patient or to protect others, this rule provides a clear constraint. Likewise in health policy, it limits what may be done. For example, even if a person's liberty is justifiably restricted, it leaves "moral traces" in that it requires the use of the least restrictive alternative.[37] Such an alternative might involve regulation of risky actions so that they could only be performed in certain areas or sanctuaries instead of prohibiting them altogether.

What is required of the risk-taker is also important. In general, as I have suggested, it is easier to justify indirect paternalism (e.g., requiring manufacturers to modify equipment) than direct paternalism. And it is easier to justify the prohibition of conduct than to require a person to undertake such actions as exercise or meditation. A policy that requires a person's active participation must meet a heavier burden of proof.

One mode of governmental nonacquiescence is passive: the government might refuse to provide funds for or to facilitate some lifestyles. This passive nonacquiescence might be justified to protect others (e.g., not funding abortion, if the fetus is believed to be a person) or to protect the agent (e.g., not funding sterilization, if it is believed to be against the person's best interest). While passive nonacquiescence is easier to justify than active nonacquiescence, much will depend on whether certain wishes can be restated as positive rights, i.e., rights to others' assistance. If so, the moral case against passive nonacquiescence may be strong.[38]

Sometimes, of course, the society chooses to underwrite or subsidize risky activities such as firefighting for the welfare of the society as a whole. But when a cost-benefit analysis indicates a net loss from certain activities, may the government withhold medical care from or tax the risk-takers to cover the costs of that care?

Within the individualistic model of risky behavior, there is a tendency to hold the individual responsible for his or her conduct and even to "blame the victim," whereas within the model of "societal constraints on individual will," there is a tendency to "blame the society." Robert Veatch holds

> that it is fair, that it is just, if persons in need of health services resulting from true, voluntary risks are treated differently from those in need of the same services for other reasons. In fact, it would be unfair if the two groups were treated equally.[39]

As a defender of the societal constraint model, Victor Sidel contends that most health and illness are socially determined and that a societal failure to prevent risky actions (such as not wearing seat belts) makes the society responsible for what happens. Finally, he grounds the societal obligation to provide health care on reparative or compensatory justice: society should help bind the wounds it has made (or has allowed to be made).[40]

Even Sidel does not claim that "all" risky behavior is socially determined, just as Veatch does not claim that it is individually determined.

But, concentrating on risky behavior that is individually determined, may the government or third-party payers withhold medical care when risk-takers need it (e.g., the cigarette smoker who develops lung cancer)? Whether medical care is conceived as a right or as a privilege, withholding it from voluntary risk-takers may be warranted in principle. Within a society, medical care may be conceived as a positive wish or need or as a positive right which enables one to claim the assistance of others and the society. In order to consider the strongest case against withholding medical care, I will assume a right to medical care.[41]

As I indicated earlier, there is a *logical correlation* between the rights and the obligations of different parties: if X has a right, Y has a correlative duty.[42] While this correlation may not hold for some duties or obligations of charity, it holds in general. In addition, there is a *moral correlation* of the rights and obligations of the same party: if X has rights, she also has certain responsibilities. X's failure to fulfill these responsibilities may result in a loss of the right. For example, although there are rights to life and to liberty, either right may be forfeited by a criminal's failure to fulfill some basic social responsibilities. As Joel Feinberg points out, according to the classic doctrine of natural rights some natural rights can be *forfeited* but not *alienated*.[43] That is, one can lose a right through one's own fault or error, but one cannot voluntarily give the right away. Obviously, a right that can be forfeited is not absolute. Is the putative right to medical care forfeitable? Can it be forefeited by an individual's failure to fulfill her responsibility to care for her health?

Several general arguments are directed against attempts to connect a right to medical care with a person's conduct. First, it is sometimes held that if a person has to "earn" the right to health care there is really no right to it.[44] But if "earned" rights depend on individual responsibility, there are many examples, including the right to drive an automobile. However, even to state the issue in terms of "earned" rights is to distort the picture. For a society could operate with a presumption that everyone in need is entitled to medical care, and that presumption could be rebutted only in cases of gross irresponsibility (e.g., where a person has taken unreasonable risks). Rather than earning a right that has not been assigned to him, a person would need to avoid forfeiting a right that he already has.

More persuasive is a second argument against a policy of holding that an individual forfeits his right to medical care if he fails to meet a certain level of responsibility. Such a policy would encounter serious and perhaps insurmountable moral and practical difficulties. It is difficult if not impossible to pinpoint responsibility for most health crises in part because of the complexity of causal links. The results of the "natural lottery," societal practices, and individual choices may be impossible to dissect. It may be easy to determine responsibility for the skier's broken leg but impossible to determine whether a person's lung cancer resulted from cigarette smoking, environmental pollution, work conditions, or heredity. In addition, the prospect of "health police" violating privacy and keeping detailed records in order to accumulate evidence of risky conduct is morally offensive.

A third argument appeals to moral considerations that transcend rights: even if irresponsible acts abrogate the right to health care, we should continue to provide that care as a matter of compassion and humanity.

A fourth argument builds on a prediction that our society will not be able to deny medical care to risk-takers because of the considerations adduced in the second and third arguments. Even if the society can agree intellectually that the right to medical care is defeasible, it will not deny critical care to people in need, regardless of the cause of the need. This prediction hinges on a judgment about the society's character or identity that makes the abandonment of identified lives in need very difficult if not impossible. A threat to withhold medical care would not be effective because it would not be credible. It is not clear, however, just how much evidence there is for this interpretation of our society's identity and character.

Sometimes this prediction buttresses an argument for meeting the right to medical care (conceived as a right to a decent minimum) by vouchers or in-kind services rather than by the provision of funds without strings attached. A policy of vouchers or in-kind services may invoke considerations of justice or fairness rather than paternalism. Suppose that society provided access to a decent minimum of medical care by cash, but that its sense of identity or character, as defined by care and compassion, would not allow it to deny critical care to those in need who had spent their money on other goods, including risky activities. If both suppositions are granted, the society ought for the sake of fairness to provide vouchers or services instead of money. When the provision of cash is conjoined with a societal reluctance, or unwillingness, to deny crisis care, some individuals will consume more than their fair share of society's resources.[45]

Even if these arguments undermine a policy of withholding medical care from risk-takers *after* they have developed ill health, they may not affect a policy of taxing risks while they are being taken. While the threat to withhold medical care might not be credible because of the society's convictions, a policy of taxation could *deter* risk-taking because the actor would pay as he takes the risks. Marcia Kramer contends that taxing cigarettes to cover the extra medical costs of cigarette smokers "cannot but discourage smoking."[46] However, possible and probable side effects of such policies need to be seriously examined. For example, raising the price of cigarettes might reduce the number of cigarettes smoked but lead smokers to smoke each cigarette longer and farther down. It might actually increase health problems.

Another obvious difficulty of such a policy is that it is feasible for only a limited number of health risks, such as cigarette smoking, but not for "activities that are harmful only when carried to excess, or activities that involve no market transactions. . . ."[47] Examples might be insufficient exercise or obesity, though a "fat tax" has been discussed.

Although Daniel Wikler is mistaken when he holds that the question of paternalism can be reduced to a question of justice in the distribution of the burdens of incompetence, the question of distributive justice is important, especially when we consider health risks. Throughout this discussion, I have argued that beneficence and respect for persons are the most important principles for an assessment of paternalism in health care. In particular, I have tried to show that paternalism is a variegated activity; that it is supported by the principle of beneficence in its several different forms; that it is limited and constrained by the principle of respect for persons; that what the principle of respect for persons requires is often unclear because people are complex and indicate their wishes in different ways over time (hence, the complexities of past, present, and future consent); that active paternalism, particularly in its soft form, can be justified even without past or future consent when a person is incompetent or has other encumbrances and when he or she is at risk of harm; that passive paternalism poses fewer problems of justification; and that beneficence and respect for persons support a variety of actions in disclosure of information, in response to attempted suicide and refusal of lifesaving treatment, and in policies toward risky actions. Throughout I have examined patterns of paternalism in health care, indicating how the metaphor of father, or parent, can illuminate both what occurs and what ought and ought not to occur in health care. We cannot adequately understand contemporary health care without the use of this metaphor, but we cannot adequately shape health care practices if this is our only metaphor. The metaphor of father or parent expresses the principle of beneficence or care, conjoined with control, but it only partially expresses the principle of respect for persons. In health care we need actions, policies, and practices that also embody this principle of respect for persons, properly interpreted to allow differential treatment for autonomous and nonautonomous persons. Such a principle will constrain and limit, but not subvert, the principle of beneficence.

Notes

1. Quoted in J. G. Freymann, "Medicine's Great Schism: Prevention vs. Cure: An Historical Interpretation," *Medical Care* 12 (1975): 525.

2. Elena O. Nightingale et al., *Perspectives on Health Promotion and Disease Prevention in the United States*, A Staff Paper of the Institute of Medicine (Washington, D.C.: National Academy of Sciences, 1978), p. 19.

3. United States Department of Health, Education and Welfare, Public Health Service, *Forward Plan for Health: FY 1977–1981*, DHEW Publication No. (OS) 76-50024 (1976). See also M. LaLonde, *A New Perspective on the Health of Canadians: A Working Document* (*Ottawa: The Government of Canada*, 1974), which stimulated much of the interest in prevention.

4. Several commentators contend that interest in containing the spiraling costs of health care was primary in the attention to prevention. See Howard M. Leichter, "Public Policy and the British Experience," *Hastings Center Report* 11 (October 1981): 32–39, and Robert Crawford, "You are Dangerous to Your Health: The Ideology and Politics of Victim Blaming," *International Journal of Health Services* 7 (1977): 663–80. The latter offers a Marxist critique of individualistic approaches to health.

5. Nightingale et al., *Perspectives on Health Promotion and Disease Prevention in the United States*, pp. 2, 21–22.

6. See Arthur L. Caplan, H. Tristram Engelhardt, Jr., and James J. McCartney, eds., *Concepts of Health and Disease: Interdisciplinary Perspectives* (Reading, Mass.: Addison-Wesley Publishing Co., 1981).

7. Milton Weinstein, "Prevention that Pays for Itself," *New England Journal of Medicine* 299 (August 10, 1978): 307–08.

8. For "statistical lives" and "identified lives," see Thomas Schelling, "The Life You Save May Be Your Own," in *Problems in Public Expenditure Analysis*, ed. S. B. Chase, Jr. (Washington, D.C.: The Brookings Institution, 1966), pp. 127–66. See also Warren Weaver, "Statistical Morality," *Christianity and Crisis* 20 (1961): 210–13. Other helpful discussions are Charles Fried, *An Anatomy of Values: Problems of Personal and Social Choice* (Cambridge: Harvard University Press, 1970) and Albert Weale, "Statistical Lives and the Principle of Maximum Benefit," *Journal of Medical Ethics* 5 (1979): 185–95.

9. Eric H. Warmington and Philip G. Rouse, eds., *Great Dialogues of Plato*, trans. W. H. D. Rouse (New York: The New American Library, 1956), Bk. 3, pp. 203–09.

10. Nedra B. Belloc and Lester Breslow, "Relationship of Physical Status and Health Practices," *Preventive Medicine* 1 (1972): 409–21, Nedra B. Belloc, "Relationship of Health Practices and Mortality," *Preventive Medicine* 2 (1973): 67–81.

11. Victor R. Fuchs, *Who Shall Live? Health, Economics, and Social Choice* (New York: Basic Books, 1974), pp. 52–54. See also Joseph L. Lyon et al., "Cancer Incidence in Mormons and Non-Mormons in Utah, 1966–1970," *New England Journal of Medicine* 294 (January 15, 1976): 129–33.

12. Allen G. Brailey, Jr., "The Promotion of Health Through Health Insurance," *New England Journal of Medicine* 302 (January 3, 1980): 51; National Heart, Lung and Blood Institute, *Proceedings of the Conference on the Decline in Coronary Heart Disease Mortality*, NIH Publication No. 79-1610 (1979); Weldon J. Walker, "Changing United States Life-style and Declining Vascular Mortality: Cause or Coincidence?" *New England Journal of Medicine* 297 (July 21, 1977): 163–65.

13. Nightingale, *Perspectives on Health Promotion and Disease Prevention in the United States.*

14. For an analysis of risk, see James F. Childress, "Risk," *The Encyclopedia of Bioethics*, ed. Warren T. Reich (New York: Macmillan-Free Press, 1978).

15. See Chauncey Starr, "Social Benefit versus Technological Risk," *Science* 165 (1969): 1232–38.

16. Charles Fried, *An Anatomy of Values*, esp. chaps. 10 and 11.

17. See John E. Ware, Jr. and JoAnne Young, *Studies of the Value Placed on Health*, The Rand Paper Series (Santa Monica, Calif.: The Rand Corporation, 1977), p. 22. In general health was valued more by women and by older, less educated, and poorer respondents. This differential evaluation within communities would have to be taken into account in order to avoid discriminatory policies. And, as Ware and Young note (p. 26), it "is possible that the relative value of health is a different construct from an absolute rating of the value of health," which the figures in the text reflect. I should also emphasize that in discussing risks to health and survival, I do not consider certain

calamity or death, which would raise different issues, some of which surfaced in the last chapter.

18. See Pearl K. Russo, "Easy Rider—Hard Facts: Motorcycle Helmet Laws," *New England Journal of Medicine* 299 (1978): 1074–76. For a discussion of some of the arguments, see Laurence H. Tribe, *American Constitutional Law* (Mineola, N.Y.: The Foundation Press, 1978).

19. John Stuart Mill, *On Liberty*, ed. Gertrude Himmelfarb (Harmondsworth, Eng.: Penguin Books, 1976). References to *On Liberty* will give the page numbers in parentheses in the text.

20. See Tribe, *American Constitutional Law*, pp. 887, 941, et passim. His discussion has greatly influenced this paragraph.

21. Bruce M. Hannon and Timothy G. Lohman, "The Energy Cost of Overweight in the United States," *American Journal of Public Health* 68 (1978): 765–67.

22. See Leichter, "Public Policy and the British Experience."

23. *Ibid.*, p. 38.

24. Nor is it possible to argue that intervention is justified because the agent's lifestyle will set a bad example and thus harm others. Henry Sidgwick notes: "I do not here take into account the tendency of a man who harms himself to harm others by bad example. For interference to protect men from the mischief of bad example is clearly 'paternal': since if we assume them adequately capable of looking after their own interests, we must assume that bad example will be on the whole deterrent rather than attractive." Sidgwick, *The Elements of Politics* (London: Macmillan, 1908), p. 133; see also Mill, *On Liberty*, pp. 150–51. But it might be possible to argue, for example, for restricting (not prohibiting) some behavioral patterns so that their display will not be so accessible to children.

25. See Amitai Etzioni, "Individual Will and Social Conditions: Toward an Effective Health Maintenance Policy," *Annals of the American Academy of Political and Social Science* 437 (May 1978): 62–73.

26. Victor Sidel, "The Right to Health Care: An International Perspective," in *Bioethics and Human Rights: A Reader for Health Professionals*, ed. Elsie L. Bandman and Bertram Bandman (Boston: Little, Brown, 1978), p. 347. Contrast Leon Kass' claim that there is a personal duty of health care rather than a right to health care. "Regarding the End of Medicine and the Pursuit of Health," *The Public Interest* 40 (Summer 1975): 11–42.

27. In a somewhat muted version, the "real will" thesis can be seen in Dan E. Beauchamp's reinterpretation of liberty as liberation: "The idea of liberty should mean, above all else, the liberation of society from the injustice of preventable disability and early death." See "Public Health as Social Justice," *Inquiry* 13 (1976): 14. In a series of important articles over several years, Beauchamp has offered several arguments for aggressive preventive programs. The above quotation, for example, also invokes the language of injustice, while he elsewhere uses the

Rawlsian contractual model to justify prevention of early death. See his "Public Health and Individual Liberty," *Annual Review of Public Health* 1 (1980): 121–36. He contends that the demands of justice and community require the reasonable restriction of lifestyle risks even if they have a substantial *voluntary* component.

28. For a discussion of "social insurance policies," see Gerald Dworkin, "Paternalism," in *Morality and the Law*, ed. Richard A. Wasserstrom (Belmont, Calif.: Wadsworth, 1971), pp. 107–26.

29. See Daniel I. Wikler, "Persuasion and Coercion for Health: Ethical Issues in Government Efforts to Change Life-Styles," *Millbank Memorial Fund Quarterly/Health and Society* 56, no. 3 (1978): 315.

30. See note 12 above. In contrast to many recent studies, the Food and Nutrition Board of the National Academy of Sciences in 1980 issued a report that there is no conclusive evidence that reducing consumption of cholesterol and saturated fats will reduce the risk of heart disease. See Victor Cohn, "Lower Fat Diet Affirmed Despite Recent Findings," *Washington Post*, Thursday, June 12, 1980.

31. Joseph Collins, "Should Doctors Tell the Truth?" *Harper's Monthly Magazine* 155 (1927); reprinted in Stanley Joel Reiser, Arthur J. Dyck, and William J. Curran, ed., *Ethics in Medicine: Historical Perspectives and Contemporary Concerns* (Cambridge: The MIT Press, 1977), p. 222.

32. John H. Knowles, "The Responsibility of the Individual," in *Doing Better and Feeling Worse: Health in the United States*, ed. John H. Knowles (New York: W. W. Norton, 1977), p. 59.

33. Tribe, *American Constitutional Law*, p. 941.

34. I am here ignoring economic factors; but see James F. Childress, "Priorities in the Allocation of Health Care Resources," *Soundings* 52 (Fall 1979): 256–74.

35. Sidgwick, *The Elements of Politics*, p. 137.

36. Wikler, "Persuasion and Coercion for Health," p. 317.

37. On "moral traces," see Robert Nozick, "Moral Complications and Moral Structures," *Natural Law Forum* 13 (1968): 1–50.

38. Many people have been puzzled by John Stuart Mill's apparent paternalism in discussing voluntarily selling oneself into slavery; see *On Liberty*, p. 173. Despite some of Mill's arguments, it might make sense to construe his refusal to allow the state to enforce a voluntary contract of perpetual slavery as passive nonacquiescence: The state should not enforce such a contract even though it should not prohibit it. Since Mill mainly opposed paternalism as active nonacquiescence, his acceptance of paternalism as passive nonacquiescence, in this case, is not as inconsistent as many claim. See also Vinit Haksar, *Equality, Liberty, and Perfectionism* (New York: Oxford University Press, 1979), pp. 253–57. Contrast Dworkin, "Paternalism," pp. 118–19.

39. Robert M. Veatch, "Voluntary Risks to Health: The Ethical Issues," *Journal of the American Medical Association* 243 (January 4, 1980):

54. While he holds that the individualist or voluntarist model is relevant, he actually defends a multicausal model.

40. Sidel, "The Right to Health Care," pp. 341–50.

41. See James F. Childress, "A Right to Health Care?" *Journal of Medicine and Philosophy* 4 (June 1979): 132–47.

42. See Joel Feinberg, *Social Philosophy* (Englewood Cliffs, N.J.: Prentice-Hall 1973) and David Braybrooke, "The Firm But Untidy Correlativity of Rights and Obligations," *Canadian Journal of Philosophy* 1 (March 1972): 351–63.

43. Joel Feinberg, "Voluntary Euthanasia and the Inalienable Right to Life," *Philosophy and Public Affairs* 7 (Winter 1978): 93–123.

44. See Sidel, "The Right to Health Care," p. 342.

45. For a similar argument, see Charles Fried, "Health Care, Cost Containment, Liberty" (unpublished paper).

46. Marcia J. Kramer, "Self-Inflicted Disease: Who Should Pay for Care?" *Journal of Health Politics, Policy and Law* 4 (1979): 138–41.

47. *Ibid.*

Cases

Case #1

One evening five victims of an automobile accident were admitted to the ward of a small rural hospital. The nurse in charge knew the woman who had been driving and her four children who were also injured. Three of the children survived, but the oldest child, a daughter, died shortly after admission. The mother suffered contusions and abrasions, but her major problem was her mental anguish about her children. The nurse asked the doctor, who was busy in the operating theatre, what she should tell the mother about the daughter's death. The doctor told the nurse to reassure the woman at all costs because she was in great distress and her husband could not be reached until the next morning. All through the night the mother constantly asked the nurse about the children. As the nurse put it, "It went strongly against my conscience to have to look her in the eye and repeat a lie of such magnitude." The doctor told the woman the truth the next day in the presence of her husband. She cried out, "Why did she lie to me?"

[Adapted from International Council of Nurses, Barbara L. Tate, project director, *The Nurse's Dilemma: Considerations in Nursing Prac-*

tice (New York: American Journal of Nursing Company, 1977), pp. 31–33.]

Case #2

The parents of a two-year-old child with Tay-Sachs disease want to have another child and seek counseling to determine the probability of the birth of a normal infant. Both parents are Ashkenazic Jews, who have a 1 in 25 chance of being carriers for this autosomal recessive condition. Since their only child has Tay-Sachs disease, it seems apparent that both parents are carriers. However, a routine medical history taken by the family physician discloses that the husband's blood type is incompatible with his being the child's father, while the mother's blood type is compatible.

Should the husband be informed that, in all probability, he is not the father of the child and that his probability of being a heterozygous carrier is 1 in 25? Should the wife be counselled separately and should the decision be left to her? Should the situation be ignored and the couple counseled as if both were carriers whose next child has a 1 in 4 chance of having Tay-Sachs disease, 2 in 4 chance of being a phenotypically normal heterozygote carrier, and 1 in 4 chance of being normal?

[Adapted from a case prepared by Joseph Benedetto.]

Case #3

Because Mrs. S., a 74-year-old widow, has had several medical problems recently, her physician decided to put her in the hospital for a battery of tests. After analyzing the results of the tests, the physician is firmly convinced that Mrs. S. has metastasized carcinoma and that she will die in six to twelve months. Neither chemotherapy nor radiation offers any reasonable chance of success.

The physician considers whether, what, and how he should tell Mrs. S. Although she has been increasingly confused and forgetful in recent months, Mrs. S. appears to be mentally competent. The physician is not sure that Mrs. S., who has been his patient for more than 15 years, would really want to know the truth, but he believes that she would. Before he presents the bad news to Mrs. S., the physician discusses the matter with her two children, who quickly and emphatically ask the physician not to tell their mother the truth: "Don't tell Momma she is going to die. Tell her these are just nonspecific symptoms of old age. Let her live out the rest of her days in peace."

[This case has been adapted from Howard Brody, *Ethical Decisions in Medicine* (Boston: Little, Brown and Company, 1976), p. 342.]

Case #4

Method and Procedure

History

Mr. X was a 65-year-old retired army officer with a history that included significant military achievement, a productive teaching and research career, and numerous social accomplishments. Medically, the patient had had frequent abdominal operations for gallstones, postoperative adhesions, and bowel obstructions. At the time of his voluntary hospitalization, he was complaining of continued abdominal pain, loss of weight, and social withdrawal.

A mental status exam revealed an oriented, intact man with excellent higher mental functions. His mood was somewhat depressed, and he was unkempt and had poor personal hygiene. He explained that because of the difficulty of controlling his abdominal pain over the past two-and-a-half years, it had become impossible for him and his wife to remain socially active. For example, to control his pain while in social situations with friends, he would often assume awkward or embarrassing postures.

The patient's reliance on Talwin (pentazocine, a weak narcotic antagonist with some narcotic-like properties) had begun more than two years prior to the current treatment. It had been initially prescribed to control pain following abdominal surgery. Mr. X was convinced that this medication was essential for the control of pain and he had spent considerable effort adjusting dosage to his optimal level of 1.25 cc, self-administered intramuscularly, six times daily. Because of the resultant excessive tissue and muscle damage, it had become difficult to find injection sites. The patient insisted that any less than 1.25 cc was almost useless and that more was of no additional value. He had read the early drug literature and was quick to cite evidence that Talwin was not addictive. In addition, Mr. X had no difficulty obtaining his medication by prescription.

Mr. X's primary goal for therapy was to "get more out of life in spite of my pain." He also verbalized the need to control Talwin, but had become highly resistant to any change in his medication regime.

The Setting

The patient was admitted to a newly opened inpatient psychosomatic ward. The therapy program of this ward used . . . methods for rearranging the contingencies for pain behavior. For example, pain verbalization was not reinforced with staff attention. . . . In addition, adjustment of pain medication was an explicit expectation of the setting, which further included individual behavior therapy programs, daily group therapy, ward government, social activities, and brief sessions for time-limited discussion of symptoms.

Training Program

Mr. X was started on a program of self-controlled relaxation. . . . [He] also learned to control his experience of pain through visual imagery. . . . Additionally, attempts were made to help him lengthen the time between injections. . . .

Drug Withdrawal

Shortly after entering the hospital, Mr. X was shifted to a time-contingent rather than a pain-contingent medication schedule . . . a four-hour interval between his 1.25 cc Talwin injections. This was essentially equal to his self-administration schedule. Although he had admitted himself to a ward where medication adjustment was an explicit expectation, he resisted direct modification of his Talwin dosage levels. He reported numerous past self-developed attempts to modify his regime, and each time he became more convinced of the importance of the medication. Once the six-hour injection interval had been reached, there seemed to be a plateau beyond which no progress was made. The staff then wrestled with the task of reducing Talwin dosage in a patient who had great apprehension about accomplishing such a goal. Our solution was to attempt withdrawal without the patient's knowledge, and while this decision was reached after much discussion with colleagues, it was thought that such a strategy would increase the probability of the patient's achieving his goal of better control over the pain and medication.

The actual withdrawal procedure entailed a gradual dilution of Talwin with normal saline at the rate of .25 cc over the four injections each day. Therefore, after five days Mr. X was receiving injections of 100 percent normal saline four times daily. The patient experienced withdrawal symptoms of nausea, diarrhea, and cramps, but he misattributed these symptoms to Elavil (Amitriptyline), which had been introduced at the same time the Talwin dilution began. The Elavil was prescribed to ease the withdrawal symptoms, and while it was not given to deceive him, the timing fortuitously caused him to misattribute these symptoms. Mr. X continued to be unaware of dosage adjustment, and his verbal report indicated that abdominal pain was relieved by injections. Elavil was discontinued after five days, but the saline was administered for three more weeks. Concurrently, self-control training was successfully continued and the interval between injections was gradually expanded to 12 hours.

Results

After three weeks of saline injections, the patient was aware of the changes in intervals, but he knew nothing of the adjusted dosage. In a special session, his therapist told him of the medication changes. Mr. X responded with a brief reaction of incredulity and some anger. He quickly indicated, however, that saline could not have been an effective agent in reducing his pain and asked that it be discontinued. In addition, he requested continued relaxation and covert imagery training and attributed the recent management of his discomfort to these techniques. In place of medication, Mr. X continued the self-control and socialization programs in the hospital for 20 more days.

At the time of discharge, the patient reported that he continued to experience abdominal pain but that the magnitude of this discomfort could be moderated more effectively with the self-control techniques than had been possible with Talwin. In addition, Mr. X had become very involved in both on- and off-ward social interactions.

A six-month follow-up found that the patient had implemented his posthospital plans, including a return to club activities, tournament bridge, and part-time teaching, and that he was still using the relaxation techniques. Mr. X was making plans for a lengthy summer excursion and was attempting to teach his wife self-control procedures to help control her migraine headaches.

Discussion

. . . The combination of our delay in informing the patient of the drug dilution schedule and his misattributing withdrawal symptoms to the side effects of a second drug permitted the use of an effective treatment program that otherwise would have been rejected as incompatible with the patient's assumptions and beliefs. However, in using a partially blind withdrawal procedure the staff chose an alternative with definite ethical implications. Mr. X admitted himself to a ward, where medication adjustment was an explicit expectation, for treatment of debilitating pain and drug dependency. However, because of his apprehension about direct intervention, we decided that informing him specifically of the withdrawal program would only increase his resistance. Therefore, withdrawal was started surreptitiously but under close medical monitoring concurrent with a self-control treatment program that he agreed was helpful. The Talwin was gradually diluted, Elavil was prescribed to ease withdrawal symptoms, and the process was reversible at any point. In short, Mr. X had been informed that a modification of his medication regime would be undertaken, but the details of his withdrawal were not specified.

Mr. X was our patient and not a subject in an experiment. We felt ethically obliged to use a treatment that had a high probability of success. To withhold the procedure may have protected some standard of openness but may not have been in his best interests. We saw no option without ethical problems. Although it is precarious to justify the means by the end, we felt most obliged to use a procedure designed to help the patient achieve a personally and medically desirable goal. Similar ethical decisions may become more common and more complex as health care professionals treat other dependencies, addictions, or self-destructive behaviors. One can only hope that the individual will be included in as much of his case planning as possible and that treatment goals will be made in an open arena where the staff can freely discuss and contribute to the decision-making process.

[This case is quoted by permission from Philip Levendusky and Loren Pankratz, "Self-Control Techniques as an Alternative to Pain Medication," *Journal of Abnormal Psychology* 84 (1975): 165–68. It is also discussed in several articles in the same issue.]

Case #5

A 60-year-old man developed myasthenia gravis which responded poorly to drug therapy. A thymic tumor was found, and thymectomy was performed. Following chest surgery, the patient remained dependent on the ventilator for three months. Over this time span he was totally paralyzed except for slight movements of his fingers, hands, and eyelids. Gradually, his neuromuscular function returned, and he appeared to be ready for weaning from the respirator. He was depressed, and had become totally dependent on the intensive care unit (ICU) staff whom he believed to be totally in command of his bodily functions. When he was able to breathe on his own for long periods (12–24 hours), he was afraid that he would die if he fell asleep while the respirator was disconnected. His insomnia agitation and sleep deprivation resulted in failure to wean from the respirator, which had to be reinstituted on two occasions. Because his physicians could find no physiological cause for his failure to wean, they decided to wean him by the method of intermittent mandatory ventilation (IMV). In this method, the mechanically delivered breaths per minute are gradually reduced until less than one breath every 2–4 minutes is required. The patient was weaned, but he was not informed until the ventilator had been totally off for a period of three days and nights during which he breathed spontaneously and slept soundly. Because of the noise from the machines, he thought that he was still on the ventilator. When his physicians and nurses told him that he was free from the respirator and ICU life, he expressed initial surprise and then broke into tears. Some hours later after his tracheotomy tube was removed, he thanked the ICU staff for their patient and understanding care. One week after his transfer from the ICU to a regular hospital room he could not remember the ICU physician who had cared for him for three months and could not recall his previous fears of asphyxial death.

[This case was prepared by Michael Rie, M.D.]

Case #6

I have been interested in the problem of informed consent for intravenous urography since 1969 when a patient of mine had a fatal reaction during urography. I was subsequently the defendant in a malpractice case which came to trial in June 1974.

The issue of informed consent was raised in my case by the plaintiff's expert witness who was a pathologist and a lawyer. He stated that "It is the standard of medical practice for a radiologist to warn a patient of adverse reactions including death before doing urography." On cross examination he was unable to give the name of even one radiologist who did this.

When I testified, my attorney asked me why I had not warned the patient of a possible reaction. I said that I did not warn the patient of a possible reaction because it does not do any good. I could have told her that there was a chance she might have a reaction and even die. After calming her down I would then have told her that she had seen two urologists in the past week and both of them had told her she needed urography. I have done 6–8 thousand urograms in the past 13 years and no one has ever had a fatal reaction. We have been doing urograms at this hospital for at least 25 years and no one has ever had a fatal reaction. Because the indications for urography were great and the chances for a reaction were remote I am sure I would have convinced Mrs. Edney to have the procedure. She would have then had the reaction and died and the fact that I warned her would have done Mrs. Edney absolutely no good.

The judge and the jury seemed to accept this argument. On cross examination I was asked whether the patient had a right to know that there was the possibility that she may have a fatal reaction. This is a difficult question to answer on the spur of the moment and you lose with either a yes or no answer.

I would have liked to have said on the witness stand in response to the question as to why I did not inform my patient—the American

College of Radiology has extensively studied the issue of informed consent related to urography and advised all radiologists of the following:
Our responsibility is to our patients and to do what is best for our
patients medically. Informing patients of risks and possible death from
urography may not be in the best interest of the patient and some
experts feel that it may be dangerous. As a member of the American
College of Radiology, I have adhered to this standard.

The Pennsylvania Radiological Society will introduce a resolution to
this effect at the next American College of Radiology meeting.

[This case is reprinted by permission from Robert W. Allen, "Informed
Consent: A Medical Decision," *Radiology* 119 (April 1976):
233–34.]

Case #7

In 1971 the Birmingham Brook Advisory Centre brought a complaint to
the Disciplinary Committee of the British General Medical Council
against Dr. Robert Browne for deliberately betraying a confidence without valid medical reason. The Centre had prescribed an oral contraceptive for Miss X, a 16-year-old-woman, described as highly intelligent,
attractive, and mature. In such cases, the Centre informs the family
doctor unless the patient forbids disclosure. Miss X granted permission,
and the Centre informed Dr. Browne, her family's physician for many
years. He then disclosed the information to Miss X's father without
getting her consent.

According to the Report of the Disciplinary Committee, Dr. Browne

> was concerned that a girl only just 16 had been placed on a con-
> traceptive pill without prior knowledge or consultation with the
> family doctor. It was a stable family with the daughter living at
> home. . . . The girl's father happened to come to the surgery shortly
> after this, and he asked him if his daughter was getting married. The
> father said that she was not, but that she had a steady boy friend and
> was still at school. Dr. Browne said he thought hard and then made up
> his mind—bearing in mind the girl's best interests, and for that reason
> solely—and handed the father a copy of the letter from the centre and
> explained what it meant. . . .
>
> Dr. Browne said that he had two motives in informing the parents.
> One was the physical hazards of the pill, and the second was the moral
> and psychological hazards. He was not standing in judgment, but with

his knowledge of the home background, and knowing the parents were sympathetic and kindly and could handle the situation with care and tact, he considered they were the best people to counsel her in their own way. He also saw psychological hazards, for if she were keeping a secret she might have a sense of guilt, which could have a harmful effect on her emotionally. He pointed out that it would have been difficult for him to contact the girl without arousing parent suspicion. The episode did not appear to have impaired his relationship with Miss X.

In reply to cross-examination . . . Dr. Browne said that his interests were primarily for the patient and for her alone. He had no other interest except what was best for her. His patient was being placed on a dangerous drug without his prior knowledge or consent with all the hazards that might involve—and steroid drugs were a particular hazard. . . .

The Committee found that, while the information Dr. Browne received was in confidence, and while he neither sought nor received the patient's permission to make the disclosure, he nevertheless did not act "improperly" in disclosing the information to the patient's father and thus was not guilty of serious professional misconduct.

[A fuller version of this case appears in Robert M. Veatch, *Case Studies in Medical Ethics* (Cambridge: Harvard University Press, 1977), pp. 131–35; quotations are from the "General Medical Council: Disciplinary Committee," *British Medical Journal Supplement,* no. 3452 (March 20, 1971): 79–80.]

Case #8

On June 9, 1979, artist Jo Roman, 62, began fashioning her "life sculpture"—a pine coffinlike box filled with personal mementos—with the help of her family and close friends. Early the next morning, having finished her project, written a farewell letter to 60 friends, and said goodby to her family, she swallowed 35 sleeping pills, washed down with champagne.

Mrs. Roman had planned her death for 15 months. It was her view that "life can be transformed into art" and that a person should "take command of making life's final brushstroke." Her original plan had been to end her life at age 75; but when she learned in March of 1978 that she had breast cancer which had spread to her lymph nodes, she decided to "make the best possible calculation of a time frame within which I might count reasonably on being able to function to my satisfaction." She said in her farewell letter that she had "concluded that suicide need not be pathological . . . that rational suicide makes possible a truly ideal closing of one's life span." Some months before her death Mrs. Roman organized a two-day videotaping session of discussions with those close to her about her "self-termination," in the hope that the tape might be used in medical training. She also completed a 250-page manuscript entitled "Exit House"—the title stemming from her proposal for a social agency to ensure nonintervention, and possible cooperation, in "gentle" suicides for the old or terminally ill who desire them.

Jo Roman was described by her friends as anything but morbid and as a talented artist with "a large lust for life." Her suicide note, which she had notarized two days before her death, detailed her plans and stated that she wanted to spare herself, her family, and friends the "ravages" of cancer; it was also intended to absolve those close to her of any complicity in her suicide. She had undergone 10 months of chemotherapy before deciding to end the treatment; during that time, she later wrote, "my medical team believed they had more right than I to command my life." An autopsy of her body showed no evidence of the spread of cancer from her lymph nodes to any vital organ.

[This case was prepared by James Tubbs from articles in *The New York Times*, June 17, 1979, and *Newsweek*, July 2, 1979.]

Case #9

John K., a 32-year-old lawyer, has worried for several years about developing Huntington's chorea, a neurological disorder which appears in a person's thirties or forties, bringing rapid uncontrollable twitching and contractions and progressive, irreversible dementia, and leading to death in approximately ten years. John K.'s mother died from this disease which is autosomal dominant and afflicts 50 percent of an affected parent's offspring. Often parents have children before they are aware that one of them has the disease. John K. and his wife have a child because of contraceptive failure and an unwillingness to have an abortion because of his wife's religious convictions.

John K. has indicated to many people that he would prefer to die rather than to live and die as his mother lived and died. He is anxious, drinks heavily, and has intermittent depression, for which he sees a psychiatrist. Nevertheless, he is a productive lawyer.

He noticed facial twitching three months ago, and two neurologists independently confirmed a diagnosis of Huntington's. He explained his situation to his psychiatrist and requested help in committing suicide. When the psychiatrist refused, John convinced him that he did not plan to act any time soon.

But when he went home, he ingested all his antidepressant medication after pinning a note to his shirt to explain his actions and to refuse any medical assistance that might be offered. His wife, whom he had not told about the diagnosis, found him unconscious and rushed him to the emergency room without removing the note.

[This case has been adapted from Marc Basson, ed., *Rights and Responsibilities in Modern Medicine: The Second Volume in a Series on Ethics, Humanism, and Medicine* (New York: Alan R. Liss, 1981), pp. 183–84).]

Case #10

Eleanor Maurer was dying for lack of blood. She was conscious, but could not speak. The blink of an eye was her only means of communicating.

It was a medical complication of childbirth—"uncontrolled bleeding," doctors said.

Mrs. Maurer, 31, daughter of retired Rear Adm. Robert H. Wilkinson, was offered a blood transfusion at Falmouth Hospital Monday.

"She was conscious and she had a tube down her windpipe," her husband, John, said Tuesday. "She was told to answer with one wink to say 'yes' and two to say 'no.' "

She blinked twice, refusing the transfusion.

And she died.

Maurer, a 30-year-old maintenance man, said he supported her decision. They are Jehovah's Witnesses, he said, and the refusal to accept a blood transfusion is justified by the Bible.

"Jehovah's Witnesses accept the Bible and we try to live by its teachings," Maurer said. "We have a great respect for life and want to try to keep living and healthy as long as possible.

"The only restriction we have to abide by is, as God told all of us in the Bible, to abstain from blood."

The Maurers' newborn child, Caroline, was reported doing well today and Maurer said he expected she would be home with him Thursday.

Hospital administrator Gerald F. Flynn said Mrs. Maurer died from "uncontrolled bleeding which could not be controlled without a transfusion. The patient refused a transfusion."

He said the doctors involved were not available for comment on the case.

Maurer said he was in the operating room until doctors discovered the bleeding. He said he left the room to go to the solarium because "I might have thrown up or fainted or something. I am not used to such things."

He said the doctors asked him four times if he would reconsider an earlier commitment he and his wife signed that banned transfusions.

He refused.

"I understood how serious it was every time," he said. "But God is serious too. He does promise resurrection and he does ask his servants to abstain from blood."

[This case is quoted from *The Daily Progress*, Charlottesville, Va., September 19, 1979.]

Case #11

James McIntyre, a 28-year-old diabetic, had been on renal dialysis at the Medical Center for a number of years. He was legally blind and could not walk because of progressive neuropathy. He had become increasingly disenchanted because of the stress on both his family's finances and his lifestyle created by his need for hemodialysis three times a week. Because of his despair and anger, his wife had ceased to be supportive and did not want to continue to transport him back and forth to the Medical Center and to attend to his needs between dialysis sessions. Mr. McIntyre came to the conclusion that continued dialysis was unacceptable for him, and, after numerous discussions with Robert Lincoln and other members of the nephrology unit and dialysis staff, he decided to discontinue dialysis. He was fully aware that this would inevitably result in his death. His only concern was that he be kept as comfortable as possible until then. Dr. Lincoln, the nephrologists, and his family accepted his request, feeling that he had made the decision freely and with full awareness of its implications.

Before Mr. McIntyre was taken off dialysis, he and Dr. Lincoln arrived at an agreement about the way in which his final hours would be handled. They decided that Mr. McIntyre would be admitted to the hospital to receive medication, probably morphine sulfate, as needed to control any symptoms that he suffered during this period. In addition, Dr. Lincoln promised to remain with Mr. McIntyre when he returned to the hospital after discontinuing dialysis. Dr. Lincoln also promised that he would, himself, administer the necessary medication to keep Mr. McIntyre comfortable. Further, he agreed not to put Mr. McIntyre back on dialysis should Mr. McIntyre request it under the influence of uremia, morphine sulfate, and ketoacidosia (the last resulting from the cessation of insulin). Mrs. McIntyre concurred with her husband's and Dr. Lincoln's decision.

Mr. McIntyre terminated his dialysis as well as his insulin and was admitted to the hospital some time later in a uremic state. He had begun to suffer cramps and severe itching, and requested medication which he was given according to the previous agreement. He slept most of the evening and that night, periodically awakening to request more medication. Dr. Lincoln and Mrs. McIntyre were with him throughout. At approximately 3 A.M. that morning, Mr. McIntyre awoke complaining of pain and, at that point, asked Dr. Lincoln to put him back on dialysis. Dr. Lincoln and Mrs. McIntyre considered this request, but ultimately decided to abide by the original agreement with Mr. McIntyre. Dr. Lincoln gave him another injection of morphine sulfate. Mr. McIntyre died in his sleep at approximately 7 A.M.

[This case was prepared by Gail J. Povar, M.D.]

Case #12

Mr. C., a single, 27-year-old athlete and former air force pilot, was severely burned in July, 1973 when his car triggered an explosion of natural gas from a leaking main nearby. His father, who was with him at the time of the explosion, died on the way to the hospital. Mr. C. was admitted with about two-thirds total-body burns—mostly third degree burns. As he later recalled, he didn't want to be taken to the hospital at all; and when he got there, "I told them again that I was burned bad enough that I didn't want them to try to do anything for me and only keep me out of pain. But they did go ahead and treat me and although they did not think I was going to make it at the time, they pulled me through." For the next nine months after his admission, Mr. C. persisted in his desire to discontinue his treatment—which included skin grafts, several surgeries, and painful daily "tubbings" and dressing changes to prevent otherwise inevitable infection. He recognized that stopping treatment would mean certain death.

In April of 1974 Mr. C. was interviewed by a hospital psychiatrist because he had adamantly refused further corrective surgery on his hands and insisted that he be allowed to go home to die. In that interview Mr. C. stated that he only wanted "a brief visit" at home and did not intend to die from infection but would "use some other means"—a difficult prospect, since he had been blinded by the explosion, his fingers had been grafted together, and his arms and legs were not fully functional. He described the excruciating pain of his daily treatments, his total loss of independence in doing anything for himself, his apparently slim chance of ever regaining much independence, and his nightmarish dreams that he was being used as a human guinea pig. He had always been athletic, he said, and even rehabilitation would mean that he could only enjoy life by "changing completely the things I am interested in." And in his own view, that end wasn't "worth the pain involved to be able to get to the point where I could try it out." Therefore, he was demanding to see his attorney in order to request a court order for his release from the hospital.

[This case was adapted by James Tubbs from a transcript of the videotape "Please Let Me Die," reprinted in Robert A. Burt, *Taking Care of Strangers: The Rule of Law in Doctor-Patient Relations* (New York: The Free Press, 1979), pp. 174–80. A version of the case appears with discussion in Robert B. White and H. Tristram Engelhardt, Jr., "A Demand to Die," *Hastings Center Report* 5 (June 1975): 9–10, & 47.]

Case #13

Two sisters, 68 and 70 years of age, and their husbands were searching for a schizophrenic daughter who had disappeared after her discharge from a psychiatric hospital. While their car waited for a stoplight, a nearby construction machine hit a gasoline line. The spraying gas exploded, leveling a city block and igniting the car.

The sisters arrived in our burn center two hours later. The younger sister had 91 percent full-thickness, 92 percent total-body burn, with moderate smoke inhalation; the older had 94.5 percent full-thickness, 95.5 percent total-body burn, with severe smoke inhalation. The burn team agreed that survival was unprecedented in both cases. Both women were alert and interviewed separately.

The younger sister asked about death directly, looking intently into the physician's eyes. When he answered, she replied matter-of-factly, "Well, I never dreamed that life would end like this, but since we all have to go sometime, I'd like to go quietly and comfortably. I don't know what to do about my daughter. . . ."

After she was made comfortable, the nurse obtained a description of the missing daughter and possible whereabouts. The social worker alerted the police to look for her, and telephoned relatives, informing them of the accident as gently as could be conveyed by telephone. The husbands were located at another burn unit. An attempt was made to arrange a final spousal conversation, but both husbands were intubated.

Meanwhile, the older sister doubted whether her injuries were as serious as reported, "I feel so good, wouldn't I be hurting horribly if I were going to die?" The effect of full-thickness burns on nerve endings was explained. The physician reiterated that we wished to do what she thought was best for her. She hedged, "What did my sister say? I'll go along with her decision." Since the patient seemed unsure of her decision, she was offered full therapy in her room with her sister. She then refused the therapy adamantly but denied that she was dying.

The sisters' beds were placed next to each other so that they could see and touch each other easily. They discussed funeral arrangements and then joked, in the next breath, about the damage done to their hair. The hospital chaplain prayed with them. By active listening, he was able to convey to the older that her husband was not to blame for the accident as she had thought. "It's good to go out not cursing him after all our years together," she said. The younger sister died several hours later after her sister lapsed into a coma; the older died the next day. The daughter was not located.

[This case is reprinted by permission from Sharon H. Imbus and Bruce W. Zawacki, "Autonomy for Burned Patients When Survival is Unprecedented," *The New England Journal of Medicine* 297, no. 6 (August 11, 1977): 309.]

Case #14

Shortly before Christmas, 1976, Otis Simmons, a 58-year-old derelict, walked barefoot in bitter cold through the streets of Manhattan to reach Roosevelt Hospital. He was hospitalized, and when his badly frostbitten feet developed gangrene, doctors ordered the infected portions amputated. They said he would lose them anyway, and if the gangrene spread it could be life-threatening. "My two legs got to stay on—I won't have the operation," Mr. Simmons countered, "I got to cure my own self." He explained what had happened: "I froze. I sat in one place 15 hours." Over objections from physicians, New York State Supreme Court Justice Hilda G. Schwartz ruled that Mr. Simmons had the right to refuse the operation. She held that the operation was not "life-saving" and that contrary to psychiatrists' findings, the invalid was competent to decide his own fate. With antibiotic treatment the infection did not spread but Mr. Simmons lost two toes on his left foot and part of his right foot. His three-month hospital bill was $29,000.

[See *The New York Times*, January 3, 1977; January 11, 1977; and April 14, 1977; and *Newsweek*, January 24, 1977, p. 77.]

Case #15

Miss Mary Northern, a 72-year-old woman, lived alone in an unheated house without electricity in Nashville, Tennessee. She was found by public officials in January 1978 to have suffered frostbite of both feet, subsequently complicated by burns from her wood fire. Reports from several concerned parties led police to go to Miss Northern's home three times; on the third visit, they entered and forcibly transported her to Metro General Hospital.

After one week of treatment, physicians urged amputation of both feet (now gangrenous) as a necessary life-saving measure. But Miss Northern could not be persuaded to consent to this surgery. Hospital officials appealed to the Tennessee Department of Human Services, which in turn petitioned the Chancery Court of Davidson County, to have Miss Northern declared incompetent to consent. Drs. Amos D.

Tackett and R. Benton Adkins submitted identical letters declaring that Miss Northern "does not understand the severity or consequences of her disease process and does not appear to understand that failure to amputate the feet at this time would probably result in her death." On January 24 Chancellor C. Allen High heard the petition and appointed Carol L. McCoy to be Miss Northern's guardian ad litem.

On January 25 Chancellor High ordered that Miss Northern was incapable of consent and that the State Department of Human Services should be designated responsible for her personal welfare, including "consenting to any necessary medical treatment." This order was immediately stayed, though, to hear testimony from Dr. John J. Griffin, who, while finding Miss Northern generally lucid and sane, also stated that,

> . . . She tends to believe that her feet are black because of soot or dirt. She does not believe her physicians about the serious infection. There is an adamant belief that her feet will heal without surgery, and she refused to even consider the possibility that amputation is necessary to save her life.

Dr. Griffin also warned of the strong possibility of post-amputation psychosis in Miss Northern's case, and advised delaying surgery for a few days (if feasible) "in order to attempt some work for strengthening her psychologically." Chancellor High reinstated his original order, with the further instruction that surgery be delayed as per Dr. Griffin's recommendation.

Ms. McCoy then filed a petition for supersedeas with the Tennessee Court of Appeals (after requesting unsuccessfully a new trial and a stay of previous orders). Two Appeals Court judges heard testimony from Drs. Tackett, Adkins, and Griffin, and then interviewed Miss Northern in the Intensive Care Unit of Metro General Hospital. It was the opinion of the Appeals Court,

> That respondent is an intelligent, lucid, communicative and articulate individual who does not accept the fact of the serious condition of her feet and is unwilling to discuss the seriousness of such condition or its fatal potentiality.
>
> That, because of her inability or unwillingness to recognize the actual condition of her feet which is clearly observable by her, she is incompetent to make a rational decision as to the amputation of her feet.

That respondent has no wish to die, but is unable or unwilling to recognize an obvious condition which will probably result in her death if untreated.

Therefore the Court upheld the intent of Chancellor High's order, but altered its specific content, deleting the words "and consenting to any necessary medical treatment," and including instructions that a responsible *individual* (Horace Bass, Commissioner of the Department of Human Services, or his successor in that office) be named "with authority to consent to amputation of respondent's feet when urgently recommended in writing" by Drs. Tackett and Adkins in "severe imminence of death." Judge Frank Drowota III added, in a separate concurring opinion, that

The applicable principle here, recognized even in authority vigorously defending the right to choose in most situations, is that "the state, as *parens patriae*, has a special duty to help the person who is incompetent to make such vital decisions as whether to submit to necessary treatment." The initial assumption must be that the patient desires lifesaving treatment, unless that assumption is contradicted by previous statements competently made. . . .

Further appeals to the Tennessee Supreme Court and the United States Supreme Court failed to win a stay of the Appeals Court's order. However, Drs. Tackett and Adkins eventually decided that amputation of Miss Northern's feet was no longer medically indicated.

[Adapted from *Department of Human Services v. Northern*, 563 S.W. 2d 167 (Tn. App. 1978), cert. denied, U.S. (1978) and from Virginia Abernethy, "Case Study."]

Case #16

A 57-year-old woman was admitted to hospital because of a fractured hip. Surgery, which involved pinning the hip, was strongly recommended but was refused by the patient. Her major reason for refusing the procedure was that she could not tolerate the postoperative pain. While she recognized that surgery could mean the difference between being able to walk and remaining bedfast, she preferred to remain bedfast but free of pain.

During the course of the hospitalization, a Papanicolaou test and biopsy revealed state 1A carcinoma of the cervix. Again surgery was strongly recommended, since the cancer was almost certainly curable by a hysterectomy. Again, the patient refused the procedure.

The patient's treating physicians at this point felt that she was mentally incompetent. Psychiatric and neurological consultations were requested to determine the possibility of dementia and/or mental incompetency. The psychiatric consultant felt that the patient was demented and not mentally competent to make decisions regarding her own care. This determination was based in large measure on the patient's steadfast "unreasonable" refusal to undergo surgery. The neurologist disagreed, finding no evidence of dementia. On questioning, the patient stated that she was refusing the hysterectomy because she *did not believe* she had cancer. 'Anyone knows,' she said, 'that people with cancer are sick, feel bad and lose weight,' while she felt quite well. The patient continued to hold this view despite the results of the biopsy and her physicians' persistent arguments to the contrary.

[This case is reprinted by permission from Ruth Faden and Alan Faden, "False Belief and the Refusal of Medical Treatment," *Journal of Medical Ethics* 3 (1977): 133.]

Case #17

A young man with a high fever, headache, and stiff neck appeared at the emergency room and gave permission for a spinal fluid examination, which the physician had advised in order to test for meningitis. The lumbar puncture confirmed a diagnosis of bacterial (pneumococcal) meningitis, which can be cured easily with antibiotics. But without treatment, it is fatal in three out of four cases, and survivors usually have severe and irreversible physical and mental impairment. But this patient refused antibiotics when the physician disclosed the diagnosis and prognosis.

[This case is adapted from Mark Siegler and Ann Dudley Goldblatt, "Clinical Intuition: A Procedure for Balancing the Rights of Patients and the Responsibilities of Physicians," in *The Law-Medicine Relation: A Philosophical Exploration,* ed. S. F. Spicker, J. M. Healey, Jr., and H. T. Engelhardt, Jr. (Boston: D. Reidel Publishing Co., 1981).]

Case #18

Mrs. G.M., a 72-year-old West Virginia housewife, became aware of breathlessness and was easily fatigued in 1970. She was known to have had a heart murmur since 1968. She consented to come to University Hospital for cardiac catheterization, which confirmed the presence of severe, calcific aortic stenosis with secondary congestive heart failure.

Because of the unfavorable prospect for survival with this lesion with nonsurgical management, the recommendation at the combined cardiac medical-surgical conference was for operation. The physician explained the situation to Mr. and Mrs. M. and recommended aortic valve replacement. It was noted that the risk of surgery was not well-known for her age group, that the early mortality was usually around 10% with 80% good functional results after three years, and that her lack of other, obvious disease made her a relatively "good candidate" for a successful surgical outcome despite her age.

Mrs. M. appeared to understand the discussion and recommendation but requested deferral of the decision and showed signs of denial of the problem. She had no other medical problems, her husband was in good health, and their marriage appeared to be a happy one. They were financially secure and enjoyed a full set of social and recreational activities. She returned on three subsequent occasions for simple, supportive attention. The physician decided not to employ psychiatric assistance or other measures to reduce her denial and began to use conversation in such a way as to reduce her anxiety associated with the decision she appeared to have made.

Comment: The distinguishing features of this situation were (a) a relatively narrow margin in favor of operation on biological grounds because of the patient's age, and (b) the relatively high-risk, complex surgery that would be required to correct the problem. In this setting the decision was shared with other members of the cardiac medical-surgical group and with the patient. In the face of the patient's resistance to operation, the following options were available to the physician: (a) Refusal to participate in further attention to the patient and referral elsewhere for supportive care; (b) more effort to manipulate the patient's attitude into conformity with the physician's; or (c) acceptance of the patient's attitude as an expression of fundamental values not to be overruled in an ambiguous situation and provision of such supportive care as the patient desired.

[This case was prepared for presentation in the Series of Medicine and Society Conferences at the University of Virginia School of Medicine and is used by permission.]

Case #19

E.S., a sexually active 26-year-old intern in Internal Medicine, requests a tubal ligation. She insists that she has been thinking about this decision for months, she doesn't want children, she doesn't like available contraceptives, and she understands that tubal ligation is irreversible. When the staff gynecologist on service suggests that E.S. might sometime marry and that her future husband might want children, E.S. indicates that she would either find another husband or adopt children. Although she concedes that she might possibly change her mind in the future, she thinks that this is unlikely and views the tubal ligation as making it impossible for her to reconsider her current decision. She has scheduled a vacation in two weeks and wants the gynecologist to perform the surgery then.

[This case is adapted from "The Refusal to Sterilize: A Paternalistic Decision," in Marc D. Basson, ed., *Rights and Responsibilities in Modern Medicine: The Second Volume in a Series on Ethics, Humanism, and Medicine* (New York: Alan R. Liss, 1981), pp. 135–36. It is discussed in the same volume by Tom L. Beauchamp, "Paternalism and Refusals to Sterilize," and Eric J. Cassell, "The Refusal to Sterilize Elizabeth Stanley is Not Paternalism."]

Case #20

Carol H., a 25-year-old married woman with a 2-year-old child, is seven months pregnant. She and her husband have decided to have their second child at home; they both feel that their relationships to each other and to the new baby will be greatly enriched by the homebirth alternative. Carol's pregnancy has been 'normal,' like her first one, and her physician foresees no complications at delivery.

However, he refuses to deliver her baby outside the hospital. While he finds both mother and fetus to be healthy, he asserts that childbirth always carries risks; and both he and the parents have a responsibility, he feels, to provide every possible medical advantage for the baby's delivery. Furthermore, the Obstetrics-Gynecology Department of the hospital at which he practices has made it clear that any physician who intentionally participates in a nonemergency home delivery will be considered remiss in his/her professional responsibility and may face loss of OB admitting privileges.

The young parents agree in part with the physician's position—i.e., they want to minimize risks somewhat by having a health professional in attendance at delivery. Since the physician will not agree to homebirth, though, their other alternative is to consult a midwife. But nurse-midwives in their state are licensed to practice only in a hospital or clinic setting, and then only under a physician's supervision. So Carol and her husband really have only two choices: they can have their baby at home, accepting whatever risks are associated with nonprofessional delivery; or they can forego their own plans and submit to the hospital's policies, even though they consider in-hospital delivery to be a controlled and relatively joyless experience.

[This hypothetical case was prepared especially for this volume by James Tubbs.]

Case #21

A 19-year-old married woman sought advice about pregnancy because of her congenital heart disease. When she was five years old, cardiac catheterization revealed that she had a ventricular septal defect, dilatation of the pulmonary artery, and pulmonary hypertension (Eisenmenger's syndrome). Physicians determined that the abnormality was inoperable, and this judgment was reconfirmed during subsequent annual examinations and another catheterization when the patient was 14. Despite this abnormality, her childhood was only moderately restricted. She married when she was 15 and used contraception for the next four years. Then she wanted to have a baby. A cardiologist and obstetrician informed her that while she could possibly have a successful pregnancy she would be subjecting herself to a 25 percent risk of death. After deliberation she and her husband decided to accept that risk. During the pregnancy her condition was carefully monitored, and she was admitted at 38 weeks with borderline hypertension and 2 + albuminuria without edema. After 11 days in the hospital she delivered a healthy infant, but she died of respiratory insufficiency six days later. Dr. John Figgis Jewett analyzes this case:

> Open-heart surgery can afford newborn infants correction of septal defects and spare them the development of secondary pulmonary hypertension, but such surgery was unavailable when this patient was born; by the time she underwent cardiac catheterization at the age of five, the pulmonary process was undoubtedly already under way, making an operation impossible at that time. But despite the inoperability of the congenital heart disease, the irreversibility of the pulmonary hypertension, and the faultless obstetrical and medical management, an argument could be made for considering this death to have been preventable. Responsibility would have to be assigned to the patient and her husband for having declined good advice. Without pregnancy, she might reasonably have survived one or two more decades. This choice, however, was clearly her moral and legal right, and one cannot measure the deficit in happiness and self-fulfillment that those added barren decades might have held.

[Adapted from John Figgis Jewett, "Pulmonary Hypertension and Pre-Eclampsis." *The New England Journal of Medicine* 301, no. 19 (November 8, 1979): 1063–64.]

Case #22

Facts in the Case

Carrie Buck was an 18-year-old girl committed to the Virginia Colony for Epileptics and Feebleminded in 1924. She was diagnosed as having epilepsy, being mentally retarded (or "feebleminded"), and being a "moral delinquent" because she had an illegitimate child. Both her mother and her 6-month-old daughter were also diagnosed as "feebleminded."

The Law

Carrie Buck was chosen to test the constitutionality of the 1924 Virginia Statute for Eugenical Sterilization. The law extended the authority of state institutions to sexually sterilize patients who "would likely become by propagation of their kind a menace to society." The provisions of the law prescribed sterilization for any inmate found to be "insane, idiotic, imbecile, feeble-minded or epileptic, and by the laws of heredity . . . the probably potential parent of socially inadequate offspring likewise afflicted." The objective of the law was to promote both "the welfare of the inmate and of society."

The Opinion

(delivered by Mr. Justice Oliver Wendell Holmes)

"We have seen more than once that the public welfare may call upon the best citizens for their lives. It would be strange if it could not call upon those who already sap the strength of the State for these lesser sacrifices, often not felt to be such by those concerned, in order to prevent one being swamped with incompetence. It is better for all the world, if instead of waiting to execute degenerate offspring for crime, or to let them starve for their imbecility, society can prevent those who are manifestly unfit from continuing their kind. The principle that sustains compulsory vaccination is broad enough to cover cutting the Fallopian tubes (*Jacobson v. Massachusetts*, 197 U.S. 11). Three generations of imbeciles are enough."

[This case was adapted by Paul Lombardo from *Buck v. Bell* 274 U.S. 200 (1927).]

A Critique of the
Gert-Culver Definition
of Paternalism

In their article, "Paternalistic Behavior," [*Philosophy and Public Affairs* 6, No. 1 (1976): 45–57], as well as in other articles,[1] Bernard Gert, a philosopher, and Charles Culver, a psychiatrist, offer a very careful and rigorous definition of paternalism. It is important not only because of its clarity and precision but also because of the authors' systematic argument and helpful examples, many from the biomedical area. They focus on "paternalistic behavior," but they do not consider behavior apart from intentions, motives, and so forth. What makes behavior paternalistic is its rationale. Thus, it is not fair to suggest that their definition of "paternalism" applies primarily to behavior as if behavior were disconnected from its reasons. Furthermore, they rightly reject the narrow focus on liberty and coercion of action that characterizes most philosophical discussions. Nevertheless, their definition suffers from several serious defects.

Gert and Culver offer five necessary and sufficient conditions for paternalism:

A is acting paternalistically toward S if and only if A's behavior (correctly) indicates that A *believes that*:

(1) his action is for S's good

(2) he is qualified to act on S's behalf

(3) his action involves violating a moral rule (or doing that which will require him to do so) with regard to S

(4) he is justified in acting on S's behalf independently of S's past, present, or immediately forthcoming (free, informed) consent

(5) S believes (perhaps falsely) that he (S) generally knows what is for his own good (pp. 49–50).

Not all these features are *necessary* for paternalism. The first condition is certainly acceptable, and the second is another way to state A's belief that his action will probably benefit S. Perhaps it would be better to state both the first two features in terms of A's intention to benefit S if his intention is understood to include the belief that S is more likely to receive a net benefit from his action than from any other available course of action or inaction. Otherwise, the agent intends to deprive S of at least the level of good that he could otherwise obtain.

It is useful to consider both the second and fifth conditions together for they suffer from the same defect. For both conditions, Gert and Culver insist, it is necessary for either the agent or the patient to have a "general belief" when, in fact, it is only necessary to have a belief regarding a particular set of circumstances. Let's start with the second condition. Its original formulation does not specify or even imply a "general belief," but in their explication of this condition, Gert and Culver insist: "[a] *general belief* in A's knowing what is for the good of S better than S does himself is required for paternalistic action . . ." (p. 50). But it is not clear why they hold that this "general belief" or conviction of general qualifications is necessary for paternalism. Surely the paternalistic agent must believe that *in these circumstances* he is more qualified, for whatever reason, than S to make a judgment about S's good and the means to realize it. Applying this second condition, Gert and Culver say that it "explains why a small child usually cannot be said to be acting paternalistically toward his parents even when he satisfies all of the other conditions" (pp. 50–51). But it is plausible to hold that a child can act paternalistically to help a drunk parent without believing that he is generally qualified to act on behalf of the parent.

The fifth condition is unnecessary for a similar reason: Agent A must believe that "S believes (perhaps falsely) that he (S) *generally knows* what is for his own good" (italics added). It is not clear that Gert and Culver actually insist S believe (or be thought to believe) that he "generally knows what is for his own good." Their discussion and examples suggest that it is sufficient for S to believe (or to be thought to believe) that he knows *in these circumstances* what is for his own good. For example, a person may believe himself to be incompetent to handle any of his affairs except for one matter that he reserves for himself, delegating all other affairs to someone else. If we override his decision-making in that one matter (say, selling more land) for his own benefit, we are acting paternalistically toward him even though he does not believe that he "generally knows what is for his own good."

Even more problematic is their third feature of paternalism: the violation of a moral rule, such as the prohibition of inflicting pain, depriving of liberty, and lying. This feature confuses the general description of paternalistic action with the various modes of paternalistic action (e.g., deception or coercion). It is true that paternalism can take a variety of modes, some of which violate more stringent or more important moral rules than others. And it is necessary to examine these various modes in order to determine whether they are justified under some conditions. But it is both unnecessary and misleading to insist that the violation of moral rules is a condition of paternalism. It is unnecessary because it is sufficient to point to the refusal to acquiesce in a person's wishes, choices, or actions. It is misleading because it does not identify in specific terms what is common to all paternalistic acts, namely, this refusal to acquiesce in a person's wishes, choices, and actions.

Gert and Culver's analysis of a case of a religious refusal of blood transfusion illustrates these points.

> Mr. N, a member of a religious sect that does not believe in blood transfusions, is involved in a serious automobile accident and loses a large amount of blood. On arriving at the hospital, he is still conscious and informs the doctor of his views on blood transfusion. Immediately thereafter he faints from loss of blood. The doctor believes that if Mr. N is not given a transfusion he will die. Thereupon, while Mr. N is still unconscious, the doctor arranges for and carries out the blood transfusion. (p. 46.)

Gert and Culver contend that "[g]iving the blood transfusion to the unconscious member of the religious sect is a paternalistic action *which does not itself constitute a violation of any moral rule,* but which does involve doing that which will require one to violate a moral rule" (p. 51, italics added). If the patient survives and regains consciousness, then the physician will have to choose between violating the rule against deception or violating the rule against causing pain. Because his initial act of providing the blood transfusion leads to one of these violations, it is paternalistic. A more adequate analysis of this case is that the blood transfusion is paternalistic because it refuses to acquiesce in Mr. N's wishes and choices on grounds of Mr. N's best interests. It is unnecessary and misleading to focus on what the provision of the blood will *lead to*, such as an infliction of pain or deception. The transfusion is paternalistic (and prima facie wrong) because it goes against Mr. N's expressed wishes and choices. The Gert-Culver analysis of this case is paradoxical. It implies that if the patient dies, no paternalistic act has been committed, for the act does not lead to a violation of one of the moral rules.

The Gert-Culver analysis of a simple example shows their circuitous and misleading route to a definition of paternalism. Suppose that a bully has bothered A's younger brother. Without telling his brother, A beats up the bully and warns him that he can expect the same treatment if he bothers A's brother again. Gert and Culver hold that this act is paternalistic because A has "*deceived* [his] younger brother by taking an action which normally would require his consent. Thus, acting without his consent counts as deception" (p. 51, italics added). This analysis is counterintuitive. If A's action is paternalistic, it is only because it occurred without the younger brother's consent (if we assume that consent would normally be required). Perhaps it also insulted the younger brother because, we might suppose, he wanted to handle it himself. Under these conditions, it might have inflicted "pain" on him. It is difficult, however, to see why the action without additional features should be considered as "deception." Perhaps Gert and Culver were led to this conclusion in order to square their intuitions about this case (that it is paternalistic) with their theory of paternalism (that it involves or leads to a violation of moral rules such as deception).

Thus, the Gert-Culver account of paternalism may be inadequate in part because of their understanding of moral rules.[2] First, they focus too narrowly on "rules," ignoring "principles" that are more general and foundational in a moral system.[3] They define paternalistic behavior in terms of specific actions that violate moral rules, failing to see that some forms of paternalistic action are morally suspect not because they violate moral rules but because they fail to respect a person's wishes, choices, and actions. The content of their moral rules does not adequately express the principle of respect for persons and their autonomy. As a consequence, their analysis distorts both the blood transfusion case and the bully case.

Their fourth condition of paternalism does, however, implicitly invoke the principle of respect for persons and their autonomy, even though Gert and Culver do not appear to believe that acting independently of S's consent is morally problematic in and of itself. It is morally problematic only if other rules such as not deceiving or inflicting pain are violated. In a later article,[4] Gert and Culver modified the fourth condition of paternalism to read: "S's good justifies him [A] in acting on S's behalf independently of S's past, present, or immediately forthcoming (free, informed) consent." This rewording makes it clear that the paternalistic agent justifies his action by appeal to S's good (the first condition) rather than some other reasons such as protecting third parties from harm. If S consents to A's action when it occurs, the action is not paternalistic; it is not contrary to S's express wish or choice. In general, this point holds for past consent and for immediately forthcoming consent, though very careful analysis of these situations is required.

Although Gert and Culver have wrongly defined paternalism, within their definition are the ingredients of an adequate definition, which they were unable to produce in part because of the distortions caused by their moral theory. While I have indicated these ingredients in my critique, it may be useful to state them in conclusion: Paternalistic action is non-acquiescence in a person's wishes, choices, and actions for that person's own benefit.

Notes

1. Gert and Culver, "The Justification of Paternalism," *Ethics* 89, no. 2 (January 1979): 199–210. See also Gert and Culver, *Philosophy in Medicine: Conceptual and Ethical Problems in Medicine and Psychiatry* (New York: Oxford University Press, 1982), which incorporates and elaborates several of these themes. I did not have access to their book when I prepared this appendix.
2. Bernard Gert, *The Moral Rules* (New York: Harper and Row, 1970).
3. For a different perspective, see Tom L. Beauchamp and James F. Childress, *Principles of Biomedical Ethics* (New York: Oxford University Press, 1979).
4. Gert and Culver, "The Justification of Paternalism," p. 199.

Index